TECUMSEH'S LAST STAND

Tecumseh (properly Tecumthe), leader of Britain's Indian allies until his death at Moraviantown. This engraving by Benson J. Lossing was supposedly based upon a pencil sketch made about 1808 by a fur trader named Pierre Le Dru. Unfortunately, Lossing substituted a uniform coat for the chief's native costume in the mistaken belief that Tecumseh held the rank of brigadier general in the British army. No fully authenticated portrait of the Shawnee leader exists. *Courtesy British Library.*

Tecumseh's Last Stand

By John Sugden

UNIVERSITY OF OKLAHOMA PRESS: NORMAN AND LONDON

For a much remembered parent,
Lily Cuthbertson Sugden, 1914–1981

Library of Congress Cataloging-in-Publication Data

Sugden, John, 1947–
  Tecumseh's last stand.

  Bibliography: p.
  Includes index.
  1. Thames, Battle of, 1813. 2. Tecumseh, Shawnee Chief, 1768–
1813—Death and burial. 3. United States—History—War of 1812—
Campaigns. 4. Northwest, Old—History—War of 1812—Cam-
paigns. 5. United States—History—War of 1812—Participation,
Indian. I. Title.
E356.T3S84   1985   973.5′2   85–40480
ISBN 0–8061–1944–6 (cloth)
ISBN 0–8061–2242–0 (pbk.)

3   4   5   6   7   8   9   10   11   12

CONTENTS

ILLUSTRATIONS

MAPS

PREFACE

THE WAR of 1812 continues to find historians, but relatively little scholarly attention has been accorded the operations of the Indians and the British on the frontier. Even those historians who directed their research solely or primarily to the conflict on the borders left the Indian and the British perspectives cloudy. As long ago as 1816 the American Robert B. McAfee provided his countrymen with a comprehensive if patriotic account of *The Late War in the Western Country*, and more recently his ground has been retraced at length by A. R. Gilpin, Frank Owsley, and others, who have provided a satisfactory reconstruction of the campaigns from the American point of view, but nothing comparable exists for other participants. The Indian history of the war, in particular, has suffered from neglect, the most notable exceptions to which are the few sketchy accounts of the Creek War and a brief but admirable dissertation by George Chalou, which regrettably remains unpublished.

This situation is somewhat surprising, considering the impact the war made on Indian communities and the fact that the Indians were a mainstay of British efforts in the Northwest and the South and were involved in one of the most strenuous of all North American Indian resistance movements. A rare solidarity linked embattled natives from the Great Lakes to the Gulf of Mexico; Tecumseh's agents fought with the Creeks and the Seminoles in the South, and Creek warriors stood in the Indian line when the

Shawnee chief made his final stand at Moraviantown in Canada. In lieu of scholarly analysis, accounts have frequently fallen prey to the indifferent primary sources that bear upon the Indians, many of which are weltered in conjecture and legend. Some of the most unreliable passages in histories of the War of 1812 have related to the British-Indian campaigns.

Of no event are these remarks more true than they are of the retreat of the Indians and the British from Amherstburg in 1813 and the subsequent defeat at Moraviantown, an engagement often called the Battle of The Thames. Despite its importance—it was the greatest disaster that befell the British and Indian armies on the Canadian border during the war—the campaign has never been treated fully, and only seldom accurately; hitherto available accounts are either brief outlines or an inextricable confusion of history and legend. Few episodes of the war generated more myths than did this retreat of 1813, many of them surviving unscathed by criticism despite the flimsiest of foundations. In part, the production of an adequate appraisal has been retarded by a paucity of readily accessible materials. Most histories have been furnished from a handful of contemporary dispatches, and the more popular of the unreliable reminiscences of veterans of the campaign.

Far more important are the minutes of the court-martial of the British commander, Henry Procter, which sat from December 21, 1814, to January 28, 1815, and accumulated some 430 large manuscript pages of testimony, most of it from the interrogation of the thirty-four witnesses called to accuse or to vindicate the defendant. This document survives in the Public Record Office, Kew, England, but has not been published, except for the statement made by Procter in his defense, which was circulated in a little-known pamphlet of 1842. The court-martial evidence was first used by Reginald Horsman for a judicious narrative, a few pages long, in his *The War of 1812* (1969), and more fully since by Pierre Berton, whose recent history of the war fails to disentangle fact from fiction in the various materials at hand. My own study has depended heavily upon the minutes of the court-martial, but it also evaluates the other relevant published and unpublished primary sources to be found in archives and libraries in Britain, the United

States, and Canada. Some of this evidence has been presented in the following pages at length, particularly when it concerns aspects of controversy. Quotations from the sources preserve the original spellings, including variations in proper names, but changes in the punctuation have occasionally been necessary in the interest of clarity.

As a contribution toward a better understanding of the British-Indian alliance in the War of 1812, I have tried to answer the pertinent questions about the retreat from Amherstburg and the Battle of Moraviantown and to document its significance for the sometimes tempestuous relationship between Britain and her Indian allies of the Northwest. The reasons for Procter's decision to abandon Amherstburg and the processes by which his force disintegrated and was overthrown are explored. While the necessity for the retreat was understood, it was inefficiently conducted. Major General Procter was not the inhumane coward so repeatedly portrayed. Although he emerges as a good peacetime corps commander with an adequate grasp of strategy, his inexperience in the field, his poor organization and leadership, and his tactical incompetence left him inadequate to a taxing situation and contributed to his defeat and disgrace. For their part, the Indians displayed varied motives and capabilities, but the most determined warriors were formidable opponents until Tecumseh's death at Moraviantown robbed them of effective leadership and the British commissariat failed to satisfy their basic material needs.

The fact rather than the manner of Tecumseh's death was important, but several reasons induced me to reopen the once celebrated question of how the Shawnee leader met his end. First, no account of the retreat could afford to sidestep the one incident that became a matter of national hearthside gossip and exercised the minds of so many for so long. Second, the analysis furnishes an interesting footnote to the history of early American politics, since candidates for public office squabbled for years for the credit of having destroyed the great Indian enemy. And, finally, some of the most vivid impressions of the action at Moraviantown are contained in the material relating to Tecumseh's death, and the few conclusions that can tentatively be deduced from them illuminate precisely that aspect about which the contemporary British records offer the least information—the battle between the Indians and the Americans. Therefore, a clarification if not a resolution of the controversy is offered in the following pages.

My last chapter assesses the importance of the campaign for the remaining months of the war. It is generally recognized that the engagement on the Thames consummated the American naval victory on Lake Erie, which had driven the British from the Detroit and dispersed their Indian allies, but that it was not so sufficiently followed up that Britain's influence in the West was extinguished. It was an enormous fillip to American morale, and by arresting the major British-Indian invasions of the Old Northwest, enabled the United States to concentrate on more decisive theaters farther east. But the effects of the campaign upon British allegiance among the Indians, although profound, have commonly been exaggerated. Most of the tribes of the Northwest continued to support Britain, many of them openly, until news of the Treaty of Ghent reached the West in 1815. Where the British showed vigor in prosecuting the war on the frontier and infiltrated supplies, Indians still rallied in force to the king. The ineffectiveness of their support after Moraviantown was largely caused by British inactivity, the vicissitudes of the supply system, and the lack of strong Indian leadership.

Among those whose assistance has made possible this study, special thanks are due the staffs of the Public Record Office, Kew, England; the British Library, London; the British Newspaper Library, Colindale; the Kingston-Upon-Hull Public Library; the university libraries of Warwick and Leeds, England; the various departments of the Library of Congress, Washington, D.C.; the National Archives of the United States at Washington, D.C.; the State Historical Society of Wisconsin, Madison; the Indiana Historical Bureau, Indianapolis; the Public Archives of Canada and the National Library of Canada, Ottawa; and the Public Library of Ottawa. I am much indebted to Lieutenant Bryn Owen and Colonel W. R. Davies of the Welch Regiment Museum, Cardiff Castle, Cardiff, Wales; R. Alan Douglas, curator of the Hiram Walker Historical Museum, Windsor, Ontario; Brian Driscoll,

British Manuscripts Division, Public Archives of Canada, Ottawa; Mrs. Alice C. Dalligan, chief of the Burton Historical Collection, Detroit Public Library; Sem C. Sutter, Susan E. Kerr, and Margaret A. Fusco of the University of Chicago Library; Sally E. Snyder, guide specialist at the Fort Malden National Historic Park, Amherstburg; Sandra Burrows of the Newspaper Division of the National Library of Canada, Ottawa; Dr. Colin G. Calloway of Bellows Falls, Vermont; Anne B. Shepherd, curator of manuscripts at the Cincinnati Historical Society; R. Le Gette Burris, museum specialist, National Numismatic Collection, National Museum of American History, Washington, D.C.; David B. Kotin, head of the Canadian History Department at the Metropolitan Toronto Library Board; and G. M. Wilson, deputy master of the Armouries, H.M. Tower of London. Finally, I owe much to my publishers for their suggestions and encouragement; to Mrs. Terri Egginton, who helped with the research and preparation of the manuscript; and to my indefatigable brother, Philip, with whom I have been arguing about Indians ever since I can remember.

John Sugden,
Kingston-Upon-Hull

TECUMSEH'S LAST STAND

1

INTRODUCTION

LATE on October 5, 1813, a group of exhausted British soldiers clattered into Delaware, a village on the Thames River [Ontario] in Upper Canada. One of them, Captain John Hall of the Canadian Fencibles, brigade major to the Forty-first Regiment of Foot, hastily concocted a note giving the British high command official notification of their first major land defeat in the War of 1812. "Sir," began Hall, addressing Lieutenant Colonel John Harvey, the deputy adjutant-general,

I am commanded by Major General Procter to acquaint you, for General De Rottenburgs information, with the result of an afair that took place with the enemy near Moravian Town this afternoon about 4 o'clock. One of the guns being deserted early in the action, the troops near it gave way and the consequence was a complete rout—notwithstanding the exertions of the general to rally them—so much so that I thought it impossible he could escape being taken—we are just arrived here. The general is so fatigued by riding from the field of battle on the other side the Moravian Town, through the Wilderness that he cannot write & I am not much better—I have the honour to etc.[1]

By European standards the Battle of Moraviantown, often remembered as the Battle of the Thames, appears a trivial affair. A handful of British regulars and their Indian allies were overwhelmingly defeated by an American army three times their number after a retreat from Amherstburg, on the Detroit River, to

3

Moraviantown on the River Thames. But succeeding the over-throw of British naval supremacy on Lakes Erie and Ontario, as it did, it intensified doubts about the ability of Britain to defend her possessions in North America. For more than a year a meager collection of Redcoats and militia, sustained by various Indian forces, had parried the thrusts of superior American armies and preserved Upper Canada from invasion. Now, as Britain's struggle with Napoleonic France was drawing toward a triumphant close and the prospect of British reinforcements for America brightened, the red line crumbled, and the United States threw off the humilia-tion of successive defeats to secure redemption in the Old North-west. The Indian alliance that had nourished the king's earlier victories seemed to have been broken.

The battle was heralded by Americans as their first important breakthrough of the war. Canada had seemed an easy conquest, and an attractive one, for many reasons. It possessed rich land and abundant resources and would have been an acquisition in itself. British intrigue with the Indians, so feared in the American backcountry, would also have ended with the fall of Canada. In addition, Canada supplied Britain with invaluable raw materials for her navy and shipping, materials essential for her war effort against France. If the United States could seize Canada, President James Madison might have commanded a means to wring con-cessions from the British and to bring the war to something of a victorious close. Never did the Americans come closer to that elusive dream of conquering Canada than in the campaign that drove the British and the Indians from Amherstburg to their defeat at Moraviantown. For years participants boasted of how they had routed the Redcoats and their savage allies, killed Tecumseh, and won their rewards in public office. It has been said that the victory helped create a president and a vice-president of the United States, three state governors, four United States senators, and twenty congressmen.

In retrospect, it can be seen that Moraviantown achieved less than the British feared or many of the Americans hoped. It did not establish American control of western Canada, nor lead to the permanent annexation of any territory by the United States. It destroyed neither British influence among the Indians nor Indian resistance to American expansion in the Northwest. It remains, nevertheless, a significant milestone in frontier history. For the first time, the Americans won a clear-cut success campaigning in Canada. By restoring their prewar position on the Detroit River they were able to prevent the British-Indian forays into Ohio, and Michigan and Indiana territories, which had rekindled the worst memories of the Revolution and the northwestern Indian war of the late eighteenth century; and after Moraviantown the area west of Lake Ontario ceased to be a theater of major mililtary operations, largely because both sides concentrated upon securing decisive advantages farther east. Consequently, the engagement marks the close of an important phase of the War of 1812 along the Canadian border.

In Indian history, the retreat of 1813 and the Battle of Moraviantown also mark a watershed. As historian Reginald Horsman has written, Moraviantown was "the decisive battle of the war on the Detroit frontier, and the decisive battle for the Indians of the whole region. It meant more to them than the loss of a single battle, for this was also their last great battle in defense of the Old Northwest."[2] The resistance of the Indians to the United States in the Old Northwest certainly survived the campaign of 1813, but its ablest leaders, Tecumseh and Roundhead, did not, and without them the Indian movement lost energy and direction. Never again were the North American Indians a substantial element in international affairs.

Defeats are not always remembered, far less commemorated, but in Canada considerable interest has continued to attend the British-Indian retreat of 1813. Most of it clung to Tecumseh, the Shawnee who commanded the Indians at Moraviantown and lost his life in the battle. Survivors of the war in the West remembered Tecumseh as its outstanding personality, investing him with a legendary status that historians find difficult to penetrate. Within a few years of the chief's death, John Richardson, a volunteer in the campaign of 1813, composed an epic poem, *Tecumseh; or, The Warrior of the West*, moved by a "generous anxiety to preserve the memory of one of the noblest and most gallant spirits that ever tenanted the breast of man."[3] Then, in 1841, funds were sought for the erection of an official Tecumseh monument, and seven years later the Canadian Board of Ordnance purchased a site for it on Saint Helen's Island, Montreal.[4] Tecumseh's specter lingered along the full line of his final retreat, in the lakeside town that now bears his name, the Tecumseh road, which passed from Sandwich to the mouth of the Thames, the Tecumseh Park at Chatham (where the Indians skirmished with the American army before the main engagement), and in the names of many buildings that were established near the old battlefield at Moraviantown—a farm, a house, a post office, a station. Proud of their hero, the citizens of nearby Thamesville in 1911 placed a granite boulder commemorating the chief close to where he was believed to have fallen, and the next year the Tecumseh Memorial Association was founded to gather money to ensure more permanent recognition in the form of a monument or a museum. The centenary of Moraviantown in October, 1913, saw thousands of Canadians congregating upon the battlefield to celebrate "Tecumseh Day." The memorial boulder was draped in purple for the occasion and crowned with a portrait of Tecumseh decorated in evergreens, while upon its flanks flags stood at half-mast. A mixed force of regulars trooped the color; a salute of fourteen guns was fired in Tecumseh's honor; and speeches (one by Dr. Tecumseh K. Holmes, president of the Kent County Historical Association) recalled his services. Eleven years later the boulder, placed upon a bronze tablet and granite pediment, was unveiled before more than two thousand persons as the center of a new Tecumseh Memorial Park.[5]

If Tecumseh was the hero of the story of the retreat as it was remembered, Major General Henry Procter, who saved his own life by flight at Moraviantown, acted the villain. He has always seemed a poor partner to the Indian leader, and commentators on the war enjoy abusing him. Tecumseh, wrote an American historian, "was as superior to . . . Proctor, as the blazing noonday sun is to a farthing rushlight."[6] Upon this trend the few dissenting voices raised in the general's defense have made little impression.[7] Procter's popular reputation had long been checkered, his victory at Frenchtown in January, 1813, earning him the hatred of his enemies as the defeat of Moraviantown accorded him the contempt of his colleagues. Literature portrayed him as a vicious but cowardly and inefficient commander and generally failed to appreciate the difficulties under which the man invariably labored. Veterans even allowed their dislike of him to influence their memories of his appearance. "Colonel Proctor," recalled one who beheld him in 1812, "was one of the meanest looking men I ever saw. He had an expression of countenance in which that of the murderer and cowardly assassin predominated; nor did he belie his appearance."[8]

This kind of writing does not advance the argument very far. Certainly, the retreat from Amherstburg cruelly exposed Procter's weaknesses as a commander and shrouded the modest talents he had used effectively in other circumstances. There is nothing, however, to suggest brutality in the general's nature, and his proverbial cowardice is a matter of interpretation. Perhaps he demonstrated a degree of moral cowardice when he endeavored to salvage his ruined career by unloading the blame for Moraviantown upon his soldiers. Only days after the action he was informing his superior officer that "the conduct of the troops was not upon this unfortunate occasion such as I have on every other witnessed with pride & satisfaction. The inclination to retreat was too strong, nor did I receive that cordial aid I sought and was entitled to. . . ."[9] The testimony presented at Procter's court-martial amply vindicates his acquittal of charges of physical cowardice on the field.

It was a verdict that failed to rescue the general's courage from public vilification. During their miserable months of captivity in the United States, British prisoners from Moraviantown nursed their resentment of their commander and mercilessly trounced him at every subsequent opportunity. While still incarcerated in Kentucky, Captain Peter Chambers told a correspondent that: "My prophecy to Colonel Harvey respecting Major General Procter has also proved but too true, he never made any exertion to rally his troops, but was one of the first who fled. My God, how anxiously do I look forward to the moment that will enable me to do my character justice. . . ."[10] John Richardson's influential reminiscences related how "mounted on an excellent courser" Procter "sought safety in flight at the very commencement of the action. . . ."[11] And Ensign James Cochran spoke of the "malign influence" and "glaring imbecility" of a general who, although an indifferent horseman, "galloped off on the first charge. . . ."[12] Procter's enemies fell upon him at the court-martial but failed to carry their point. The slander stuck nevertheless, and numerous stories depicting Tecumseh's disgust with and humiliation of the general have fed upon the latter's supposed deficiency of courage. The passion was understandable, but after the best part of two centuries it is time for a fairer assessment.

In the following pages, an attempt has been made to provide a reconstruction of the retreat of Tecumseh and Procter that is consistent with all the surviving evidence and places the event within the wider context of the British-Indian operations of the war. The story must begin in the summer of 1813, when American naval and military forces were being mobilized for another attempt upon Canada and to test again the army that held the Detroit frontier from its fortress of Fort Malden at Amherstburg.

2

A PROLOGUE: AUGUST AND SEPTEMBER, 1813

*I entreat your excellency to send me
the means of continuing the contest.*

AMHERSTBURG was a small town in 1813, perhaps no more than one hundred and fifty neat and largely wooden houses of recent construction with a public storehouse, on the Canadian side of the Detroit River at the head of Lake Erie. Immediately to the south lay the farm of Colonel Matthew Elliott, an Irish veteran of the Revolution who was still in the service of the British Indian Department. A few hundred yards to the north and also facing the river stood Fort Malden, the most important British fortress west of Lake Ontario. Governor Isaac Shelby of Kentucky, who saw Malden that September, considered its defenses to be formidable, but as recently as May, 1812, only a month before the outbreak of the war between Britain and the United States, it had been described by His Excellency Sir George Prevost, captain general and governor in chief of Canada, as "a temporary field work in a ruinous state."[1] The shape of an irregular pentagon, with bastions at the five corners, and embrasures, it was surrounded by a deep ditch and two rows of heavy pickets and supported by a small redoubt close to the riverbank. Amherstburg was Britain's principal port on Lake Erie. Flanked at opposite sides by Fort Malden and the town, a small dockyard, guarded by blockhouses, overlooked the channel that ran between the shoreline and Bois Blanc, a thickly wooded island about a mile in length that rose some fifteen feet from the Detroit River. The island afforded Amherstburg additional security, for blockhouses

9

and batteries had been erected at both of its extremities, standing sentinel upon the entrances to the passage leading to the harbor.

Two principal lines of communication served Amherstburg. A road from the town passed north, beyond Malden and the nearby Indian council house, and hugged the riverside unless swinging away through thick woods to use bridges over the tributaries of the Detroit. It reached the small settlement of Sandwich, home of the district jail and courthouse, situated opposite the American town of Detroit, and proceeded beside Lake Saint Clair to the mouth of the River Thames, a waterway that stretched through the wilderness toward the head of Lake Ontario.[2] More convenient was the other route by Lake Erie to Lake Ontario by way of the Niagara River. Unfortunately, the war had closed part of this thoroughfare in May, 1813, when the Americans secured control of the Niagara frontier, and thereafter the British ships had been compelled to ply between Amherstburg and Long Point, a haven on the northeastern shore of Lake Erie from which new supply lines had been developed overland to the head of the lower lake. All of these routes, however, by the Thames, Niagara, and Long Point, merely took up a tortuous chain of communication that led through Lake Ontario and the Saint Lawrence River to Quebec.

On September 10, 1813—a fateful day for this remote outpost of the Empire—the British Right Division had dominated the Detroit frontier from Fort Malden for more than a year, since August, 1812, when the American army had surrendered Detroit. It still had a substantial, if insufficient, force in the vicinity. The division consisted primarily of the Forty-first Regiment of Foot, one battalion of which had been stationed in Canada for many years; a second, commanded by Lieutenant Colonel William Evans, was shipped from Europe late in 1812 and had been arriving on the frontier throughout the summer.[3] In support were small details from other corps, revealed by a return of that September as 30 men of the Royal Artillery, 23 of the Tenth Royal Veteran Battalion, 15 from the Royal Newfoundland Regiment, 51 of the Canadian Light Dragoons, and 8 members of the Canadian Artillery.[4] These forces were dispersed in three posts. Lieutenant Colonel Augustus Warburton of the Forty-first had 298 men at

Fort Malden and Amherstburg, painted by Margaret Reynolds about 1813. On the left is Bois Blanc Island, and across the channel from it are Fort Malden and the dockyard. *Courtesy Parks Canada: Fort Malden National Historic Park.*

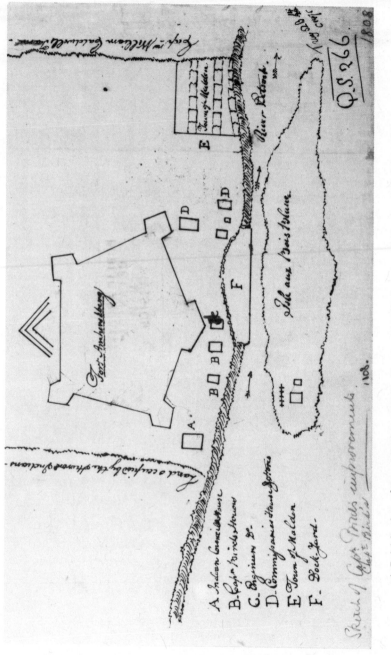

A British plan of Fort Malden, 1808. *Courtesy National Map Collection, Public Archives of Canada.*

The uniform of an officer of the Forty-first Regiment of Foot, about
1813. The officer's shako is black, trimmed with gold, with a red and
white plume. The tunic is red with gold facings, a white shoulder strap,
and a scarlet sash. The trousers are gray and the footwear black. Such
uniforms were probably worn by the second battalion of the regiment,
which reached the frontier just before the retreat from Amherstburg.
Officers of the first battalion still would have been attired in the old red
uniforms with silver facings. *Courtesy British Library.*

Fort Malden, Brevet Major Adam Muir of the Forty-first occupied Detroit, in Michigan Territory, with another 68, and the balance of the division was at Sandwich under Lieutenant Colonel Evans. There too, at his headquarters, was stationed the controversial Colonel Henry Procter, brevet major general, overall commander of the entire complement of 881 officers and men.[5] On the morning of September 10 an additional 152 men of the Forty-first and 97 of the Royal Newfoundland Regiment were serving with Britain's naval squadron on Lake Erie.

Although they were charged with an important mission, these guardians of Canada's western border, their condition was not the best. Specie was in short supply, and provisions were expensive and scarce. The pay of both the civilian artificers of Amherstburg dockyard and the troops was in arrears, and the men had been unable to buy necessities. They lacked salt, and the once-resplendent uniforms of the Forty-first Regiment, scarlet coats with gold, silver, or black-and-white facings, were ragged and in need of essential replacements.[6] By September 22, 110 of the Right Division were returned as sick. Moreover, all was far from well between Procter and his officers, and the discord was beginning to undermine discipline and cooperation within the ranks.

A Welshman, Henry Procter was some fifty years of age in 1813 and had devoted the bulk of his life to the army, having entered the Forty-third (Monmouthshire) Regiment in 1781 and purchased promotion until he received his commission as a captain more than eleven years later, on November 30, 1792. As a lieutenant at Kilkenny he had courted a clergyman's daughter, Elizabeth Cockburn, and married her on May 19, 1792, in a union that produced several children, at least three daughters and a son. Procter had later transferred to the Forty-first Regiment stationed in Canada and had become a lieutenant colonel in 1800. He became a colonel of the army in July, 1810, and in both ranks he earned the reputation of a good disciplinarian and considerably improved the appearance and order of his corps. Towns in which he served voiced regret at his leaving. Thus, on July 19, 1805, the magistrates of the District of Quebec in Quarter Sessions published their approval of Procter and his soldiers, "expressing their perfect approbation of the very becoming conduct of that regiment during its long stay in this garrison, which must be attributed to the zeal of the commanding officer and good discipline of the 41st Regiment. . . ."[7] Six years later, when the corps was detailed from Montreal to Upper Canada, a similar spirit prevailed:

Montreal, August 5. [1811] The departure of the 41st Regiment of Upper Canada excites in this city the greatest regret; and we are indebted to Colonel Proctor, the officers, and all those who compose that respectable corps for the politeness we have received; and the peace and security we have enjoyed during their stay here; we, therefore, present publicly our most sincere thanks for their meritorious conduct, and assuring them that our sincere wish is, their prosperity.[8]

Although he was a competent administrator, Procter's weakness was his scant experience in the field. During the campaign against Detroit in 1812 the operations had been directed by Major General Isaac Brock, a younger and more daring officer, and although Procter had led his army in three expeditions since that victory, they constituted a total of less than seven months of service. Even more disturbing were the general's relations with his immediate subordinates, Warburton and Evans, both new arrivals who found their commander aloof and uncommunicative, courting a small coterie of officers in which they were not included. In September, 1813, Procter's "private pique," as one observer called it, had placed him on such poor terms with his second- and third-in-command that he deliberately kept them ignorant of important decisions respecting the management of the division.[9]

Although many of the guns of Fort Malden had been turned over to the naval squadron to complete the armaments of the vessels, the Right Division still possessed a formidable battery that September: 12- and 18-pound carronades, some 24- and 6-pound long guns, and an 8-inch howitzer, in addition to the field train, which consisted of two 6-pounders, three 3-pounders, and a 5½-inch howitzer.[10] But the "strongest arm"[11] of the military force defending western Upper Canada was the American Indian army of several thousand warriors camping with their families in the neighborhood, to the perplexity of the British commissariat. William Jones of the Indian Department believed that "as nearly as I can recollect there were above 10,000 souls, exclusive of children at the breast."[12] They lived in scattered bands, some about Fort Malden, some with Tecumseh, the celebrated Shawnee chieftain, on Grosse Isle with its sheltered bays near the American side of the Detroit River, and others in Michigan Territory at Brownstown, near Detroit. According to American intelligence, 1,630 braves were assembled at Brownstown—100 Winnebagoes, 150 Kickapoos, 80 Shawnees, 100 Sacs, 800 Potawatomis, 200 Ottawas, 60 Muncey Delawares, 40 Senecas, and 100 Ojibwas.[13]

The Indians had been drawn beneath the British banner for many reasons. The most steadfast hated the Americans on account of the seizure of Indian land in the Northwest. The Miamis, on the other hand, had found neutrality impossible once the war had begun. Others were simply seeking provisions, presents, and plunder. They were certainly valuable fighting men, durable, skillful and ferocious, adept in ambuscade and stratagem. Provisioned and armed by the Indian Department, they were capable of maintaining a protracted offensive. Nevertheless, the Indians were also a volatile force, eager for immediate returns, and likely to tire and defect in the absence of tangible progress and the trophies of war. The pursuit of scalps and booty sometimes militated against the achievement of strategic objectives.

Nor were the tribesmen invariably efficient upon the actual field of battle. They had been raised in numerically weak societies in which every warrior was also a hunter and a producer, and they knew the military and economic value of their menfolk. Unwilling to squander the lives of their warriors, they fought best in cover from ambush and typically gave way when a hard pounding promised heavy losses; rarely would they storm fortifications. Then, too, the loose authority structure among the Indian bands and the cultivation by the tribesmen of a proud personal independence rendered them unamenable to discipline. Unsupported by gazetted ranks backed by the articles of war and the machinery of a state, the authority of the Indian chief depended largely upon the amount of public support his policies could command and upon his own powers of personalilty and leadership. His role was to influence, to inspire, and to persuade, rather than to order and instruct. Not surprisingly, the British found difficulty in controlling their Indian allies, and their repeated and embarrassing inability to prevent the warriors from robbing and murdering prisoners and civilians had fed American fury. In the most recent attempt to restrain the natives from gratuitous killing, a board of British officers recommended at Saint David's on July 20 that the Indians be paid five dollars for every prisoner they delivered.[14]

The Indians did not regard themselves as subordinates of the British. They were independent allies, reaching their decisions in band, tribal, and intertribal councils. The small staff of the British Indian Department, headed by the venerable Colonel Matthew Elliott, acted as advisers to the Indians, as intermediaries between the chiefs and the British commanders, as distributors of rations and presents, and as interpreters. The most effective single human instrument in maintaining the British-Indian alliance was the great Shawnee chief, Tecumseh (Shooting Star). In September, 1813, he was about forty-five years of age and at the zenith of his power. For years Tecumseh had zealously devoted himself to uniting the Indian tribes in resistance to the remorseless advance of the American frontier, and in the British alliance he saw his last opportunity to save the lands of his people. Encouraged by British promises of support for Indian claims, he had worked with energy and determination to convince the warriors that only with British assistance could they defeat the United States. The "great dependance" of the Indians, as his brother, the Shawnee Prophet, called him, Tecumseh equally enjoyed the admiration and confidence of his white allies.

"I wish we had Tecumseh here to help us out of our difficulties," wrote Charles Askin to his father from the troubled Centre Dvision of the British forces at the head of Lake Ontario in 1813.[15]

Major General Procter certainly appreciated the value of this Indian leader. As early as November, 1812 he had explained that the efforts of the British Indian Department were impeded by jealousies between Elliott and Thomas McKee, which he attributed to the former, and that:

I was struck forcibly with the imbecility of the Indian Department on my first arrival at Amherstburg. We are indebted to McKee and much more to the Chief Tecumthe for our Indian arm. He convinced the Indians that our cause was thiers and his influence & example determined and fixed the Wyndots whose selection determind every tribe. . . .[16]

Two years later the general acknowledged that Tecumseh's "example and talents governed the councils of his brethren."[17]

Second in importance only to Tecumseh was Roundhead (Stiahta), the leader of the militant faction of the Wyandots. Since 1806 he had been associated with Tecumseh in the formation of the intertribal confederacy, and he was a committed opponent of the United States whose notoriety had been enhanced by his capture of General James Winchester at the battle at Frenchtown in January, 1813. Although an able and respected chief, Roundhead lacked some of Tecumseh's authority and in the Shawnee's absence had found difficulty in managing the Indians on an expedition to Fort Wayne in September, 1812.[18] Of the other chiefs the most influential were Main Poc (Withered Hand) and Naiwash. The former, a boorish Potawatomi, had a primitive sense of Indian unity and a predilection for raiding the Osages, but he, too, had been brought into the movement led by Tecumseh, his brother the Prophet (Tenskwatawa, the Open Door), and Roundhead, and he had spent the winter of 1811–1812 forging an alliance among the Illinois Indians. He remained sullenly hostile to the United States but was to prove an unsteady ally to the British.[19] Naiwash, who headed the pro-British Ottawas, cuts a more shadowy figure in contemporary records. He survived the War of 1812 and settled for a time on Turkey Island, near Sandwich, before retiring with his people to a quiet obscurity on the Miami River in Michigan Territory.[20]

On September 10, 1813 the fates of Amherstburg and Fort Malden once again hung in the balance, but the decision did not rest with the military force under Procter and Tecumseh. A tiny squadron of six vessels—the brigs *Detroit* and *Queen Charlotte*, two smaller craft, the *Lady Prevost* and *General Hunter*, and two gunboats, *Chippawa* and *Little Belt*—seriously undermanned and poorly equipped, had been led out of harbor the previous day by acting

Commodore Robert Heriot Barclay to challenge the American squadron for mastery on Lake Erie. Barclay was not an experienced officer. He was barely twenty-seven years of age and had held the king's commission for eight of them. Still officially a lieutenant, for he did not become a post-captain until 1824, he had been acting commander on the lakes for a mere four months, during which time he had seen no action. The empty left sleeve of Barclay's uniform proclaimed him a man of courage. He had served at Trafalgar, lost an arm attacking a French convoy some three years afterwards, and none doubted that he would now do his duty.[21]

About noon on September 10 the distant thunder of guns was heard in Amherstburg, and spectators gathered at accessible points on the shoreline to gaze southeast across the lake toward the Bass Islands, some thirty miles away, where thick columns of powder smoke obscured a desperate encounter between the rival squadrons. More than three hours later the guns fell silent, but none at that distance could determine the outcome. Lieutenant Colonel Warburton, the second-in-command of the Right Division, watched the engagement from an eminence roughly fifteen miles below Amherstburg and agreed with a number of other observers that the British squadron appeared to have been victorious. But the wind that blew fair for Amherstburg on the tenth and eleventh brought no word from Barclay, and on the eleventh vessels were detected working down the lake under enemy flags. A member of the Indian Department, reconnoitering in a canoe, confirmed the worst fears: the British had lost the battle of Lake Erie.[22]

When the decisive battle on the lake was fought, the war was already fifteen months old. Declared in Washington on June 18, 1812, it had long been brewing. The outbreak of an earlier and greater conflict in Europe led to France opening her trade to neutrals in 1793 and providing the expanding American marine with new outlets for commerce. In attempting to exploit it, American merchants ran afoul of Britain, which was locked in combat with revolutionary France and wielding her naval supremacy to cripple French trade. After the short-lived peace of Amiens was ruptured in 1803, the economic warfare between the two principal belligerents intensified. Bonaparte tried to close Europe to shipping from British ports and declared vessels operating according to the regulations of the British Admiralty liable to seizure. Britain, on her part, placed hostile coasts under a close blockade and ordered that ships trading with France must sail through British ports and under British license. American merchantmen were caught in the middle; either they abandoned their European trade or forfeited the protection of one of the two combatants.[23]

Among minor aggravations was the Admiralty's insistence on Britain's right to stop neutral vessels in search of contraband and British deserters. In 1807, *H.M.S. Leopard* fired upon the American *Chesapeake*, killing three of her men, after the captain had refused to permit the British to take off suspected runaways. Such incidents whipped up a clamor in the United States for the vindication of national honor. Eventually the Americans replied with a number of economic measures of their own: a law in 1806 curtailing the importation of certain British goods; an embargo act the following year that forbade American ships to sail to foreign ports, thus depriving Europe of materials and markets; a nonintercourse act of 1809 that restored American commerce to all except Britain and France; Macon's Bill Number 2 of 1810, which reestablished trade with the belligerent powers but offered to reimpose the nonimportation act against either one, depending upon which was prepared to lift its restrictions upon American shipping; and in 1811 a renewal of the nonimportation law against Britain when France appeared to relax her strictures. These measures, which were much to the commerical disadvantage of the United States, failed. Other irritants, among them a view that the British in Canada were encouraging Indian resistance to American settlement of the Northwest, may have fed the rising war fever produced by maritime grievances and commercial restrictions. But the Admiralty's Orders-in-Council remained at the core of the difficulties. Ironically, they also antagonized British manufacturers, hungry for raw materials from America and were revoked by the government on June 23, 1812, after the declaration of war by the United States but before news of it had reached Britain.

Britain was most vulnerable in Canada. Involved in the war with France, she had few resources to spare for the defense of her North American possessions. The white population of the United States was then about six million, twelve times that of Canada, and before the end of April, 1812, the American government had authorized the raising of 36,000 regulars, 50,000 volunteers on a year's service, and 100,000 federal militia to serve for up to six months. Nearly 700,000 men were enrolled in the state militias. By contrast, Sir George Prevost could count upon only 8,125 regulars and an estimated 71,000 militia to defend a front almost two thousand miles long, from Halifax, Nova Scotia, to Fort Saint Joseph on Lake Huron. The greater part of his men, most of the regulars and about 60,000 of the militia, were stationed in Lower Canada. At the terminus of the tenuous supply line from Quebec lay Upper Canada, remote, in areas almost isolated, its security dependent upon a friendship that had been cultivated with the disaffected Indian tribes of the Northwest.[24]

For many of the Indians the war was more than an exercise in misunderstanding, commercial rights, and national pride. These warriors were taking up the tomahawk in defense of their lands, their cultural identity, perhaps even of their survival. South of the Great Lakes tribal hunting grounds had been under perennial pressure from settlers, land speculators, and empire builders, and the governor of Indiana Territory, William Henry Harrison, had recently exceeded all caution by extinguishing Indian title to more than a hundred million acres between 1802 and 1809.[25] Such cessions struck further blows at a native economy already harnessed to the vagaries of white markets by the fur trade. Encouraged by the availability of trade goods and the lure of improved material standards of living, the Indians had abandoned and forgotten traditional skills and crafts and had overexploited the fur-bearing animals and intensified intertribal squabbling over hunting territories. Relinquishing land not only reduced the range over which the Indians could hunt but preceded the advance of the farming frontier, which drove away the game animals. The collapse of the land-extensive aboriginal hunting economy augured well for the white settlement of the Northwest, and the United States was willing to preside over it. A "civilization" program, promoted alike by Indian agents and missionaries, was attempting to transform the tribesmen into farmers so that their surplus lands could be released. Dispossession, a crumbling economy, social change, the loss of the fulfillment and freedom of the hunting life, the schism between nativists and "progressives," all were forces creating tension in the Indian country before the War of 1812. This was an issue of survival for some of the native communities, ravaged by disease and drunkenness and debauched to the brink of extinction. In little more than a century, for example, the Illinois Tribe was transmuted from one of the most populous of Indian nations into a diminutive band of paupers.[26]

The most explosive reaction to the Indian problem in the years preceding the War of 1812 was the growth of a resistance movement led by the Shawnee brothers, Tecumseh and Tenskwatawa, and the Wyandot chief, Roundhead. While Tecumseh preached the need for intertribal unity, his brother spearheaded a revivalist cult that revitalized Indian culture and values and condemned debasing influences from the whites. William Henry Harrison was alarmed at the growing power of Tecumseh and Tenskwatawa, and organized an expedition to their village on the Tippecanoe, Indiana Territory, but an indecisive battle in November, 1811 failed to crush Indian militance.[27] It was this group of embittered tribesmen that provided the nucleus of Britain's Indian alliance. In the summer of 1812 the outbreak of war found Tecumseh, Roundhead, Main Poc, and their followers at Fort Malden to facilitate the earlier British victories, successes which in their turn portended a shift in the balance of power in the West that encouraged additional warriors to rise on behalf of the Redcoats. Other Indians, especially those recruited from the Mississippi region, rallied to the British for plunder and scalps. Not a few, their villages destroyed by American armies rooting out enemy sources of supplies and shelter, found the British commissariat an immediate means of repairing their broken livelihoods.[28] By July, 1813, Tecumseh and the British agents Matthew Elliott and Robert Dickson had been able to muster nearly four thousand braves for an invasion of the American Northwest—Sac, Fox, Kickapoo, Win-

Tenskwatawa, The Shawnee Prophet, younger brother of Tecumseh and leader of the religious revitalization cult among the Indians before the War of 1812. In 1814 he succeeded Tecumseh as the principal chief of the confederated Indians, a part for which he displayed no talent. This is a copy by Charles Bird King of a portrait made about 1824 by J. O. Lewis. The original, considered by Lewis Cass to be a "striking likeness," has disappeared. *Courtesy Thomas Gilcrease Institute of American History and Art, Tulsa, Oklahoma.*

nebago, Menominee, Sioux, Ojibwa, Wyandot, Shawnee, Delaware, Ottawa, Miami, and Potawatomi.

Upper Canada was to have need of the Indians in the first months of the war. President James Madison rightly realized that could the United States but concentrate upon capturing Montreal and severing the communication line along the Saint Lawrence, the British would be compelled to relinquish their territory above that river and Upper Canada would fall. But his forces were not yet up to full strength in the summer of 1812, and the New England militia, upon whom an ambitious strike at Montreal must depend, were among the least reliable of the American soldiers; indeed, the war was to awaken fears for New England's loyalty to the Union. Furthermore, westerners were spoiling for an invasion of Upper Canada, a task that appeared both easy and rewarding. The capture of the Canadian West would enhance the glory of American arms and perhaps also the president's reelection prospects later in the year, and it would extinguish British interference with the Indians. Whatever the thinking in Washington might have been, the first battles were certainly fought along the borders of Upper Canada.

The American offensive of 1812 was, however, ill conceived and badly managed and it grandly misfired. A precarious control of Lakes Erie and Ontario by the British provincial marine enabled Prevost and the commander in Upper Canada, Major General Isaac Brock, to consolidate their slender resources upon the narrow frontiers of Detroit and Niagara, and along the Saint Lawrence. Aided by the Indians, Brock succesfully fended off an invasion across the Detroit and miraculously induced Brigadier General William Hull, the American commander, to surrender his army at Detroit in August. About two months later the United States suffered another serious defeat when an attack on the Niagara front was repelled at Queenston with considerable loss to the invaders in killed and captured. A third assault, directed against the Saint Lawrence, dissipated before it even reached Canada.

Britain's successes in 1812 placed renewed emphasis upon the western theater in the following year, for the Americans were determined to expunge the national humiliation of Detroit and

remove the threat of British-Indian incursions from the Northwest. Brigadier General William Henry Harrison was named
commander in chief of a new army to consist of ten thousand men
in all, regulars, rangers, and militia. "Old Tippecanoe" envisaged
an early winter campaign, but an advance force of a thousand men
was destroyed by the British-Indian army at Frenchtown in January, 1813 and the invasion was postponed. In the spring it was the
British and the Indians who mounted an offensive. They besieged
Harrison and his soldiers at Fort Meigs, on the Maumee River, and
cut to pieces an American relief force, but were unable to make
further progress and retired upon Detroit and Fort Malden.

One consequence of the imperative in the West was that America's war effort of 1813 remained hamstrung by a faulty strategy
geared toward dividing resources among several fronts, rather than
concentrating them for a thrust into Canada's vitals. Nevertheless,
some lessons had been taken to heart, among them the realization
that unless the United States exercised naval control of the lakes the
conquest of Upper Canada would be expensive and bloody. Gradually the stage was prepared for the Battle of Lake Erie. Stimulated
by the capitulation of Hull's army in 1812, the Americans began to
assemble squadrons for service on the lakes, and before the year ran
out ships were being constructed for Lake Erie at Presque Isle (Erie)
and for Lake Ontario at Sackets Harbor. When Oliver Hazard
Perry, master commandant, arrived to supervise the Lake Erie
operation the following March he found two brigs, a schooner, and
three gunboats already laid down.[29]

Despite Britain's penchant for naval warfare, the Americans
possessed the local advantages in this race for supremacy on Lake
Erie. Resources were relatively close at hand: the American base on
Lake Ontario, Sackets Harbor, drew upon the New York region,
while Erie possessed reasonable communications with Philadelphia
through Pittsburgh, as well as with Lake Ontario. The United
States also showed greater munificence in manning their squadrons. Perry brought one hundred men with him in March and
received substantial reinforcements shortly before the battle with
Barclay in September.[30] By comparison, the British effort appears
to have been almost dilatory, hampered by a lack of foresight,

difficult communications, inadequate resources, and a number of misfortunes in war. In 1812, Sir George Prevost, to whom the provincial marine was responsible through the army quarter-master general's department, seems to have recognized the necess-ity of reinforcing his small squadron on Lake Erie, but in-comprehensibly ordered only one schooner to be built at Amherst-burg. He did, however, request that the Admiralty assume responsibility for the lakes service and that it dispatch experienced seamen and a post captain to Upper Canada to man the vessels.[31] Whitehall responded in March, directing the Admiralty to shoul-der part of the burden but permitting the army to retain the duty of providing basic supplies. Admiral Sir John Borlase Warren, com-mander in chief of the American station, received instructions to assist the squadrons on the lakes, and Sir James Yeo, a naval officer, was appointed to accompany reinforcements of seamen for Canada.

Warren's immediate reaction was to order Lieutenant Barclay to Lake Ontario and stores to Quebec, ready for shipping up the Saint Lawrence as soon as the ice cleared.[32] Yeo found Barclay at Kings-ton when he arrived from England with 486 men in May. Taking command on Lake Ontario, he sent Barclay with a surgeon and twenty-three men to Amherstburg to supervise the force on Lake Erie. The new acting commodore found his command in a depress-ing condition. A brig, the *Detroit*, was building, and a number of small vessels—the *Queen Charlotte*, the *General Hunter*, the *Chippa-wa*, the *Eliza*, the *Colonel Myers*, and three transports—were already in commission, but there was a deficiency of ordnance, stores, and seamen. Barclay appealed to Yeo for help and became openly critical of his superior's indifference to the plight of the Lake Erie squadron when his call was unanswered.[33] Nevertheless, there was logic in assigning priority to Lake Ontario since the fall of the British army's Centre Division, which held Niagara, would have severed Amherstburg's communications with Quebec and rendered it untenable in any case.

Procter and Barclay began to bombard their superiors with letters that betrayed an increasing air of desperation. The latter considered that his best course was to attack Presque Isle to destroy the American squadron in embryo, but the lack of men and stores and the inability of the Right Division to spare soldiers aborted the expedition. On his part, Procter pleaded for seamen, regulars, provisions, Indian goods, and specie. Writing to Prevost, he said, "I entreat your Excellency to send me the means of continuing the contest. I do not expect the least assistance from the Centre Division. . . ."[34] Prevost relayed the requests to Warren: "a less re-enforcement than two hundred seamen would be of little avail, and with it I should feel confident in the means of successfully opposing the American flotilla on both lakes."[35]

Several other developments were concerning Procter in the summer of 1813. The most important was the deteriorating situation in the center. There, neither side could establish a clear supremacy on Lake Ontario, and both used their squadrons to attack enemy positions. The British raided Sackets Harbor, the American naval base, but York, on the northern shore, was ravaged in return, twice in four months. Worse, the Centre Division was driven from the forts on the Niagara frontier and retreated to Burlington at the head of the lake, where it grimly maintained itself against further attacks. In such circumstances the reluctance of Yeo, Major General Francis de Rottenburg, lieutenant governor of Upper Canada, and Brevet Brigadier General John Vincent of the Centre Division to release valuable resources for Lake Erie is understandable.

Procter was directly threatened, therefore, by the forces Perry and Harrison were mobilizing against him, and threatened indirectly by the possible overthrow of the Centre Division and the Right Division's communications capacity with the Saint Lawrence. He was also worried about the fidelity of his Indian allies, who alone gave him the strength to oppose an American army. Several hundred warriors, the immediate followers of Tecumseh and Roundhead, would probably remain firm, even in adversity, but there were recurrent doubts about the bulk of the Indians, especially if the tide of war turned against the Crown. The means to humor the tribesmen were unfortunately diminishing. Procter lacked specie, but some of the chiefs had apparently been used to receiving a stipend of ten to twenty dollars a month.[36] Provisions and arms were also in short supply. In June, Procter admitted that the Indians "are not half fed, and would leave us if they were not warm in the cause."[37] By September such shortages, exacerbated by the wastefulness of the natives, had become critical.[38] Nor could Procter call upon the presents the British periodically distributed to mollify the Indians, for although Prevost commanded the purchase of two hundred guns in Montreal that July, the annual shipment of Indian gifts from England did not arrive in Quebec until the end of August, and more than a month later they had still not reached the head of Lake Ontario.[39] To inspire Indian confidence Procter pressed for the second battalion of the Forty-first to be sent forward as soon as possible, and in July employed his allies in an unsuccessful expedition to the Miami which failed to enhance British prestige.

A symptom of these difficulties were the defections noticed among the natives from about June 16. Before August was out nearly all of the Indians recruited by Robert Dickson from the upper lakes and the Mississippi, including the Sioux and the Menominee, had left the Detroit for home, and Dickson himself— the man the Indians called "the Red Head" because of his auburn hair—had been ordered to the British post of Michillimackinac to help provision them. Elliott was not displeased to see the backs of these warriors, accusing them of having "nearly ruined the country by killing the cattle & robing the inhabitants," but their departure reduced Tecumseh's army of about four thousand braves to about two thousand.[40]

Amid all his distractions, Procter grasped the first priority. Everything, the maintenance of supplies, the loyalty of many of the Indians, and British control of the Detroit frontier itself depended upon Barclay's preservation of naval superiority on Lake Erie. Yet the plan to forestall Perry's ship-building program by raiding Presque Isle foundered for want of men, ordnance, and stores and the failure of de Rottenburg and the Centre Division to cooperate, and Barclay remained starved of materials and professional seamen.[41] At the end of August only an acting captain with his servant had arrived to reinforce the twenty-four professional sailors Barclay had first brought with him to Amherstburg, and when the *Detroit* was launched as flagship of the squadron there were few guns or stores "and not a man to put on her."[42] Procter was compelled to place soldiers in the ships and to strip Fort Malden of part of its battery.[43]

The British were reaping the rewards of complacency and suffering from the difficult communications between England and North America and between Quebec and Upper Canada. There had been insufficient provisioning before the winter of 1812–1813, and when the ice freed the Saint Lawrence in May new problems beset the movement of supplies to the lakes. The capture of Fort George by the Americans in May prevented Britain shipping provisions from Lake Ontario to Lake Erie by the Niagara River, and a difficult route had to be developed as an alternative, from the head of Lake Ontario to Long Point by land or by way of the Grand River. For Procter there was the additional complication that the Centre Division was in a position to intercept supplies intended for the Right Division, a temptation that de Rottenburg, himself in a tight corner, presumably found hard to resist. Lamenting his isolation on the western flank, Procter told Prevost's adjutant-general that "being situated at the extremity of a long line, I do not feel the full effects of His Excellency's consideration for me; the aid intended never reaches me undiminished from some circumstance or another."[44] Nor was he exaggerating. When the Americans raided York in April, for example, valuable ordnance, naval stores, and ammunition awaiting shipment to Amherstburg were captured.[45]

Prevost no less than Procter spent his patience upon the problem. He did what he could. Most of the Forty-first Regiment of Foot was pushed forward from the head of Lake Ontario to Malden, and specie, clothing, and some supplies were dispatched. Unfortunately, the guns and naval stores lost at York could not be readily replaced, and when twelve 24-pound carronades were eventually ordered up to Fort Malden in August to replace the battery used to arm the *Detroit* it was too late.[46] The efforts of the commander of the forces to summon trained seamen for Barclay were also futile, except in the instance of a few Yeo was instructed to send from Lake Ontario. His request of June 24 to Warren for two hundred or more sailors from the North American fleet took nearly two months to find the admiral in the Chesapeake on August 21. In response, first the crew of the *Indian* sloop and then 110 volunteers from the *Marlborough*, a total of 220 men, were directed to Quebec. Upon receiving further representations from Sir George, Warren dispatched two battalions of marines to Canada. None of these veterans served Barclay, for the first reinforcements, the complement of the *Indian*, did not reach Quebec until October 1 and another ten days failed to produce more.[47] By then the battle of Lake Erie had been fought and lost. Prevost had also appealed to the colonial secretary, Henry, Earl Bathurst, for seamen on July 20, with little more success. Although three hundred sailors were sent from England in August, it was November before the first consignment arrived in the Saint Lawrence. In the meantime, however, fifty-three sailors in the troopship *Dover*, apparently also from Europe, independently reached Canada, anchoring in Montreal on August 22 before proceeding upriver. Yeo planned to enlist them for service on Lake Ontario, but promised to release the same number of his existing complement for Barclay as soon as the reinforcements arrived. Again, the recruits were too late, for September 6 saw them still short of Kingston.[48] The only forces to reach Amherstburg before Barclay made his fated cruise were those Prevost ordered the Centre Division to provide from Yeo's squadron. One group of sailors, forty-one in number, left Burlington early in August and joined Barclay on September 5, and an additional fifty seamen with their petty officers were released on August 29. The last were too late to participate in the battle, and it is doubtful if Barclay and Procter even learned that they were on their way before the Lake Erie squadron sailed on September 9.[49]

Enmeshed in these difficulties, the British suddenly lost their grip on Lake Erie. Barclay relaxed his desultory blockade of Presque Isle in July, and Perry was able to bring his vessels over the bar and assemble his warships and transports among the Bass Islands. Within a month he was cruising on the lake, appearing off Hartley's Point three miles below Amherstburg, on August 24, and blockading the Canadian port before quitting the station on the twenty-sixth. Times had changed. Now the British were on the defensive and frantic for their communications with Long Point.[50]

Sir George Prevost, captain general and governor in chief of Canada during the War of 1812, by S. W. Reynolds. *Courtesy Public Archives of Canada* (C–19123).

Lieutenant Robert Heriot Barclay, acting commodore on Lake Erie, whose defeat on September 10, 1813 precipitated the British retreat from the Detroit frontier. From a photograph of a portrait showing Barclay in 1809, once in the possession of the family. *Courtesy John Ross Robertson Collection, Metropolitan Toronto Library* (T30961).

John Richardson, a volunteer with the British Right Division on its historic retreat of 1813, as he appeared in later life. This portrait is the only remaining authentic likeness of any British soldier who fought at Moravian-town. *Courtesy Public Archives of Canada* (C–31606).

"Provisions and stores of every description" were needed at Amherstburg and Fort Malden, Barclay reported to Yeo, for "there was not a days flour in store, and the crews of the squadron . . . were on half allowance of many things, and when that was done there was no more. . . ."[51] Presumably Procter and Barclay knew that cattle, flour, shoes, and other provisions were on their way to Amherstburg by way of the River Thames, but the roads were difficult and slow and Perry had only to pass up the Detroit River into Lake Saint Clair to threaten these supplies at the mouth of the Thames. Bulkier items, as well as the only convenient access to victuals, depended upon the more vulnerable route by Lake Erie to Long Point, upon which Amherstburg was then primarily subsisting. The chances were that even if the collapse of food supplies had not been imminent, the British squadron would have had to fight for their much-needed naval ordnance and stores. These commodities had at last arrived at Burlington, and Lieutenant Colonel John Harvey wrote Procter on August 28 that they would be sent to Long Point as soon as it was learned that Barclay was coming for them. Probably the commodore was not in possession of this information when he determined to "risk everything rather than abandon my post without a struggle."[52]

Procter's only consolation was that Indian confidence in the British remained resolute, for the time being, despite the unsettling machinations of the American commander, Major General William Henry Harrison. The United States had enlisted about four hundred friendly Delaware, Shawnee, Wyandot, Seneca, and Mingo Indians for service, and Harrison suggested that a deputation from them might be able to sow disaffection among their British brethren. The influential Wyandot were selected for the mission. At the same time Perry was sent to demonstrate off Amherstburg to undermine enemy morale.[53] Both of these ploys were substantially unsuccessful.

On August 22 the pro-American emissaries, seven Wyandots and a Seneca, put their views to a general council of the British Indians at Brownstown, in the presence of Matthew Elliott, captains Thomas McKee and Billy Caldwell of the Indian Department, and Captain Peter Chambers of the Forty-first.[54] Dwelling upon the preparations of the United States to attack the British by land and sea, the envoys solemnly beseeched the tribesmen to withdraw from the contest for the sake of their families:

We salute our Father and our Brethren and return thanks to the Great Spirit who has been pleased to allow us to meet here at this council. General Harrison desires us to address the chiefs that having taken into consideration the long time the different nations have been separate has sent this deputation to speak with their friends.

He has selected seven Hurons and one Seneka to tell (as he always intended to do) their brethren who is alongside of their British Father that he is now ready and that his fleet are also prepared at Sandusky Bay. There are from eleven large ships ready. He wishes the chiefs to take pity on their women and children and seriously consider their situation and listen to what has been said. He wishes those chiefs who will listen to his words to come to talk with him and those who wish to stand before him like men, he will meet them.

Those nations who have any wish to treat may come forward seein[g] my force come and return unmolested. Your English Father deceives his children very much.   He never informs them of the battles that have been fought below. [He] has made three attempts on our forts but has not succeeded. This is the time if any chief of the tribes will step forward and take him by the hand.[55]

White wampum was offered by the delegates in the council as a symbol of goodwill, but none cared to take it. On the following day Roundhead, in his last public service, returned the answer of the British allied Indians. Three versions of it survive. According to the contemporary minutes made by Elliott, the Wyandot chief was brief and blunt. "We are happy to learn your Father [Harrison] is coming out of his hole as he has been like a ground hog under the ground and will save us much trouble in walking to meet him. We recommend you to remain at home and take no part in the war." A year later Billy Caldwell remembered that "the answer of our Indians was that they would never take the Americans by the hand as long as their Father's [the king's] vessels swam on the lake."[56] The fullest, if least reliable, version was received after the war by Lewis Cass, governor of Michigan Territory, from a family of mixed-blood Wyandots who had been present at the council.

Brothers, the Wyandots from the Americans, we have heard your talk, and will not listen to it. We will not forsake the standard of our British Father, nor lay down the hatchet we have raised. I speak the sentiments of all now present, and I charge you, that you faithfully deliver our talk to the American commander, and tell him it is our wish he would send more men against us, for all that has passed between us, I do not call fighting. We are not satisfied with the number of men he sends to contend against us. We want to fight in good earnest.[57]

There can be no doubt that Roundhead was his truculent self, and that the British were pleased by the result. "Nothing," reported Chambers, "could be more noble than the behaviour of our Indians."[58] Elliott was also at pains to ensure that the council was not without British counterpropaganda. The Americans, he said, were the deceivers, for far from enjoying success in the war, they had just lost four large vessels and suffered a reverse on Lake Champlain. To salvage something from their embassy, the American messengers conferred privately with some of the British Wyandots after the council had dispersed and were informed by Walk-in-the-Water (Mayar or Mey-ye-ra) that while he dared not accept the white wampum openly, he would defect to Harrison when the Americans advanced. In his dispatch, Harrison consoled himself in the opinion that Walk-in-the-Water was "the principal chief of the British Wyandots." In fact he was the leader of a single group of Wyandots who resided at Brownstown and had been impressed into British service in 1812, remaining uneasily in harness ever since. Roundhead's militant faction of the tribe, which evidently dwelt on the Aux Canard River near Fort Malden, appear to have had no private intercourse with the American delegation.[59]

If the Wyandot mission had little success, Perry's appearance off Amherstburg with nine sail on August 24 or August 25 had even less. The peace embassy, which included the Wyandot leaders Skootash and Between-the-Logs, was still at its post when the naval display occurred and carried tidings of its effect back to Harrison and to their own chief, the Crane (Tarhe). Anthony Shane, a half-blood then serving with Harrison's Indians, recalled their report. When Tecumseh saw Perry's ships, he said, he made

strong representations to the British, urging them to leave port
and give battle.[60] A similar story has been given by Harrison's
biographer, Moses Dawson, who may have received the information from the general himself. The emissaries were on Bois Blanc
Island

in conversation with Tecumseh when the American fleet came in sight.
Tecumseh appeared much rejoiced at their appearance, and assured the
American Wyandots that the British fleet would soon destroy them. The
many thousand Indians who were on the island (Bois Blanc) hastened to
the shore to witness the conflict; but no motion or preparation was visible
in the harbour of Malden. Tecumseh launched his canoe, apparently
much mortified, and hastily paddled over to the British fortress. Upon his
return he made known to the Indians that the big canoes of their great
father were not yet ready, but that the destruction of the Americans must
be delayed for a few days.[61]

However much truth these reminiscences contain, the Indians
were sufficiently unimpressed by Perry's demonstration to permit
Procter a day or so later to write Prevost that: "I have reason to
believe that the Indians will heartily oppose the enemy; and that
we stand rather high in their opinion, tho' they observe the
enemy's fleet on the lake, possessing the command of it."[62] He was
right. Although most of the warriors from the Far West were now
turning homeward, some like the Sac head chief Mitass ("a splen-
did man" according to Ensign Cochran) remained to support the
Indians recruited from the state of Ohio and from Indiana and
Michigan territories. They were bristling for a fight, eagerly
awaiting another American thrust at Fort Malden. Elliott did not
doubt that they would give Harrison "a warm reception" or that
"the issue will prove favourable to us." The only justification for an
American belief that the British and their allies were in confusion
and discord lay in a complaint of the latter that the Redcoats, with
their main strength at Sandwich, were too far from Amherstburg
to reinforce the Indians there in the event of an attack: "they say the
business must be over before he [Procter] would arrive to render any
assistance."[63]

The temper of the Indians was not an important consideration in
promoting Barclay's decision to engage Perry's squadron. With

supplies almost exhausted, he determined to clear his communications with Long Point and sailed at three o'clock on the
afternoon of September 9 with six vessels. In the number of ships
and guns, and in the weight of metal of both carronades and long
guns, Barclay was inferior to his adversaries, but during a hard-
fought battle the following day his men gave a good account of
themselves; forty-three were killed and ninety-two (including
Barclay) were wounded aboard the British squadron before it
surrendered. Nevertheless, the palm went to the equally gallant
Perry. Jubilantly he announced to Harrison, who waited with an
army generally composed of Kentucky militia, that his path to
Canada was finally open.[64] In Baltimore, *The Weekly Register*
reported: "All was gratitude to the Supreme Disposer of events for
a victory that humanity may rejoice at, as relieving a wide and
much exposed frontier from the scalping knife, and leading directly to peace, at least in that quarter. We can hardly attribute too
great importance to this victory."[65]

3

THE PAINFUL DECISION: SEPTEMBER, 1813

I . . . hope I shall be fairly judged . . . .

HISTORY has little clemency for those without the advantage of hindsight, and it seldom acknowledges that decisions that may have been fully appropriate to ascertained circumstances can, by misadventure, produce the most unfortunate of consequences. Many who have freely traduced Major General Henry Procter for the retreat that followed Barclay's defeat have accorded but scant attention to the situation in which the Right Division found itself in September, 1813. Some have unfavorably contrasted Procter with his predecessor, Isaac Brock, quite forgetting that Brock possessed what Procter did not, naval superiority on Lake Erie. Some have condemned Procter for retreating and others for not retreating quickly enough. A few have quoted with approval a passage from the reminiscences of the American secretary of war, John Armstrong, which vilifies the British commander for failing to hold Fort Malden but has few suggestions explaining how he could have summoned the resources to do so:

Procter's situation at Malden . . . made necessary on his part, a prompt retreat to Vincent [of the Centre Division], unencumbered with baggage; or, a vigorous defence of the post committed to his custody. By adopting the former, he would have saved seven hundred veteran soldiers and a train of artillery, for the future service of his sovereign; by adopting the latter, he would have retained the whole of his Indian allies . . . ; given time for the militia of the interior to come to his aid; had the full

39

advantage of his fortress and its munitions—and a chance, at least, of eventual success, with a certainty of keeping inviolate his own self-respect, and the confidence of his followers. Taking a middle course between these extremes he lost the advantages that would have resulted from either.[1]

This tidy analysis leaves unprobed the most pressing aspect of the strategical problem confronting Procter after the battle of Lake Erie, which was the difficulty in maintaining an advanced position at Fort Malden when cut off from supplies. By defeating Barclay, Perry had secured at a stroke the mobility to sever Procter's communications with the head of Lake Ontario. The supply line by Lake Erie from Fort Malden to Long Point was open to total disruption by the American squadron, in the event of which Procter would have been dependent upon the long and difficult route along the River Thames. Unfortunately, by passing up the Detroit strait into Lake Saint Clair and the mouth of the Thames, Perry's vessels could sever even this artery. Furthermore, they might sail eastward along the northern shore of Lake Erie and intercept supplies on the Thames at a number of other points. A road, free of obstacles, ran from Port Talbot on the lakeside to Delaware on the Thames, while another, which would have required cutting, led from Pointe Aux Pins to the Thames. By either the Americans could have sliced communications along the river and isolated a British-Indian force at Fort Malden or on the lower Thames.[2] Harrison and Perry were not ignorant of these roads. In October the secretary of war advised Harrison to make use of the route from Pointe Aux Pins to intercept a British retreat, and by that time the general had already been alerted to it at Fort Malden by Lewis Bond, formerly a prisoner of war of the British. When the American army eventually occupied Sandwich, Harrison and his officers also considered cutting off the enemy's escape by means of the road from Port Talbot, but they abandoned the idea because of the inadequate water transport at their disposal and the uncertainty of the navigation of Lake Erie in that season of the year.[3]

In these circumstances an energetic naval campaign alone could have made Amherstburg and Fort Malden untenable by a large military force. The British-Indian army consisted of nearly a thousand British, with some of their families, and more than ten thousand Indians, and it consumed about fourteen head of cattle and as much as seven thousand pounds of flour a day. Victualing such a multitude had become a nightmare for the deputy assistant commissary to the British army, Robert Gilmore, and swallowed most of his time ("I find more expected of me than all my abilities and zeal can perform . . ."). By September 5 the provisions in the storehouse had been reduced to a mere three hundred bushels of corn and forty barrels of flour. Of livestock there was rather more, sufficient perhaps to have lasted the army about two to three months, but it could not readily have been replenished.[4] Such demands were not capable of being satisfied by the resources of the neighboring countryside alone. The American side of the Detroit was destitute of provisions, and later in the year the United States lost soldiers almost daily trying to garrison it.[5]

Across the river the western district of Canada was scarcely better. It boasted good soil; it produced corn, wheat, oats, peas, and grass and it sustained animals, but the farms had been ill attended in 1812 and 1813, when men had been enlisted with the militia, and the military and naval establishment had already taxed them hard. In 1813 the wheat harvest had been reaped in August, but little of it could be converted into flour; the streams had recently been too low for the mills, while the dams of the two principal mills, owned by John McGregor and Christopher Arnold on the Thames, had been damaged earlier in the year by excessive rain. The corn harvest was not gathered before the beginning of October, and beef and pork were in short supply. The British-Indian army was therefore dependent upon what it could bring from outside. There, true, some supplies were still to be had. Colonel Thomas Talbot of the Canadian militia believed that he could have victualed the Right Division from Port Talbot until the local mills could produce enough flour, and he shipped some provisions to Muncey Town on the Thames. During the last days of September, Gilmore also procured some flour from Port Talbot, but these were the very sources vulnerable to American naval attack.[6]

This was a situation that demanded stringent measures. Barclay

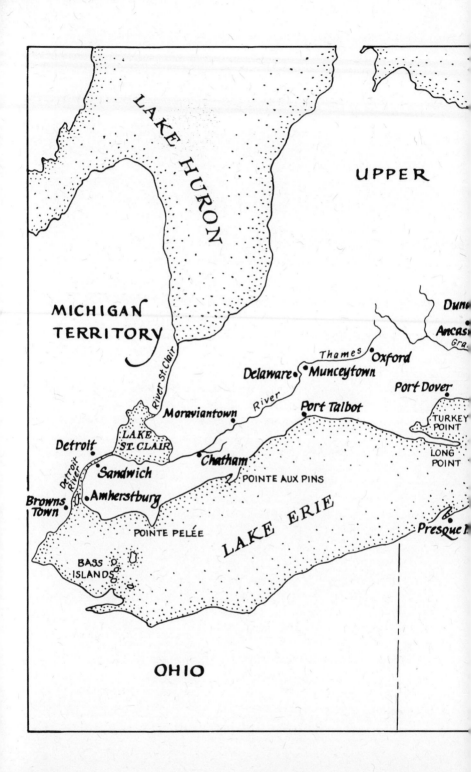

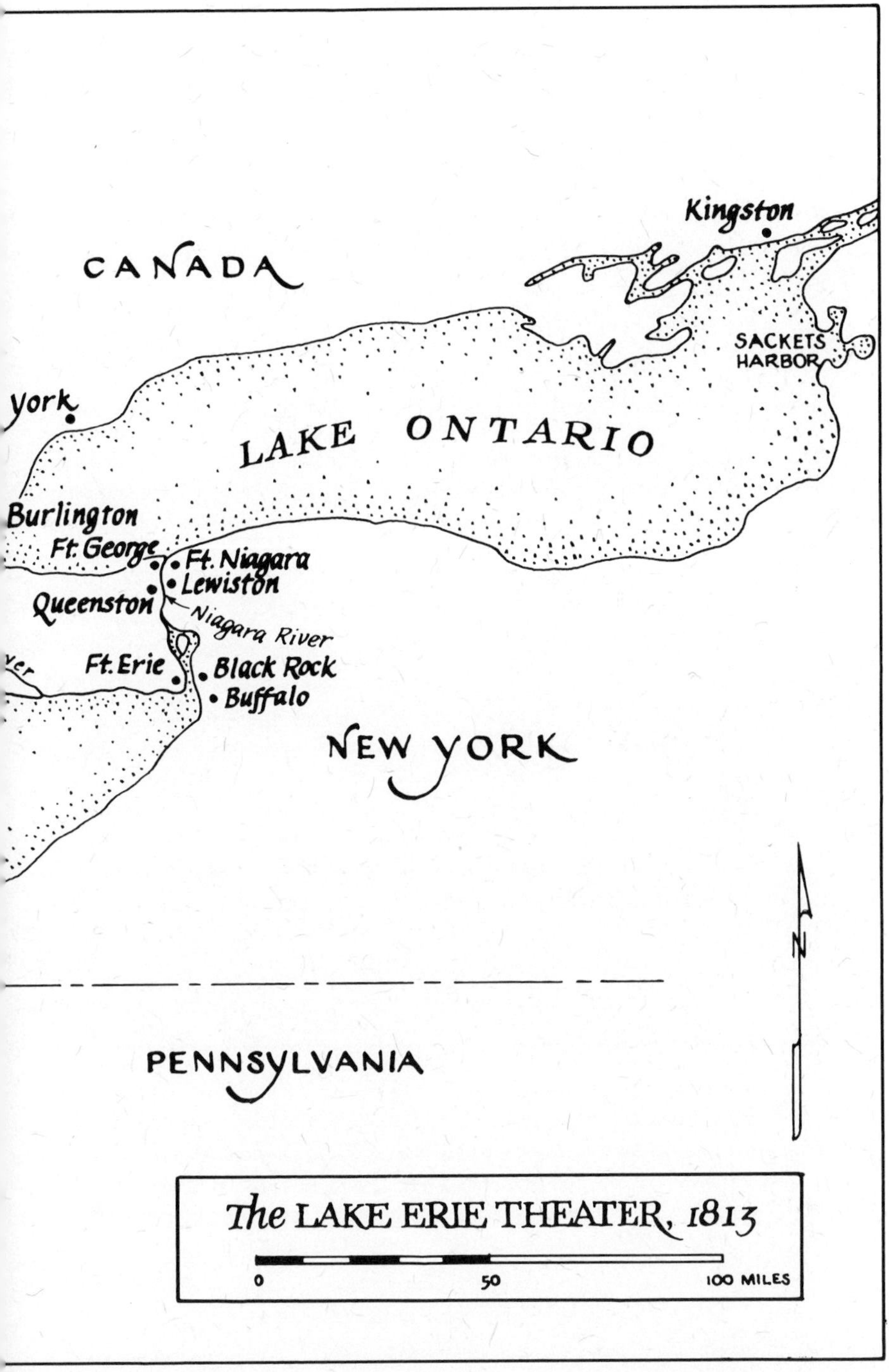

CANADA

Kingston

SACKETS
HARBOR

York

LAKE ONTARIO

Burlington
Ft. George
Ft. Niagara
Lewiston
Queenston
Niagara River
Ft. Erie
Black Rock
Buffalo

NEW YORK

N

PENNSYLVANIA

The LAKE ERIE THEATER, 1813

0   50   100 MILES

was driven to try his strength with Perry on September 10, and three days later Procter placed the western district of Upper Canada under martial law to facilitate the requisition of provisions.[7] Whether Perry had the means or the inclination to paralyze Procter's supply system completely is open to doubt; the Americans made little enough of their occasional superiority on Lake Ontario. But it would have taken a foolishly courageous commander to attempt to hold Fort Malden in the face of these difficulties. Procter had to retreat. It was the only sensible decision, as some appreciated at the time. The *Montreal Gazette* explained Perry's triumph:

This misfortune, together with the distress to which the brave Gen. Proctor has been reduced for want of provisions, must oblige him to evacuate the country which . . . Brock obtained from the enemy. . . . We are afraid that we may now comfort ourselves with the reflection, that in the country above Niagara, we have lost all but "our honour," and that what men could do under existing circumstances Barclay and Proctor have effected.[8]

More than a year later, when the general's conduct was examined in a court-martial, a rigorous prosecutor condemned Procter for not abandoning Amherstburg and linking with the Centre Division at Delaware or the head of Lake Ontario immediately after learning of Barclay's defeat.[9] Something may be said for this opinion, but an immediate retreat so far up the Thames would have incurred problems of its own. The first concerned the disposition of the Indians. It was by no means clear whether they would accompany the British upon any kind of withdrawal, and since they furnished more than twice the number of fighting men fielded by the Right Division their goodwill was not a matter about which Procter could be complacent. The general fully recognized the fragility of Indian confidence in the British. Fresh in the memories of the tribesmen was the infidelity of the Redcoats in both of the previous wars. At the end of the Revolution, a conflict in which the Indians had served the Crown well, Britain had ceded tribal land south of Canada to the United States without granting their allies the dignity of a consultation. A second betrayal occurred in 1794, during the Northwestern War in which the Indians, encouraged by Britain, defended their lands north of the Ohio against the infant republic. After their final defeat at the Battle of Fallen Timbers, the warriors sought sanctuary in a British post, Fort Miamis, but found the gates closed against them. Bitter were the recollections of both events, which stamped Britain as a frail friend in times of difficulty. Procter's movements were going to be judged in this light. The Indians were fighting for their land south of the Great Lakes, and by retiring deep into Canada the Right Division would inevitably awaken fears that once again the warriors were to be left to the mercy of a renascent American army.[10]

One of the few citizens of Amherstburg in whom the natives reposed implicit regard was Colonel William Caldwell. He had fought shoulder to shoulder with them during the Revolution, ever since 1776, and shared with them some of their greatest successes, including the rout of a Kentuckian army at Blue Licks in 1782. Indian women had borne him sons. As anxiety among the tribesmen grew, Caldwell was consulted by the Indians about the British intentions. Caldwell testified:

> The Indians seemed to be very uneasy, and many of my acquaintance[s] of the Indian cheifs came and told me that the Indians would be very lazy to move down with their families to such a remote country as Canada, and that that was not agreeable to the speeches that came from their Father to them, which were that they should be supported. At that time we told them that it was owing to the loss of our fleet and the great scarcity of provisions. They said to me this is like the peace of 1783, and again alluded to 1795 [1794] and said this is the second [third] time we have been decieved by our Father.[11]

None appreciated the Indian suspicions more than General Procter ("if we are drawn off from the Thames, especially before the Indians settle thereabout, they will look on us as deserting them:—which I conceive we cannot do, in honor or policy . . .").[12] He knew that a retreat was now necessary, but was at a loss as to how the Indians could be persuaded that the British intention was not to abandon them. Further, he lacked the courage to inform them of the fate of Barclay, aware that many of the Indians, fearful of being found on the losing side or hungry for the spoils of war, were ardent in the British cause only as long as the Crown was victorious. With his peculiar facility for mishandling people, Procter shrank from facing the chiefs. His secretiveness, in fact, simply aggravated the mistrust. The Indians had seen the ships sail and heard their guns; two of their braves had even volunteered to accompany the squadron, and when they failed to return and Procter had nothing to impart about them, the warriors began to credit their allies with every kind of duplicity.[13]

Had Procter adopted from the beginning a candid and determined stance and advanced the logic of a temporary retreat, he might have carried his points with greater conviction; he would also have enjoyed the support of the more committed chiefs. Roundhead and Tecumseh considered the alliance to be the ablest instrument for furthering their cause, and both were intelligent leaders capable of appreciating the strategical problem before them if it had been explained. According to a Shawnee prisoner of the Americans, Masalemata, the death of Roundhead about this time shook the loyalty of the Miamis and the Wyandots, but the balance were in a fighting mood and Tecumseh held remarkable sway with them. Instead, the general postponed the inevitable, if unpleasant, meeting with the Indians and fed their anxiety and suspicion. Some observers believed that the resentment of the natives grew to be so great that had the Right Division attempted to fall back as far as the upper Thames or beyond, the Indians could have turned their fury upon the inhabitants of Amherstburg or even the troops themselves.[14]

There were other reasons that counseled against a precipitate retreat toward the head of Lake Ontario. It would have invited the Americans to land their army at Long Point on Lake Erie and threaten the rear of the harassed Centre Division and the stores at Burlington, a maneuver the enemy had both foreseen and considered. The only safeguard against it was the presence of the British and Indians in the West, for had Harrison moved against Long Point, leaving Procter and Tecumseh undefeated on the Detroit or the lower Thames, he would have exposed the American frontier to a counterattack.[15] Another point, made by Procter only afterwards in justification of his general conduct, emphasized the undoubted importance of restoring British naval superiority on Lake Erie. Most of the military and naval stores at Fort Malden and Amherstburg were difficult to remove because the Thames was unnavigable to any but small craft beyond a few miles above Chatham. The command of the lower Thames, at least for some time, might help to save stores that would otherwise be lost and "thereby facilitate the recovery of a naval ascendency on Lake Erie. . ."[16]

Finally, lingering in Procter's mind were fears for his professional image. The British-Indian army numbered about three thousand men, sufficient to stand against the enemy with reasonable chances of success, and Tecumseh and his Indians were spoiling for an encounter with the Long Knives. With such a force at his disposal, Procter would surely have incurred a degree of public censure if he had abandoned the western district without fighting a battle or catching a sight of his adversaries. This may have been one of the reasons why the British remained at Amherstburg until September 23 and did not leave Sandwich until Harrison's forces had actually landed on Canadian soil. Procter certainly had no doubt that his reputation was on trial. "I feel the weight of my responsibility," he said, expressing his uneasiness to Prevost. "I shall act to the best of my judgement and hope I shall be fairly judged."[17]

Once the retreat commenced, only two realistic options were open to Procter. One was to withdraw to the Centre Division at the head of Lake Ontario, in which case the prospects for action would have been slight and probably no more than the hard core of the Indian allies would have remained in consort. The alternative, which Procter chose, was to fall back to the Thames so that the most immediate threat to the British supply line, between the mouth of that river and Fort Malden, could be obviated, and then to review the possibilities of making a stand with his full force. Preparations would also have to be made for a further retreat, should the British and Indians be defeated. This strategy, not at all injudicious, emerges fairly clearly from the contemporary evidence. On September 12, Procter wrote de Rottenburg that he intended retiring to the Thames, "preparatory to any other move-

ment that may be found requisite. . . ." He had requested
provisions to be sent forward to him, and Colonel Talbot had been
instructed to repair "the road . . . thro' the Wilderness," a wood
along the upper Thames between Moraviantown and Delaware.[18]

The following day Procter conferred with some of his officers at
Sandwich. Captain Matthew Charles Dixon of the Royal Engineers
understood that Procter planned to make a stand against the
Americans at about the location of John Dolsen's farm on the lower
Thames; Lieutenant Felix Troughton of the Royal Artillery understood that works were to be erected a little more upriver, at the
forks of the Thames near Chatham.[19] Procter also addressed a letter
to Prevost explaining that he could not permit the enemy to obtain
possession of the Thames, but that he had "delayed a few hours in
the expectation of learning the views and wishes of the Indian
body. . . ."[20] On September 21 he more frankly declared his
determination "to fall back and make a stand on the Thames. . . .[21]

Although the general later complained that some of his officers
regarded the scheme to defend the lower Thames as "visionary,"
Procter's mistakes were made less in the realm of initial planning
than in his subsequent direction of a retreat that had become
necessary.[22] The most questionable facet of his thinking bore upon
the proposed site for the stand, near Dolsen's or Chatham on the
lower reaches of the river. Conceivably Moraviantown or Delaware,
farther upriver, offered more defensible positions, but would the
Indians accompany the British so far? Afraid of provoking a mass
defection of warriors, which would strip him of any chance of
overthrowing his enemy, Procter considered the lower Thames to
be the preferable scene of a battle.

Because the mail was slow Procter did not benefit from the
advice of his superiors when he decided to evacuate Fort Malden
and withdraw to the Thames. Their letters did not reach him in
time. Their appraisals of Procter's position were not dissimilar to
his own, however. On September 17, Lieutenant Colonel John
Harvey, the deputy adjutant-general, wrote Procter that de Rottenburg, who commanded the army in Upper Canada, did "not
clearly see the necessity or expediency of your immediately retiring
from your present position . . ." because Barclay's defeat "cannot

affect you so immediately as to make any precipitate retrograde movement necessary." Perry's vessels must have suffered extensive damage in the long battle of Lake Erie, and time would be required to refit them. During the respite, Procter ought to court the Indians. Harvey continued:

This interval you will employ in looking well at your situation in communication with Tecumseth, and the Indians, in ascertaining the impression which this disaster has produced on them, and in concerting with them the measures best calculated to lessen the consequences of that disaster—concentrating on making such a disposition of your remaining force as may prove to them the sincerity of the British government, in its intention not to abandon them, so long as they are true to their own interests.[23]

De Rottenburg's assumption that Tecumseh would have been treated frankly was unfortunately misplaced, but Procter's reluctance to abandon Fort Malden in haste found some support with his superior. Not until the end of the month did de Rottenburg go further, when he notified Procter, through Harvey, that the Centre Division intended taking up a position at Burlington, near the head of Lake Ontario, and that Procter might join it there if he chose.[24] While he did not order the Right Division to retreat, he confided to Prevost that "I think it is now high time he [Procter] should seriously endeavour to bring his force in connection with mine provided the Indians will permit him."[25] These letters reveal some sensitivity on the part of de Rottenburg to the difficulties of the garrison at Fort Malden, for while he plainly considered it Procter's duty to retire upon Lake Ontario, he acknowledged the existence of obstacles. Unlike Procter, he did not envisage an engagement between the American and British forces, a view that hindsight might label prudence.

This last was not the opinion of his excellency, the governor in chief. Sir George Prevost's fullest instructions were issued by the adjutant-general, Major General Edward Baynes, on September 18, before the news of the Battle of Lake Erie had reached headquarters. They were consistent with Procter's assessment, counseling withdrawal only as a last resort and the use of every opportunity to resist an enemy advance. As Baynes wrote:

The superior resources of the enemy have indeed enabled him to render our situation critical and difficult; but it still does not amount to that point as to render a retrograde movement indispensable and until that is the case it should be avoided by every possible exertion and devise. Should, however, such a measure become unfortunately unavoidable, it is His Excellency's express commands that it be not resorted to untill its necessity and the mode of carrying it into effect has been previously well weighed and considered. . . . Every position which the country affords is to be occupied and defended so that the enemy be made to pay dearly for every step he advances. All retrograde movements are to be resorted to with reluctance and they are to be as limited as the circumstances which cause them will admit and they are never to be hurried or accelerated unless warranted by circumstances of peculiar urgency.[26]

Upon learning of Barclay's disaster, Prevost admitted that Procter could not now be expected to hold Fort Malden. It might become "requisite" for him to establish a "nearer connection" with de Rottenburg.[27] But this did not entail an evacuation of the western district by the army, for Earl Bathurst was simply informed that Procter might be compelled to reduce the length of his communications with the head of Lake Ontario by retiring to the Thames.[28] Procter's letter of September 21 announcing his intention to stand on the Thames elicited Prevost's approbation on October 6:

I entirely approve of your determination . . . of your making a stand upon the Thames . . . . I recommend to you to persevere in the conduct you are observing, of conciliating the Indians by every means in your power, and you may hold out to them the assurance of receiving a liberal allowance of presents, as soon as you shall reach a position where they may be forwarded with safety—a large supply of them have arrived from England, of the very first quality, and will be sent on towards the head of the lake.[29]

Two days later Prevost apprised Bathurst that Procter would "make a stand and connect himself with the Centre Division provided the Indian warriors are faithful to their promises; otherwise he will be obliged to continue to retire towards the head of Lake Ontario. I trust he will be enabled to make the enemy pay dearly for any attempt to press upon him in his retreat to that position."[30] These documents attest to the unanimity between Procter and Prevost. A retreat was inevitable, but the district would not be surrendered without resistance; and if the Right Division was defeated it would resume its march, if necessary as far as the head of Lake Ontario. Their analysis was not implausible, and it is nothing against it that the result proved disastrous. The fault lay not in the plan itself, but in its execution, and the problems began to surface within days of the battle of Lake Erie.

Barclay's defeat had introduced circumstances that Procter should have discussed forthrightly with his officers and the Indian chiefs, resassuring the latter of his determination to support them. A suitable place for a stand on the Thames could have been strongly fortified and the full resources of the allied army concentrated behind it to maximize the prospects of victory. There were grounds for optimism in this respect. Ample time remained for the British to erect works and prepare a far stronger battery than the field guns later brought up the Thames by Harrison's army. The Indians had proven their worth in bush fighting many times, and an effort could have been made to raise the militia in force.

It was unfortunate that Procter did not handle his uncomfortable situation with more tact. On September 13 he instructed his engineer, Captain Dixon, to begin dismantling Fort Malden and removing stores, cautioning him to proceed quietly so that the Indians would not become alarmed. Lieutenant Troughton of the Royal Artillery received orders to send ordnance and stores to the forks of the Thames, where Procter intimated he desired to erect works. But neither Tecumseh nor the British second- and third-in-command, Lieutenant Colonels Warburton and Evans, were notified of the general's intentions, and the Indians had not even been told the result of the battle on the lake.[31]

Later it was claimed that Procter had called a council for the purpose of consulting the Indians and was awaiting the assembly of the chiefs, but that he desired to begin the work of evacuation in the meantime. Captain John Hall of the Canadian Fencibles, who served as brigade major and subsequently as his commander's most important apologist, testified that Procter sent him on the twelfth

"with Colonel Elliott to Tecumseth to arrange with him a council
of the Indians as soon as possible," and that the fifteenth was set as
the earliest convenient time. Gathering the Indian spokesmen
from both sides of the Detroit River took time, but until they
could be convened Procter was hardly able to confer with them
adequately.[32] If this statement had been true, it would not have
excused the general of a severe error in judgment; his awareness of
the suspicions of the Indians had not prevented him from beginning his preparations for the retreat without consulting Tecumseh
and other important chiefs, nor even his own senior officers.
Unfortunately, the truth puts Procter in a poorer light still. He set
the retreat in motion without even troubling to summon the
Indians for discussion. Elliott's contemporary dispatch clearly
states that a meeting was only arranged after the natives' suspicions
had been aroused and at the request of Tecumseh and his chiefs. It
must be concluded, therefore, that Procter was simply unwilling
to confront an unpleasant duty and allowed matters to simmer
until Tecumseh brought them to a head.

The upshot of Procter's underhanded proceedings was predictable. Upon Dixon's orders Lieutenant John Le Breton of the Royal
Newfoundland Regiment set to work dismantling Fort Malden on
September 14. "While we were at work in the course of the day,"
Le Breton recalled, "several Indians came in and appeared to
examine it in a very suspicious manner . . . ." Warburton's staff
adjutant also arrived, desiring to know by whose orders Le Breton
acted.[33] The sequel was described by Warburton himself:

> On the morning of the 14th I was informed by my staff adjutant that
> part of the facing of the fort was thrown into the ditch and that Tecumseh
> had gone off in a violent passion to Colonel Elliott. I sent for Lieutenant
> Troughton and asked him not to take away the guns until I should hear
> from General Procter. . . . I did accordingly write to Major Genl. Procter
> and received for answer that he had a perfect right to give any secret orders
> that he thought proper . . . . Colonel Elliott came to me and said that if
> some previous arrangements were not made with the Indians before a
> council took place they might cut the wampum belt and no man could
> answer for the consequences.[34]

Upon this Indian initiative, runners called in the warriors for the famous council at Amherstburg, in which Tecumseh delivered his most quoted speech to Procter.[35] It was one of two councils, the dates of both of which are uncertain. The earliest source, a dispatch by Matthew Elliott, states that they occurred on September 17 and September 19, but his dates are not free from error for he has the British subsequently retreating from Lavalle's on the twenty-third instead of the twenty-seventh.[36] In December, 1814, Warburton believed that the first council took place on the seventeenth or the eighteenth and the second about the twentieth.[37] Procter and Captain Hall maintained that they were held on the fifteenth and the eighteenth, and a member of the Indian Department appears to have concurred. It seems likely, however, that General Procter would have tried to minimize his negligence by suggesting the earliest dates possible for the conferences, and that they did in fact occur on the eighteenth and the nineteenth. It is known that it was in the first council that Tecumseh gave his celebrated address, and that the whole matter was settled in the second. Bearing this in mind, it should be noted that a copy of Tecumseh's speech found by the Americans in Procter's papers is endorsed with the date September 18, and that an American prisoner stated that he visited Fort Malden on the nineteenth, the same day that the British agreed on the principles of the evacuation of the fort with Tecumseh.[38]

The first conference was staged in the council room at Amherstburg, a large, lofty building with a vaulted roof.[39] British officers, both regular and militia, grouped themselves around the walls, while the Indians made a colorful array in the center. After hearing a British proposal to retreat, Tecumseh rose to deliver a reply that witnesses unanimously declared to have been remarkable. An early account obtained from participants reported that

nothing could be more striking than the scene which then presented itself. The rest of the assembly seemed to wait with the deepest attention for the delivery of his [Tecumseh's] answer; whilst, holding in his hands a belt of wampum, or beads, which, by their colours and arrangement, form the Indian record for past events . . . he proceeded to address the British general in a torrent of vehement and pathetic appeal . . . .[40]

John Richardson, a young volunteer in the Forty-first, confused the events of the two councils into one when he wrote his reminiscences, but he furnished a vivid portrait of Tecumseh:

Habited in a close leather dress, his athletic proportions were admirably delineated, while a large plume of white ostrich feathers, by which he was generally distinguished, overshadowing his brow, and contrasting with the darkness of his complexion and the brilliancy of his black and piercing eye, gave a singularly wild and terrific expression to his features. It was evident that he could be terrible.[41]

Flavoring his laconic but energetic and expressive tirade with indignant gestures, the Shawnee chief fulminated against his British allies:

Father! Listen to your children; you see them now all before you. The war before this our British Father gave the hatchet to his red children, when our old chiefs were alive. They are now all dead. In that war our Father was thrown on his back by the Americans, and our Father took them by the hand without our knowledge, and we are afraid our Father will do so again at this time. Summer before last, when I came forward with my red children, and was ready to take up the hatchet in favor of our British Father, we were told not to be in a hurry—that he had not yet determined to fight the Americans.

Listen! When war was declared, our Father stood up and gave us the tomahawk, and told us he was now ready to strike the Americans, that he wanted our asistance; and that he certainly would get us our lands back which the Americans had taken from us. Listen! You told us at that time to bring forward our families to this place. We did so, and you promised to take care of them, and that they should want for nothing, while the men would go to fight the enemy—that we were not to trouble ourselves with the enemy's garrisons [forts]—that we knew nothing about them, and that our Father would attend to that part of the business. You also told your red children that you would take care of your garrison here which made our hearts glad. Listen! When we last went to the Rapids, it is true we gave you little assistance. It is hard to fight people who live like ground hogs.

Father listen! Our fleet has gone out, we know they have fought; we have heard the great guns; but know nothing of what has happened to our Father with one Arm [Barclay]. Our ships have gone one way, and we are much astonished to see our Father tying up every thing and preparing to run the other, without letting his red children know what his intentions are. You always told us to remain here and take care of our lands; it made our hearts glad to hear that was your wish. Our Great Father, the King, is the head and you represent him. You always told us that you would never draw your foot off British ground; but now, Father, we see you are drawing back, and we are sorry to see our Father doing so, without seeing the enemy. We must compare our Father's conduct to a fat animal that carries its tail upon its back; but when affrighted, it drops it between its legs and runs off.[42]

When Samuel Saunders, the interpreter, gave Tecumseh's description of Procter, laughter among some of the British observers suggested a certain enjoyment of the general's discomfort. The Shawnee chief may have even employed a more colorful phrase than the official record intimated. John McCormick, who was present, recalled in 1863 that Tecumseh alluded to Procter's "tall bushy tail," a statement supported by the contemporary diary of Lewis Bond, which states that the chief contrasted Procter with "an animal with bristles and a long tail which he could curl over his back and appear big . . . ." Bond was not at the council but obtained accounts from witnesses.[43] Tecumseh thundered on:

Listen Father! The Americans have not yet defeated us by land; neither are we sure that they have done so by water; we therefore wish to remain here, and fight our enemy should they make their appearance. If they defeat us, we will then retreat with our Father. At the battle of the Rapids last war [1794] the Americans certainly defeated us; and when we retreated to our Father's fort at that place the gates were shut against us. We were afraid that it would now be the case; but instead of that we now see our British Father preparing to march out of his garrison.

Father! You have got the arms and ammunition which our Great Father sent for his red children. If you have an idea of going away, give them to us, and you may go and welcome for us. Our lives are in the hands of the Great Spirit. We are determined to defend our lands, and if it is his will, we wish to leave our bones upon them.[44]

The close of Tecumseh's animated performance, Richardson remembered, was like an electric shock to the Indian spectators, who rose to their feet with a shout of approval and menacingly brandished their tomahawks. Procter's policy of witholding information from them had reaped its reward in suspicion and inflamed tempers.[45] After enduring Tecumseh's diatribe, Procter promised a reply in another council to be held shortly. As he acknowledged later, he was searching for a means of redeeming himself with the Indians:

Colonel Elliott and the other individuals of the [Indian] department were directed in the mean time, to use their influence with Tecumseth and the other chiefs. On my arrival at Amherstburg [for the second council], I found Colonel Elliot alarmed beyond measure, having wholly failed in his endeavours to convince or persuade the chiefs. He told me to prepare myself for consequences the most unpleasant, and that on my expressing my determination to retreat, the great wampum belt, in the centre of which was the figure of a heart and at each end that of a hand would be produced in the council, and in our presence cut in two, figuratively expressing our eternal separation. I then resolved myself to state to Tecumseth, the reasons that had determined me. In the presence of Lieut. Colonels Warburton, Elliot and my own staff and several others, with the aid of a map, I so thoroughly convinced him of the expediency of the measures proposed, and of my determination not to desert the Indian body, that when the council had assembled, in the course of two hours, he had brought the greater portion of the chiefs and nations into my proposal, and effectually prevented any opposition of moment.[46]

This critical episode is more fully treated by Captain Hall, who acted as aide to Procter:

On General Procter's arrival opposite the fort at Amherstburg on the morning of the 18th September, he met Col. Elliott of the Indian Department, the Colonel appeared to be very much agitated. He desired the general to prepare himself for consequences of the most serious nature if he persisted in his retreat to Dover without the consent of the Indians. On General Procter's desiring him to explain himself, he observed that the great wampum belt was to be produced at the council & cast in two in the centre. That one end was to be delivered to us, and that they would retain theirs as an emblem of eternal separation or words to that effect.

Colonel Elliott further remarked that he had been threatened to be tomahawked. About this time the 2d in command Col. Warburton came up to the genl. & the general asked if he had seen Tecumseth agreeable to promise. He replied, no, "on reflection not knowing the promises made to the Indians he had declined interfering," or words to that effect. The general then desired that Tecumseth might be sent for & proceeded to the staff adjutant's quarters. A table was placed on the outer court towards the garden and a map was spread upon it, and on Tecumseth's arrival the general pointed out to him on this map the situation of Amherstburgh, the Detroit side of the river and the country around it. This was explained by Col. Elliott in the presence of several officers. The general observed to Tecumseth that the enemy's gun boats or vessels passing up the River Detroit would completely intercept any communication with the Indians on Grosille and those on the Detroit side of the river and prevent our giving them any supplies or assistance in case the enemy should advance on the Michigan side. That by proceeding to the River Thames with their vessels or gun boats they could place themselves in our rear and compleatly cut off our retreat & intercept our supplies. Tecumseth asked many questions and made several shrewd remarks in reference to the map. On the generals assuring Tecumseth that he would not retreat beyond the River Thames or Dover he appeared perfectly satisfied and requested permission or time to confer with the other chiefs. I think two hours were given him for that purpose and when the council met the general had delivered his speech and assured the Indians that he would not retreat beyond Dover, that he would make a stand there and share his fate with them. They appeared to be overjoyed at the information. It had a very lively effect upon them.[47]

In his conversation with Tecumseh, one he should have held long before, Procter promised that the forks of the Thames near Chatham would be fortified. Two 24-pound guns were to be placed upon the high ground opposite the forks, and the location was indicated to Tecumseh on the map. In addition, Procter said presents would be available for the Indians at the same place.[48] Armed with these pledges and a better appreciation of the military situation, Tecumseh returned to his followers and carried the decision to retreat with them. As a result, the ensuing council between the Indians and their allies lacked animosity. Procter, speaking through Elliott, affirmed that he intended retiring to the forks of the Thames, which he would fortify, and where "we will mix our bones with their [the Indian] bones." The tribesmen seemed satisfied and for the moment the alliance appeared to have been saved.[49]

Procter cannot be absolved of poor judgment in this crisis, though. At his subsequent court-martial the prosecution contended that

the indignation of that brave and superior man [Tecumseh] and the suspicions of the Indians in general arose entirely from a want of frankness and candour in Major General Procter . . . nor is there any reason to believe that if the necessity not only of retreating but of leaving them behind for the present had been fairly and candidly explained to them, . . . there would have been any serious opposition to the measures.[50]

There was some truth in this. Tecumseh understood the need for a retreat, once the facts had been put to him, and his ability to influence the other chiefs indicates that had Procter been more ingenuous he could have persuaded the Indians to make a stand at some defensible position on the Thames without breeding so much mistrust. And one mistake had led to another. To allay the fears in the Indians that he had needlessly inflamed, Procter committed himself to making his stand in a specific location, near the forks of the Thames, at Chatham, a position he had not, it appears, satisfactorily reconnoitered. A member of the Indian Department later maintained that in the council the natives objected to retiring as far as Moraviantown, but there is little to indicate how strongly the protest was made. Procter's rashness in promising to fight near Chatham was pregnant with further difficulty.[51]

More than this, the Indians remained unsettled. They knew nothing of Procter's early resolution to give battle on the Thames, but they had seen him preparing to withdraw without a word, and as far as their information went he had only agreed to stand in response to the protests of Tecumseh. An identical opinion was rife among the British soldiers, who later spread the story that Tecumseh had forced Procter to fight. Unconvinced by Procter's promises, many in the Indian camps reconsidered their position in the days that passed between the second council at Amherstburg and

Shabbona, also known as Chambly or Shaubena, photographed in 1857. An Ottawa by birth, he eventually became the leader of a band of Potawatomis living on the Illinois River. Shabbona joined Tecumseh in 1807 and probably accompanied him on some of his journeys to unite the tribes of the Northwest. He was at the Battle of Moraviantown. *Courtesy Chicago Historical Society* (ICHi–15034).

Sha-wa-wan-noo or John Naudee, as he appeared in 1858. When this photograph was taken the chief, variously described as an Ojibwa or a Shawnee, was living on Walpole Island in the Saint Clair River. A veteran of Moraviantown, he died in 1870. *Courtesy British Library.*

Four Legs, a Winnebago chief, ally of Tecumseh, shown in this lithograph made by Lehman and Duval from a portrait painted by J. O. Lewis in 1827. He seems to have fought at Moraviantown, and may have been the Four Legs who died at Fort Winnebago in 1831. *Courtesy Library of Congress.*

the commencement of the retreat on September 27. Eventually, between a thousand and twelve hundred warriors actually accompanied the Right Division, some eight hundred or more either drifting back to their scattered villages or remaining about Detroit.[52] The most serious loss was the Potawatomi Tribe. A few Potawatomis, like Shabbona (Burly Shoulders) and Bad Sturgeon (Nuscotomeg), whose personal loyalty to Tecumseh was strong, retreated with the British, but most remained in their villages along the Rouge and Huron rivers or defected soon after the withdrawal began. A thousand to twelve hundred Indians were reported to be in the neighborhood of Detroit on September 30 under the leadership of the Potawatomi chief, Main Poc. If these warriors had abandoned Tecumseh, they were not all prepared to shake hands with the Americans, although some Ottawas, Ojibwas, Miamis, and Potawatomis did solicit forgiveness for their misdeeds. Main Poc remained surly, and when the American army later left Sandwich to pursue the British and their allies up the Thames, they left about seven hundred men under Colonel Duncan McArthur to disperse pillaging Indians about Detroit and to prevent attacks on Harrison's communications.[53] Nevertheless, the British-Indian alliance was crumbling, and only the more determined warriors followed Tecumseh in the wake of the Right Division. A Canadian newspaper wrote that it was

an example of fidelity, under the most trying circumstances of which those who denominate themselves civilised, have rarely been found capable. Yet these are the people, whom some persons would have us believe that England is about to abandon! We venture to assert that not one inch of the territory belonging to Great Britain, or of her allies in this war, will ever be abandoned to the United States.[54]

Legend has encrusted Tecumseh's last days in Amherstburg, much of it in stark contrast to the picture illuminated in contemporary records. Thomas Verchères de Boucherville, a French-Canadian at Amherstburg, was the source of one of the stories. More than thirty years after the retreat he remembered attending a banquet held soon after the evacuation of Amherstburg by the Baby brothers, Jacques, Jean Baptiste, and Francis, presumably at the former's imposing brick residence in Sandwich. Present also were Procter, Muir, and other officers of the Forty-first, Elliott, Tecumseh, and Sheriff William Hands:

Tecumseh was seated at my left with his pistols on either side of his plate and his big hunting knife in front of him. He wore a red cloak, trousers of deerskin, and a printed calico shirt, the whole outfit a present from the English. His bearing was irreproachable for a man of the woods as he was, much better than that of some so-called gentlemen.

The first courses had been served and disposed of when there came a knock on the dining-room door and a sergeant entered, who . . . announced that the [American] fleet was at this moment coming up the river, though there was but a light breeze and it was making very slow progress. Tecumseh did not understand all that was being said but he arose from the table and had the words of the sergeant explained to him by Colonel Elliot's interpreter, a man named Cadotte, who was waiting in an adjoining room. The chief turned pale and placing a hand on each of his pistols addressed General Procter in these words: "Father, we must go to meet the enemy and prevent him from coming here. We are quite numerous enough. We must not retreat, for if you take us from this post you will lead us far, far away, perhaps even to the shores of the great salt lake, and there you will tell us Good-bye forever, and leave us to the mercy of the Longknives. I tell you I am sorry I have listened to you thus far, for if we had remained at the town we have just left [Amherstburg] we could have taken our stand behind the great sandbanks of Father Elliot's point; here, without any doubt we could have prevented the enemy from landing and kept our hunting grounds for our children. Now they tell me you want to withdraw to the River Thames and there entrench yourself and build bakehouses for the soldiers. I am tired of it all. Every word you say evaporates like the smoke from our pipes. Father, you are like the crawfish that does not know how to walk straight ahead."

As soon as the chief concluded this harangue, all hurried to pack up preparatory to retreat that same day to the River Thames. The fleet had already reached Turkey Island, halfway up the river.[55]

As it stands this account makes little sense, although it has often been quoted. Obviously Tecumseh's words cannot have been remembered accurately after more than three decades, and the narrative, which was finished on April 15, 1847, exhibits confusion in a number of areas. Amherstburg was abandoned on September 23,

1813, and four days later, when the news reached Sandwich that the American squadron was preparing to land troops on the Canadian side of the Detroit, the British withdrew toward the Thames. It is to September 27, therefore, that Verchères refers. At that time Francis Baby was not even in Sandwich, for on the twenty-fifth he had been sent forward to repair roads and bridges toward the Thames and did not return before the retreat had commenced. When he met the Right Division on his way home on the twenty-seventh, it was already at Lavalle's, nine or ten miles from Sandwich. Again, on September 27, Tecumseh had, of course, become party to Procter's plan of campaign and many of the Indians had been persuaded by him to retreat with the British army. He was therefore unlikely to have spoken to Procter in the manner recounted. The most obvious explanation of the narrative is that Verchères confused the banquet with Tecumseh's reproof to Procter in the earlier Amherstburg council.[56]

Having said this, it is also probable that Tecumseh's acceptance of the need to retreat did not extinguish his zest for combat. It was not in the man's nature to permit a challenge to rest unanswered, and the news of Harrison's approach may have rekindled the chief's martial appetite. In this respect, Verchères's story would not merit much credence were it unsupported. The American press, however, published a fragment of a letter purportedly written by a captain in the British dragoons that colors the supposition that Tecumseh was not fully reconciled to withdrawing without an engagement. It was dated at Detroit on September 26, addressed to the officer's parents in England, and was reputedly discovered among Procter's papers that were captured at the Battle of Moraviantown. The Indians, explained the soldier,

have declared they will not budge one inch further, and remind us of our general having promised to conquer or leave their homes with them; as we are now completely in the savages' power, we are obliged, in a great measure, to act as they think proper. The celebrated chief Tecumseh dined with me last Friday, and assured me his Indians were determined to give battle the moment the Americans approach.[57]

An examination of the letter suggests that the date may have been misprinted, for the statements about the declared intentions of both Tecumseh in particular and the Indians in general seem inconsistent with the circumstances of September 26. They would have been thoroughly applicable to the Indian position ten days earlier, on September 16.

Another popular tale was given by Anthony Shane, the mixed-blood Shawnee, to Benjamin Drake in 1821. By it Tecumseh became so disgusted with Procter that he informed the Shawnees, the Wyandots, and the Ottawas that he was returning home to leave the British to fight their own battles. He complained that the reinforcements promised by the British in 1812 had not appeared, and the Indians, like dogs in snipe hunting, had always been sent ahead to start the game. Although Tecumseh's decision was accepted by his immediate audience, upon hearing of it, the Sioux and the Ojibwa prevailed upon the Shawnee chief, as the instrument of their unification, to persevere with the alliance. Tecumseh remained depressed and remarked to his friend, Jim Blue-Jacket, that while the Indians would follow the British, he doubted whether they would return.[58] Shane may have been sincere, but he was not with the British-Indian army and at best transmitted mere hearsay with this anecdote. Nor does it ring true to Tecumseh's character. The Indian hero must often have experienced frustration and perhaps despair, but he had nothing to gain for his cause, to which he was devoted, by leaving the only allies who could help him contest American encroachments in the Northwest.

A story even more improbable can be found in the Mary Ruth Lacey Papers of the Burton Historical Collection at Detroit. It is contained in a typescript entitled "Incidents of the War of 1812" attributed to one "Hamtramck," probably John Francis Hamtramck (1798–1858), and appears to have been written about 1858. According to this story, Procter consulted Tecumseh about engaging the American army, and the chief referred the matter to a prophet, White Pigeon, who dreamed that as Harrison's forces landed the Indians should fall upon their flank and rear while the British attacked in front. It is difficult to discern why such obvious tactics required the intervention of a prophet, and Procter certainly did not confer with the Indians about the possibility of attacking Harrison's men while they were being disembarked. The episode must be assigned the legendary status that so frequently obscures the activities of the celebrated Shawnee chieftain.[59]

When General Procter promised Tecumseh that he would occupy the forks of the Thames near Chatham, he had only the flimsiest knowledge of the area. Its potential for defense had been complimented late in the eighteenth century by Lieutenant Governor John Graves Simcoe, who had invested it with a blockhouse, and it may have possessed a strong local reputation.[60] A contemporary description of the area suggests some features that may have attracted Procter's attention:

> About 15 miles up the river Thames, is the town of Chatham, situated in a fork of it, on a very desirable spot, so well protected, and so central, that as the population increases, it will doubtless become a large and flourishing place; a blockhouse was erected here by His Excellency Major-General Simcoe, and it was made a depot for the the fine whale boats, which were built by His Excellency's directions. Indeed it possesses many advantages; the point is extremely well suited for the launching of vessels, and the river is sufficiently deep for those of any size; so that a secure arsenal, and building place, and an excellent dock might be made in the lesser branch of the forks, upon which there is now a mill. . . . Its greatest disadvantage is the bar across the embouchur into Lake St. Clair; but that is of sufficient depth for small craft rigged, and for large vessels when lightened . . . .[61]

To discover more about the forks, Procter had sent Captain William Crowther to inspect them and to erect barracks and ovens and prepare canoes along the line of retreat. Although Crowther apparently reported back favorably on September 18, other information indicated that the choice of the forks for a stand had been premature. Colonel Thomas Talbot of the militia, responding to a letter from the general, explained that the position at Chatham was vulnerable because of a road from its rear to Pointe Aux Pins on

Lake Erie, and that Moraviantown, farther upriver, was a better place to fight.[62] In consequence, Crowther was ordered out again on September 25 to examine the road to Pointe Aux Pins and was told by John Dolsen, a local farmer, that it had not been cut. Attempting to trace it, Crowther discovered that it disintegrated into a swamp of black mud decorated with stands of beech and oak. It was his opinion that an army with cavalry and guns would have to blaze a path to pass it.[63] Equipped with this information, Procter was prepared to rest content with his choice of a battle-ground.

There was still no doubt that a more extensive retreat might become necessary, and Procter instructed Talbot to repair the roads through the Wilderness, on the upper Thames, and to gather provisions for his force. The colonel not only improved the road as far as Oxford, but cut another path from Port Talbot on Lake Erie to low Muncey Town, some twenty-eight miles upriver of Mora-viantown. Evidently he intended facilitating the passage of sup-plies, but he additionally provided another means for the American navy to annoy British communications.[64]

The scene was now set for the retreat. By the eighteenth Troughton had sent all ordnance and stores at Amherstburg up the Thames, and the next day the artillery was taken from Fort Malden, except for an obsolete 18-pounder that was destroyed and left on the beach. The guns in Detroit were dismounted and removed on September 23–24. Before the British finally left Sandwich on the twenty-seventh, the whole of their artillery had been sent to the Thames, apart from most of the field train, which was to accompany the army on its march. The 3-pound field guns, however, were loaded onto wagons and transported to Chatham, presumably for mounting at the forks.[65] September 22 saw the last of the stores from Detroit and Sandwich shipped up to the Thames, and the plundered dockyard at Amherstburg was fired. The follow-ing day Warburton burned the public buildings in the town and withdrew its garrison to Sandwich.[66] Fort Malden, for more than a year the first bastion of Britain's defenses in the western district of Upper Canada, was a smoking ruin when Harrison's army reached it nearly a week later.

The Right Division concentrated at Sandwich, opposite Detroit, where the officers were briefed each morning at Procter's
house. They had many duties to attend to before the frontier was
completely abandoned. Some American prisoners were escorted to
Burlington; cattle were rounded up and hay was brought from
Amherstburg to be sent forward as forage for horses; instructions
covering provisions and the repair of roads and bridges required by
the army were given; and the sick and noncombatants, the latter
including Procter's wife and children and some citizens of Amherstburg, with their personal baggage, left for the Thames.[67]
Struggling along with the civilians was an aged, white-haired
man, blind and infirm, with particular cause to fear falling into
American hands. He was Simon Girty, "the white savage" whose
participation in Indian raids during the Revolution had made his
name anathema in Kentucky.[68] After the twenty-second the retreat was partly delayed by the Indians, who slowly brought
forward their families and possessions. By September 21 they
began to cross from Michigan Territory and Grosse Isle to make
their way to Sandwich, but the last warriors who accompanied the
retreat did not move to the Canadian side of the Detroit River until
September 29, when they fell into the rear of the British column.[69]
Tecumseh seems to have been camped with the Indians of Grosse
Island, who probably crossed to the Canadian bank about the
twenty-second, and appears to have been at Sandwich five days
later. Billy Caldwell, who left Detroit for Sandwich on the twenty-
seventh, at least recalled speaking to the Shawnee chief that day.[70]

Considering Procter's shortage of manpower and that he was
moving closer to his sources of supply, it seems surprising that in
those last days on the Detroit he did not call upon the militia to
help defend their country. About eight thousand white settlers
lived between Amherstburg and Moraviantown, a mixture of
French-Canadians and old Tories, the latter inveterate opponents
of the United States and the former more loyal to the Crown than
many supposed. There were also a few recent immigrants from
south of the border whose reliability might have been in greater
doubt. Possibly Procter believed that the response from the militia
would have been poor at a time when the corn was due for

harvesting, or perhaps, as one historian has inferred, he remembered that the 460 or so militiamen who had accompanied his expedition to Fort Meigs in May had not proven themselves a valuable asset.[71]

Among those who held opinions on the militia question was Robert Reynolds, at thirty-two years of age one of the earliest settlers of Amherstburg. In the years after the war, Squire Reynolds was one of the most persistent informants about the campaigns on the Detroit River; Coffin, Draper, and Lossing all found him at his post with a willing supply of anecdotes. He regarded Procter as a soldier of mediocre qualities and maintained that the general had disputed with Tecumseh the value of the militia during the Amherstburg council. Procter insisted that they were unreliable, Tecumseh that having been among them he was confident that they would fight provided that they were not drawn too far from their unprotected families. This last may have been a serious objection to recruiting militia about Amherstburg or Sandwich because a retreat to the Thames would have left their homes exposed to reprisals. Reynolds's tidbit was possibly nothing more than another legend on the theme of Procter versus Tecumseh, but it may suggest reasons why the general did not afford the militia an opportunity to reverse his opinion of them.[72]

The British soldiers finally turned their backs on the Detroit on September 27, 1813. That morning Ensign Benjamin Holmes of the Canadian Light Dragoons—at the beginning of a career that would lead him to the post of collector of customs at Montreal—was stationed with a party watching below Amherstburg when he saw a number of vessels out on the lake. Waiting long enough to determine that he was witness to the invasion of Canada, at 10:30 A.M. he scribbled the first of three reports proclaiming the long expected approach of the enemy. His second was dispatched at two o'clock in the afternoon and estimated the American forces at upwards of three thousand men.[73] A third message, issued late in the afternoon, reported Harrison landing his men at Caldwell's Creek, but unfortunately it has not been preserved and there was some subsequent controversy about its contents. Holmes declared that in it he gave the enemy strength at five thousand to six thousand men, a point Procter peremptorily denied, claiming that "at no time during the retreat had I reason to suppose that the number of the enemy was greater than three thousand men."[74] There was no doubt, however, that now the campaign had begun in earnest. After notifying his superiors, Holmes withdrew to Sandwich, pausing en route to destroy the bridge over the River Aux Canard, one of two spanning tributaries of the Detroit River between Amherstburg and Sandwich. The other, Turkey Bridge, was burned the following day by a detail Holmes led out to retrace his steps.[75]

In the meantime, Procter acted quickly upon receipt of Holmes's reports and got his main body under way toward the River Ruscom the same day. Warburton marched the bulk of the division out of Sandwich late in the afternoon of the twenty-seventh, camping for the night some nine or ten miles away at a settlement called Lavalle's, while Muir destroyed the public buildings in Detroit and pulled his force across the river, eventually linking up with the rest of the force the following morning.[76]

It was a bitter moment for the men who had held the Detroit frontier against such odds for fourteen months, and none felt it more keenly than did Tecumseh and Colonel Elliott. The Shawnee saw it as the beginning of the end of his dream of an Indian resurgence in the Old Northwest; for Elliott it meant the loss of virtually all he had. He was in his mid-seventies, and had fought a lifetime for the British and Indians in the West. After the Revolution, the Elliotts had settled at Amherstburg, and their prosperous farm at Elliott's Point testified to decades of effort. Now it would fall into the hands of the Americans, and the veteran Irishman was too old to begin again.[77] Major General William Henry Harrison expected his enemies to turn out in force to oppose the landing of his two thousand regulars and three thousand militia, but his men poured into Amherstburg about four o'clock in the afternoon and reached the smoking, empty shell of Fort Malden unmolested. They were resentfully observed at a distance by the forlorn figures of Elliott and the Shawnee chief.[78] Many years after the war had ended, one of the American soldiers remembered his arrival in Amherstburg. "All had fled," he wrote, "but the brave Tecumseh.

The citizens told us that he sat on his faithful charger, at the head of the street, and looked till he saw the van of our army entering the suburbs below. He then turned his horse with a sigh, and as the Americans entered one end of the town, he slowly rode out of the other."[79]

Harrison marched north from Amherstburg toward Sandwich, halting briefly at two small tributaries of the Detroit to repair the bridges Holmes had destroyed. He reached Sandwich on the twenty-ninth and waited there for three days until Colonel Richard Mentor Johnson's regiment of mounted Kentucky infantry joined him. Then, on October 2, leaving men behind to guard his communications, to protect equipment, and to discourage prowling Indians, "Old Tippecanoe" led a command of some thirty-five hundred from Sandwich in pursuit of the British and Indian army.[80]

4

FROM SANDWICH TO MORAVIANTOWN:
SEPTEMBER 27 TO OCTOBER 5, 1813

*Everything left to chance and all our movements
directed by . . . the enemy.*

As if to proclaim the darkening
affairs of the Indians and their allies, heavy rain began to fall on the
morning of September 28 and it lasted for more than a month.
Within days the roads, already cut by the wheels of baggage carts
and carriages that had preceded the army, were reduced to mud.
Although it was not cold, the soldiers were sodden and miserable
and had little thought for the excellent country along the line of
retreat, which consisted of occasional farms alternating with marsh
and luxuriant woods of maple, poplar, chestnut, hickory, elm,
ash, beech, oak, walnut, and wild cherry. They dwelt instead upon
their wet clothing, insufficient in the face of the impending
Canadian winter, and the doubtful supplies of food. Five men
deserted from Muir's detachment at the very onset of the march. [1]

General Procter spent the night of September 27–28 in the rear
of his army, between Sandwich and Lavalle's. In the morning he
sent instructions forward ordering the troops to remain in their
quarters because of the rain, but before the message reached
Warburton the men had already begun their march to the River
Ruscom, some fifteen miles farther, where they established another camp. On the twenty-ninth the division labored another fifteen
miles across a swampy and difficult plain until they reached Louis
Trudelle's farm on the south bank of the Thames, about three miles
from its mouth. During the day Procter had overtaken the column
in his carriage, but when the men arrived at Trudelle's the general

was missing; he had driven upriver, leaving instructions directing Warburton to establish quarters. Accordingly, the second-in-command bivouacked at Trudelle's and, receiving nothing more from Procter, suffered the soldiers to spend the whole of the next day, the thirtieth, idling in camp. Thus it was that on the first three full days after quitting Sandwich the Right Division had made only thirty miles.[2]

Procter was in time much criticized for his dilatory retreat, and particularly for permitting the army to remain inactive for a whole day at Trudelle's. In his defense he pleaded that a fast march would have left the Indians, who were well to the rear, even farther behind. Although his message of the twenty-eighth, enjoining Warburton to remain at Lavalle's, mentioned only the rain in justification of the order, Captain Hall, who had written it, testified that Procter's main concern was that the Indians and their families should not be allowed to fall too far back. Such an occurrence, Procter said, would have "produced a mischievous effect on the minds of the Indians" by sustaining the impression that they were being deserted. The general had anticipated that the Indians would have been able to catch up with the division while it remained at Lavalle's, and when he learned that the troops had broken their camp there he sent Colonel Elliott a letter of explanation and promised that the army would await the Indians on the Thames.[3] Evidently the agent passed this information to Tecumseh, for the chief was believed to have referred to Procter's letter during a conversation with Elliott at Pike's Creek and to have used the enigmatic words, "There is no place for us."[4]

This evidence satisfactorily explains the division's halt at Trudelle's on the Thames from September 29 to October 1, but it hardly acquits the general of considerable carelessness. There was surely a need for at least part of the force to hurry forward to fortify a defensive position, and Procter should not have left his army encamped at Trudelle's, devoid of defenses or instructions, in the knowledge that Harrison, with at least equal strength, was close behind. Had the American general not delayed at Sandwich, the British and Indians might have been overtaken and compelled to fight in very adverse circumstances. As it was, Warburton lay

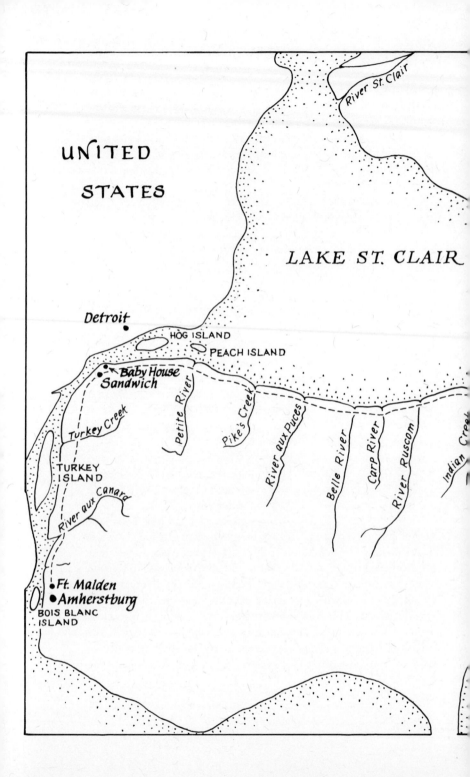

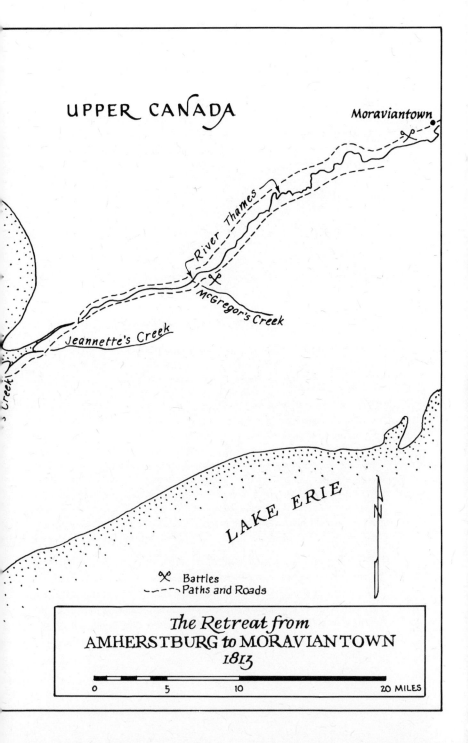

UPPER CANADA

Moraviantown

River Thames

McGregor's Creek

Jeannette's Creek

Creek

LAKE ERIE

N

✕ Battles
------- Paths and Roads

The Retreat from
AMHERSTBURG to MORAVIANTOWN
1813

0   5   10   20 MILES

inactive while the Indians gradually joined the division. The vanguard of the Indian force passed Warburton, but most of the warriors and their families did not arrive at Trudelle's until the evening of the thirtieth and stragglers were still filing in on the following day.[5]

Tecumseh and Elliott were in the very rear of the retreat, scouting the American advance and moving on stragglers. When Sandwich was evacuated, Elliott dispatched his Indian goods to a place called McIntosh's, where he distributed them to some of the tribesmen.[6] The next day he joined Tecumseh at Sandwich, now empty of British soldiers, and they rode to the farm of Colonel Francis Baby of the militia, situated on the Detroit River northeast of Sandwich. Casting his eye over the manifest destruction that had visited Baby's property during the American invasion of 1812, the injured buildings, fences, and orchards, Elliott may briefly have contemplated the fate of his own farm south of Amherstburg, now also in enemy hands.[7] Colonel Baby recalled:

> As I was getting ready to join the army Colonel Elliot and Tecumseth came to my house. Tecumseh requested of me to stay till the next morning [September 29] till we saw the enemy to which I consented. On the 29th early in the morning we sent a scout to see where the enemy was, and he returned in about an hour and a half and told us he had seen the enemy at Turkey bridge repairing that bridge which had been destroyed. We mounted our horses and proceeded to Belle River where we staid that night. On the 30th we proceeded from Belle River to the Thames and overtook on the way a great number of Indians. Some of them were preparing to encamp at the River Raskam, on which I told Colonel Elliott and Tecumseh that it would be much better to hurry them on to the Thames, for fear of the enemy overtaking them, which was done. We got on the Thames that night, and all the Indians that were by water got in that night.[8]

On the morning of October 1 the camp at Trudelle's was alarmed by a report that American vessels had been observed about the mouth of the Thames. Procter was still absent, reconnoitering upriver, and Warburton took upon himself the responsibility for resuming the retreat. An express was sent after the general with the latest tidings, while the army filed some nine or ten miles along the south bank of the Thames to cross the river by scows and camp in the barns of the farm of Matthew Dolsen and his son John, some five miles below the forks at Chatham. The Indians accompanied the British, but chose to quarter on the south bank of the river, opposite Dolsen's, rather than use the ferry. Only after the forces had taken up their new station did General Procter, recalled by Warburton's herald, rejoin his troops to take command.[9]

To investigate the reports of an American presence in the Thames, Procter detailed Ensign Holmes to scout the back trail, and early on October 2 he set out himself downriver with Captain Hall, not purely with purposes of reconnaissance in mind. Rumors were filtering among the Indians that the general had forsaken his army, and Tecumseh was known to have asked Elliott, "What is taking this other man [Procter] away, our father?" To this the agent had returned the unsatisfactory reply, "We do not know what he is gone for."[10] According to another remark of Elliott, passed on the following day, Tenskwatawa had declared that he had a mind to strip the epaulets from Procter's shoulders.

Disillusionment may not have been confined to the Indians, for a diarist of the retreat recorded that while the troops were quartered at Dolsen's some of the officers urged Warburton to remove Procter from his command.[11] But these were strong words and probably no more than rumor. Ensign James Cochran considered the story "twad[d]le" and condemned the soldiers who propagated it. "No such idea was ever brooched by any man with an ounce of brains," he declared. "Who would volunteer to 'bell the cat?' Geale and Muir were a brace of chattering geese."[12] Notwithstanding, Procter's excursion downriver on the second was certainly designed partly to allay the fears of the Indians, who could see for themselves that their "Father" was not a man to shirk danger. It did nothing to improve Procter's relations with his officers. The general almost reached the mouth of the Thames and discovered that the rumors of American vessels in the river were unfounded, for only one ship could be seen riding at a distance on Lake Saint Clair. When Procter returned to his division it was with a poorer opinion of the judgment that had allowed his subordinates to recall him without ascertaining the truth of the reports they had received.

The home of Jacques Baby at Sandwich. Built about 1797 by Alexander Duff, this house was purchased in 1807 by Jacques Baby. The officers of the British Right Division were entertained at the Baby house. This photograph by F. Neal, taken for Norman Gurd, shows the house almost a century later in a renovated condition. *Courtesy British Library.*

The Francis (François) Baby house, built in 1812 on the Canadian shore of the Detroit River, opposite the fort at Detroit and above the town of Sandwich. Tecumseh and Matthew Elliott spent their last night on the Detroit frontier at Baby's house. It was heavily damaged by fire in 1850, and rebuilt and altered beyond recognition after Baby's death in 1852. In this ink drawing, Sandra J. Pardy of Windsor recreates the appearance of the house as viewed from the northwest at the time of the war of 1812. Because of gaps in the evidence, certain details, notably the porch treatment, are tentative. Now being restored, the building houses the Hiram Walker Historical Museum. *Courtesy Mrs. Sandra J. Pardy.*

Dolsen's farmhouse on the northern bank of the River Thames about 1891. The house had been reshingled and had new floors and windows, but preserved the appearance of the building that served as the headquarters of the British for nearly two days of their retreat up the Thames. *Courtesy Library of Congress.*

These misgivings did not justify the general's deplorable treatment of his second-in-command during the following two days. What had previously appeared to be an unwillingness of Procter to impart information seems to have solidified into a steadfast determination to leave Warburton, Evans, and Muir ignorant of his intentions. During the army's stay at Dolsen's from October 1 to the third, these officers learned nothing from Procter, even when the general altered his plans on the evening of the second and rattled away in his calash the following morning for yet another reconnaissance upstream. Such circumstances simply promoted greater disunion, for speculation bred when none had the knowledge to contradict. It was said, for example, that Procter's absences from the division owed something to the presence at Moraviantown of Mrs. Procter and her children, who had gone forward with the noncombatants. There was, perhaps, some validity in this, but Procter was principally interested in intelligence since his earlier attempt to scout upriver had been frustrated a little beyond Dolsen's by the false report that Perry's vessels had entered the Thames. Now he considered that a second investigation was necessary, but he did not believe it worthwhile to make his officers privy to his intentions.[13]

Procter was deficient in one of the most important ingredients of a commander—leadership. Unlike Brock and Tecumseh, he inspired neither love nor respect in his followers. He stood distant and uncommunicative, incapable of drawing the officers into his plans and developing the teamwork and confidence necessary for success. No less serious, he was also proving himself to be dilatory and negligent. The protracted sojourns up the Thames were not only irresponsible, leaving as they did the division in the hands of these bereft of instructions or information, but the trips should have been unnecessary at that stage of the campaign. Procter had been committed to a retreat since September 11 and had Indian support for it before the twentieth, yet Chatham, the ground designated for the stand, remained without a thorough inspection, let alone preparation, as late as October 2. It is true that the division's solitary engineer, Captain Dixon, had been sick between September 24 and the morning of October 2, but it would be

surprising if there was not another officer in the division capable of
assessing a military position and executing instructions as to its
fortification, even if the effort consisted merely of siting and
mounting guns and building breastworks. Both of the general's
weaknesses, in communication and in foresight, soon paid their
reckoning.[14]

On October 2, while the troops were still lingering at Dolsen's,
Procter finally ordered Dixon to examine the forks at Chatham.
Dixon testifed:

> I looked at the ground & when I returned in the evening, I told the
> general, I did not think it a very favorable position to occupy as it was so
> very confined in space, surrounded with wood and on the opposite side of
> the river to where we were. As the general seemed anxious, that some-
> thing should be done there or at Dolsan's, I mentioned to him that I
> prefered Dolsan's; tho' I did not in the most trifling degree recommend
> either. The general put several questions to me, as to the possibility of
> maintaining the position at Dolsan's by occupying the houses & other
> trifling defences. I told him that we might do that of course, that it would
> impede the course of the enemy a little but did not venture to recommend
> the position.[15]

Possibly Dixon's memory of the affair was defective, for Lieutenant Allan McLean, aide-de-camp to Procter, believed that the
engineer reported that although Chatham was a good position, it
would require too much time to be placed in a satisfactory state of
defense; Dolsen's, where a number of wooden buildings were
available, was preferable. Procter claimed that Dixon's sole reason
for condemning Chatham was its lack of barracks as shelter for the
soldiers from the rain.[16] Still, after receiving the report late on the
second, the general convened a meeting that included Elliott,
Brevet Major William Derenzy, Captain Crowther, and Captain
Troughton (but not Warburton, Evans, or Muir, the three senior
subordinates) and declared that in view of Dixon's pessimism about
the forks he would defend Dolsen's instead. Crowther was
appointed assistant engineer with directions to prepare defenses at
Dolsen's under Dixon's supervision.[17]

Procter was held fast in a trap he had himself snared, first, by
promising the Indians that a stand would be made near Chatham,

and second, through denying the division the necessary time to erect appropriate defenses. He could renege upon his word to the Indians only at the expense of their confidence, and now that the forks had been found unsuitable, he was compelled to select the only alternative site on the lower Thames to prove to Tecumseh that he was acting in good faith. Despite what was said by some of the witnesses at Procter's subsequent court-martial, Dolsen's was not wholly devoid of natural advantages. The main road that fringed the north bank would have facilitated the movement of the British artillery, for example, to cover the fords upstream that threatened the British flank and made an attack across the Thames without boats difficult. Unfortunately, the best cover for the Indians, who felt insecure in the open, was on the south bank, where a path threaded its way through a thick wood that extended to opposite Moraviantown, and here the Thames, which averaged sixty to eighty yards in width between Trudelle's and Chatham, could have been employed by the enemy gunboats to ferry men past Dolsen's and land them upriver on the left of the British defense. Perhaps Procter sensed the increasing need for a fall-back position when he left camp with Dixon early on the third to inspect the ground at Moraviantown, which Colonel Talbot had already given his recommendation. [18]

Behind him was a smoldering and somewhat ludicrous situation. Warburton commanded, but knew nothing about the revision of Procter's strategy and still assumed that Chatham, rather than Dolsen's, was to be defended. Elliott had been informed of the changes, but not Tecumseh. In any case, the general's lethargy had left insufficient time to prepare either position, although Captain Crowther in his new capacity of assistant engineer did his best. He had been furnished with instructions by Dixon, who had then accompanied the general to Moraviantown, and set about cutting loopholes in some log buildings near the river and establishing a battery, but discovered that while the division's entrenching tools were some seven miles upriver at a place called Bowles's, there were neither boats nor wagons to collect them. Applying to Warburton for assistance, he was told that it was too late to erect batteries because the enemy had been reported close by and the men were getting under arms. Crowther considered that he could have carried out Dixon's orders had he the entrenching tools at Dolsen's, but the sudden approach of the Americans made the task now insuperable. [19]

For the second time Warburton was confronted with news of the enemy's advance in the absence of General Procter. On the evening of October 2, Ensign Holmes had been ordered from Dolsen's to pick up a detail of the Forty-first, ferry across the Thames, and backtrack to the Belle River, where an ammunition wagon awaited recovery. On his return journey he was to destroy two bridges. Holmes crossed the river and had proceeded some seven or eight miles downstream when he was captured by the American advance guard, along with a dragoon and nine men of the Forty-first. It was the news of this misfortune, brought in by one of the dragoons, that reached the British camp early on the third and signaled Harrison's approach. Warburton, certain that his moment had come, formed the Right Division for battle. [20] He said later:

> I sent the boats five miles higher up the river to Bowles's and took up a position on the banks of the river on one side—and directed Colonel Elliott to go or send a message to Tecumseth that I trusted he would defend the other bank of the river. In less than half an hour after the troops were formed, Colonel Elliott came to me with a message from Tecumseth mentioning his determination to retire upon the forks as that was the place where a stand was promised to be made. Having consulted with the officers . . . and having with me but 300 of the 41st, about 30 artillery and a few dragoons, I determined to retire also to the forks.
>
> On the arrival of the troops there Tecumseth was haranguing the Indians on the opposite bank of the river in a loud and violent manner. Colonel Elliott shortly after came over to me crying and stated that from what he had heard if something could not be done he would not stay to be sacrificed. I understood that the passion of Tecumseth was caused by not finding the forks of the Thames fortified. I told Colonel Elliott that I could not make any movement at that time and the men accordingly lay in their arms all night. . . .
>
> Early on the morning of the 4th Colonel Elliott came over from the Indians with a message from Tecumseh to say that he was determined to retire on the Moravian Village. I nevertheless waited at the forks until about ten or eleven o'clock as I expected that General Procter would join

the division there. As he did not come nor send any message, and the Indians were then skirmishing with the Americans, I called in the picquets and moved, and shortly after I received a message from Major General Procter to retire to him at Bowles's.[21]

Warburton's resume of the events of the third and the fourth is accurate. Upon receipt of word of Holmes's capture, he sent word to Procter and placed the troops under arms and positioned his guns. The first ground adopted, a few hundred yards from Dolsen's, was abandoned because it appeared unsuitable for the Indians, and a second was chosen about one and a half miles from Dolsen's in a wood facing the river. Tecumseh and his men remained, however, on the southern bank of the Thames and were unwilling to cooperate. Some of the warriors slid downriver to skirmish with the enemy vanguard, but the chiefs were in no mood to fight at Dolsen's when, as they thought, a fortified position awaited them at the forks.[22] Accordingly, the tribesmen retreated to the forks and found to their chagrin that no works had been erected. Three or four guns lay dismounted on the south bank of the river, and nearby a hut had been filled with boxes of arms.[23] The ensuing fury of the warriors is understandable. As far as they knew only Tecumseh's attack upon Procter at Amherstburg had induced the British to agree to a stand at all, but now the promises the Shawnee had wrung from Procter had been found worthless. Elliott reported that the Indians expressed their contempt of the Redcoats in "very strong language" and apparently understated the case. According to Walk-in-the-Water, Procter's life was threatened; Elliott's certainly was ("I will not by God sacrifice myself," he told Warburton). Nor was the temper of the Indians improved when Tecumseh and Naiwash requested through Elliott that the Right Division cross the river and join the Indians because the Americans were advancing along the southern, rather than the northern, bank. Warburton replied that he would do all in his power to fulfill any promises Procter had made, but that boats were not available for him to reinforce his allies.[24]

Chatham, misleadingly called a "township," consisted of no more than "a solitary hut and little plantation" four or five miles upriver of Dolsen's, situated at a fork formed by McGregor's Creek running west into the River Thames.[25] The mouth of the creek was unfordable but it was served by a wooden bridge that enabled the few travelers who used the south bank of the Thames to pass above. About a mile up the creek was another bridge, located close to John McGregor's mill, an edifice that had sat upon the southern bank of the stream for many years, one of the first mills the district had seen.[26] It was not far from this mill that the Indians camped on October 3 and discussed the perfidy of the British. A retreat to Moraviantown was decided upon, perhaps because some were acquainted with the area and recognized its potential, or possibly for no better reason than that Procter had gone there.[27] When Warburton was informed by Elliott the following morning, in accordance with the wishes of the Indians that he too should retire to Moraviantown, he set the Right Division on the march to Bowles's about ten o'clock, regulating its pace along the way to protect a number of squaws who had been sent forward by the warriors to retreat with greater safety among the troops. A rear guard under Muir was formed to fulfill the function previously held by Ensign Holmes.[28]

In the meantime, Tecumseh and Naiwash endeavored to obstruct the American advance with a hastily improvised rear-guard action at McGregor's Creek. The planks of the lower bridge were torn up and cast into the stream; the upper bridge was burned, along with McGregor's mill, which would probably have provided the enemy with cover and food. As the thick columns of black smoke rose above the woods, the Indians secreted themselves in the timber and covert on the north bank of the creek, within the fork, and a few warriors and British occupied a small house across the Thames itself from which they could annoy the American flank with musketry. Given the time to hand, the Indians did the best they could, but against the full weight of the enemy they could attempt nothing more than a holding action.[29]

It lasted less than two hours. Harrison's forces, consisting of nearly three thousand men, were luckily informed by a woman they encountered on the trail that the Indians were waiting to dispute their passage over McGregor's Creek. The Americans advanced cautiously in battle formation in the early light, over undergowth, morass, and fallen trees. In the vanguard rode Colonel Richard Mentor Johnson's regiment of a thousand mounted volunteers, fanning out to form a front along the creek, while the rest of Harrison's militia under Governor Isaac Shelby of Kentucky gave support in the shape of a drawn bow, facing both McGregor's Creek and the Thames itself. Because the angle of the fork sheltering the Indians was acute, the warriors near the mouth of the creek saw the Americans first and opened a heavy fire upon Captain Benjamin Warfield's company as it ventured dismounted toward the damaged lower bridge. Johnson's right, commanded by the colonel himself, soon came upon the stream opposite the Indian left at the upper bridge and the action became general.

Seizing upon the Indians' weakness, Harrison, who was attended by Commodore Perry near the fork, directed Major E. D. Wood's artillerymen to clear the enemy from the opposite side of the lower bridge with his two 6-pound field guns. The task was quickly accomplished, and about twenty of Warfield's men were able to cross by the naked sills of the broken bridge to shelter behind the north bank of the creek and provide additional covering fire. A few of their colleagues then rescued some of the planks from the river and sufficiently restored the bridge to permit the passage of guns and men. Unable to withstand the pressure longer, the few hundred Indians defending the creek between both bridges gave way, setting fire to a house stocked with muskets near the upper bridge before they retreated. Their opponents fell hungrily upon the considerable booty that remained in the vacated positions and salvaged many, and perhaps all, of the arms in the small arsenal after extinguishing the flames. The operation had cost Harrison three men killed or fatally wounded and three to six injured, but the loss he had inflicted upon Tecumseh's followers, if any, is unknown.

One Indian interpreter, J. Baptiste Boismier, had a fortunate escape, either during or shortly after the skirmish. Unable to sustain the pace of the retreating warriors because of a swollen knee, he sheltered for the ensuing night in a house. When he awoke the following morning he discovered that the hiding place was surrounded by American soldiers, but boldly striding among them, Boismier passed himself for one of their number until he could slip away into the forest. Since the enemy were now between himself and Tecumseh, the interpreter was unable to rejoin his friends and made his way back to Pike's Creek where he lived for nine months unknown to the Americans. Eventually Boismier was able to return to the British, then at the head of Lake Ontario, to relate his adventures.[30]

After the skirmish at McGregor's Creek, Tecumseh continued to fall back up the Thames for the rest of October 4. His men had been shaken by the recent evidence of British unreliability and many of the warriors were deserting, convinced that the Redcoats had no intention of supporting them. Captain Billy Caldwell of the Indian Department later denied that this was so, but to little purpose. Testifying in Procter's defense at the court-martial in January, 1815, Caldwell maintained that only a few Wyandots under Walk-in-the-Water and some Delawares abandoned the British on account of the broken promise to fortify and defend Chatham.[31] The former were in any case of dubious value. Walk-in-the-Water had already advertized to Harrison his intention to desert the British, and apparently took the opportunity to do so with about sixty warriors on the morning of October 4. Elliott reported that a small number of Shawnees likewise accepted American offers of friendship.[32] These remarks minimize the seriousness of the Indian losses, however. At Dolsen's on the third Tecumseh had some twelve hundred warriors in attendance, but two days later he fought at Moraviantown with little more than five hundred. It is difficult to accept Caldwell's proposition that such attrition was due entirely to the hurried retreat from Dolsen's that prevented some braves with their baggage and noncombatants from keeping pace with the division.[33] Disillusionment with Procter probably played its part. Indian fears at Amherstburg had been reassured by a pledge to stand at the forks, and Tecumseh must have risked some of his personal credibility in persuading his followers to accept it. The British had now let them down and the darkest suspicions flamed anew. Although the resolute core of tribesmen still remained, some fifteen hundred warriors had been shed by the British between September 10 and October 4, taking with them what slender hopes there were for an eventual victory.

General Procter learned of the retreat from Dolsen's shortly after midnight on October 4. He had arrived at Moraviantown late the previous day, just before dusk, having been overtaken on the way by an express carrying news of Holmes's capture. This had caused Procter no apparent alarm. "Very well," he told the herald, after reading the message, and continued his journey. After examining the ground at Moraviantown, Procter satisfied himself that it was defensible, told Dixon that he would station the troops there, and retired for the night. A second messenger from Warburton, Captain Thomas Coleman of the Canadian Light Dragoons, shortly arrived and insisted upon waking the general to inform him of the retreat from Dolsen's and the ugly disposition of the Indians. "Retire from Dolsen's," muttered Procter, "I never intended they should." When Coleman expressed a belief that provisions and supplies had now been sent forward to Bowles's, above the forks, the general replied tersely, "Then they must be sent back again." He soon had Coleman on the return journey with word that he would rejoin his army later that morning. Coleman reached Warburton before daylight on the fourth, at about the same time that Procter finally left Moraviantown in his carriage, having ordered Dixon to begin the job of preparing the ground for defense.[34]

The Chatham crisis represents Procter at his most culpable, and the full consequences of his ineptitude extended far beyond the alienation of the Indians. Since the British had intended fighting at Chatham valuable stores, including ammunition and ordnance, had been shipped from Amherstburg or Sandwich and deposited at the forks or at Bowles's, a few miles upriver. Above Bowles's the river was also unnavigable to large vessels and goods that were difficult to transport farther had had to be disembarked there. All of these resources were imperiled by the sudden retreat of the British, who had not the means to remove them. Captain Chambers lamented how "perfectly useless" they were once Warburton withdrew from the forks on the fourth, but "had the fortifications gone on as was originally intended," he added, "the principal part of the ordnance would have come into use."[35] The division arrived

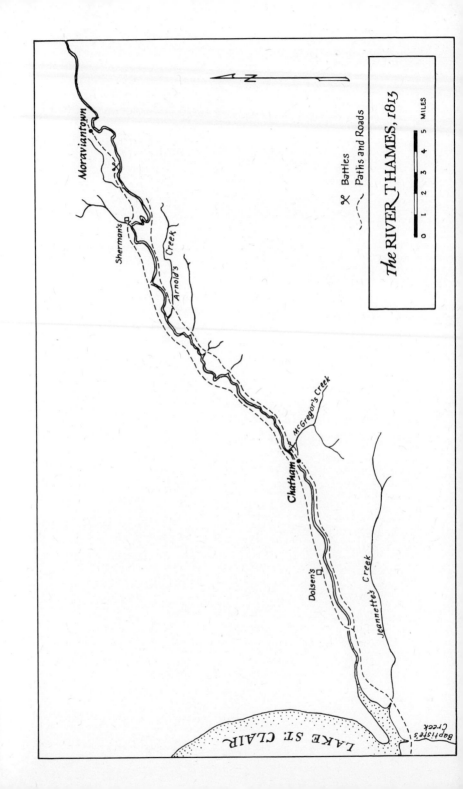

the RIVER THAMES, 1813

✕ Battles
-- Paths and Roads

0 1 2 3 4 5 MILES

Moraviantown

Sherman's

Arnold's Creek

McGregor's Creek

Chatham

Dolsen's

Jeannette's Creek

LAKE ST. CLAIR

Baptiste's Creek

at Bowles's to find Procter already busy directing the destruction of surplus materials. Two vessels, one the schooner *Ellen* of fifty-nine tons burden, laden with ammunition and military stores, were scuttled across the river to check the progress of Harrison's gunboats, while the entrenching tools and some ammunition were loaded into light craft and sent upstream. The field train, including the 3-pound guns, accompanied the army by road.[36]

After helping to destroy the stores, Procter retreated with his division to the farm of Lemuel Sherman (Shearman), below Moraviantown, and directed the troops to camp there after their march of fifteen miles. The rear guard bivouacked at Richardson's, a settlement within one and a half miles downriver of Sherman's. Without any justification and with almost compulsive irresponsibility, the general then took his customary leave of the soldiers and returned to his wife at Moraviantown, where he spent the night of the fourth to the fifth.[37] It was a critical time when the consequences of the previous day's work were still materializing, and Procter had no business consigning his command to a surrogate whose judgment he had already found grounds to suspect. Fresh disasters were even then striking at the crumbling morale of the British troops. For a time they had escaped short rations. At Sandwich, Procter had ordered ovens to be built at Dolsen's and Sherman's and depots to be established at various places.[38] His soldiers eventually marched from the town with two days' provisions, both pork and biscuit, and found fresh victuals to hand when they reached the River Ruscom; substantial numbers of cattle were driven ahead of the division.[39] The commissariat began to stumble on the morning of October 4, when the army retreated so rapidly from the forks that meat brought onto the ground could not be cooked, and the little bread that was rescued from the ovens at Dolsen's was insufficient to go round.

The column was also disappointed when it camped at Sherman's later in the day, because orders for the baking of bread in the ovens there seem to have been sent too late to allow anything to be done. These difficulties spilled into October 5, the day the soldiers were expected to march from Sherman's to Moraviantown and perhaps to engage the enemy. The failed bread supply had not been repaired, and after three oxen had been butchered it was discovered that the meat could not be prepared because cooking utensils had been packed and sent to Moraviantown. Quartermaster Matthew Bent and Assistant Commissary Robert Gilmore were hurriedly dispatched upriver to prepare bread, potatoes, beef, and cabbage at Moraviantown for the anticipated arrival of the troops later in the day. Unfortunately, few of them ever reached that position; they fought their battle with the Americans en route, fortified that day with little more than a drop of whiskey and having been inadequately provisioned for more than fifty hours.[40]

This appalling situation was yet another result of the hasty retreat from the lower Thames. Bread left behind at Dolsen's was not replaced at Sherman's, and for one reason or another no meat was served. To add to the vexations, early in the morning of the fifth another serious blow was delivered to the reeling British-Indian forces. The boats in which the spare ammunition and the entrenching tools had been sent upriver from Bowles's were captured, along with ninety-four men, including eight to twelve artificers. Both Warburton and Procter should have foreseen this possibility because the distances traveled by the boats along the twisting river were far greater than those demanded by the relatively straight road along the north bank over which the Right Division marched. Despite the assignment of twenty additional men to the boats, they soon fell behind on October 4. Captain Peter Chambers, fresh from the destruction of stores at Bowles's, rejoined the army at Sherman's after dark and reported the plight of the boats to Warburton, and the second-in-command and Evans were additionally alerted to the danger by Sergeant John Grant. Nevertheless, Warburton dallied until daylight before dispatching Chambers with some dragoons to ride downriver to the rescue, by which time it was too late. Although he salvaged some of the men, Chambers found that most of the boats had been captured; he returned to the division with the further alarming news that the enemy, upwards of three thousand strong, was advancing. The retreat had become a rout.[41]

The Americans might well have congratulated themselves upon their latest coup. Procter's army was already depleted in man-

Major-General William Henry Harrison commanded the American invasion of Canada in 1813. *Courtesy BBC Hulton Picture Library.*

Richard Mentor Johnson in later life, by John Neagle. Johnson raised the mounted regiment of Kentucky volunteers who served under Harrison in the campaign up the Thames. Wounded at Moraviantown, Johnson was subsequently championed as the man who shot Tecumseh. *Courtesy The Corcoran Gallery of Art, bequest of Mrs. B. O. Tayloe.*

Governor Isaac Shelby of Kentucky, who responded to Harrison's personal invitation to command the militia during the invasion of Canada. The experience closed a distinguished career of active service on the frontier, *Courtesy British Library*.

power; now much of its ammunition was lost, and with the lack of entrenching tools had disappeared the means of erecting any but rudimentary works at Moraviantown or elsewhere. The general wrote an urgent request for supplies and ammunition to the Centre Division the same day, but it was too late to affect the imminent conflict, and the men had to be told on the battlefield to manage with what ammunition they had.[42] Probably more could have been done to save these valuable commodities. They might have been sent more safely by road had spare wagons been available, but none were to immediate hand. Some wagons were apparently stranded on the south bank of the Thames, prevented by high water from using the ford near Arnold's mill above Bowles's, and others, regettably, had been used to convey surplus baggage to Moraviantown and other places.[43] Warburton's lethargic response to the warnings he had received about the boats and Procter's absence also contributed to the disaster. Neither had anticipated the difficulty, although the meandering state of the river must have been known and several heavily laden wagons at Sherman's might have been discharged of their baggage and requisitioned to transport essential supplies.[44]

As the British troops fell in for the march from Sherman's to Moraviantown that fateful fifth of October, great must have been the consternation of their officers at the swelling tide of misfortune. Yet the matter had rested to a large extent in their own hands. They had been harried from Dolsen's, the forks, and Sherman's, the odds mounting daily against them, without any appreciable show of foresight or preparation. "Never was a country lost so shamefully as this has been, and will be," complained a York chaplain as the facts about the retreat became known, "not the smallest vigour displayed—no plan of the campaign— everything left to chance and all our movements directed by those of the enemy. Our generals appear not only ignorant of the art of war but destitute of common sense."[45] Now the day of reckoning had come. Warburton waited until Chambers returned to report the loss of the boats and the approach of the enemy, and then between ten and eleven o'clock put the column hastily into motion, "all . . . bustle and confusion."[46] Only four or five miles upriver was the village of Moraviantown.

William Conner, by J. Cox. An Indian trader in Indiana Territory before the War of 1812, he accompanied a Delaware contingent with Harrison's army in 1813 and identified Tecumseh's body on the field of Moraviantown. *Courtesy Indiana Historical Society/Library of Congress.*

A similar foreboding haunted the remaining Indian allies as they fell back after holding the Americans for a useful two hours at McGregor's Creek on the morning of October 4. Tecumseh's vision of an Indian renascence in the Old Northwest was fading with the fallen Canadian leaves. A few of the Indians, including women and children, traveled with the British and camped on the night of the fourth at Sherman's, but the majority were still across the river, moving ahead of the horsemen in the American vanguard.[47] After the skirmish at the forks they were seen in large numbers passing upriver of a farm above Chatham where Hugh and Sarah Holmes lived with their four sons and three daughters. Young Abraham Holmes was then sixteen years of age, and he rose early the following morning to try to catch a glimpse of the celebrated Tecumseh. Scampering for two miles up the Thames, he reached Christopher Arnold's mill, situated on Arnold's Creek just above its junction with the river. Tecumseh was there, conversing with Joe Johnston, a neighbor whose familiarity with the Indians had given him a facililty in their languages, and reprobating his allies for failing to fight at Chatham. As Holmes recalled at the age of eighty-five:

Tecumseh, as I remember well, was a man about five feet eight or nine inches high full chested and erect of dignified demeanour grave countenance and earnest in conversation. He wore buckskin leggings and a shirt of the same material that reached to the knees and was secured at the waist with a belt. He wore a large silver brooch [medal?] at the neck but no other silver ornaments and was altogether a man of superior bearing and intelligent looking beyond others of his race.[48]

During the engagement at the forks the Indians had destroyed McGregor's mill, probably because it offered their adversaries shelter and food. But Tecumseh had no wish to inflict unnecessary suffering upon civilians and had spent the night of the fourth and fifth near Arnold's to prevent his mill, reputed the best on the lower Thames, from undergoing a similar fate. When Holmes saw the chief in the morning he was waiting for Indian stragglers to pass him. Harrison's mounted militia, too, were not far behind, for Holmes left Tecumseh at Arnold's but found the American horsemen already at his father's farm when he reached home. Johnston later told the boy that Tecumseh stayed at Arnold's until he saw the Americans approaching, when he mounted his bay pony and galloped upriver.[49] He may have crossed the Thames by a ford two miles beyond Arnold's Creek, the same used by Harrison's army between nine and twelve noon later that morning, but there was another ford above Moraviantown, which appears to have served most of the Indian force sometime on the fifth. Certainly, the warriors were with the Right Division on the north bank of the river in time for the battle in the afternoon.[50]

Tecumseh's last day has almost inevitably been the subject of innumerable stories, and the settlers of the Thames, in revering his memory, enriched the lore that obscured it. As James B. Gardner, who toured the region, wrote in 1832: "Every peasant has a legend to tell. Almost all, of adult years, have seen the 'Great Red Chief,' and many deal largely in the marvellous respecting his progress, his exploits, his daring chivalry and personal peculiarities."[51] Among the locals who remembered Tecumseh was Christopher Arnold, who owed the survival of his mill to the Shawnee leader. Arnold had served in the militia during the campaigns earlier that year and, according to his grandson, confirmed that the chief and other Indian headmen spent the night before the battle of Moraviantown at the Arnold house. In the morning Tecumseh tarried for stragglers:

It was arranged that Tecumseh should watch for the Yankees under a large tree on the road about half a mile from the mill, while Capt. Arnold was to watch for their coming on the mill dam. If Arnold saw them first he was to throw up a shovel of earth. When Arnold first saw them he looked for Tecumseh, who had been standing beside his white horse with his elbow on its withers, but the chief was on his horse and the animal was running at full speed. The Americans gave chase, but the fleet-footed pony was too speedy for his pursuers. Tecumseh kept to the road until he reached the Hubble farm; he threw a bag which contained some flour Capt. Arnold had given him into Hubble's yard. He then rode to the river bank some distance further up the stream to a spot where a squaw awaited his coming. He at once got into a canoe, his white pony swimming by the side, and was quickly passed to the opposite bank, thus throwing his pursuers for a time off the trail.[52]

Another of those who reportedly saw Tecumseh that morning was the son of George Ironside, a British trader and storekeeper at Amherstburg who probably accompanied the retreat and whose wife was a niece of Tecumseh. The trader's paternal grandson recalled how his father, Robert, in 1813 fourteen years of age, used to speak of the chief's last affectionate farewell to the Ironside family on the morning of his final battle. Mrs. Ironside had lost one of her children, George, in the hurry of the retreat, and Tecumseh himself found the child and restored him to his mother. He told her to waste no time in moving forward, and to keep her children together; there would be a battle, and Tecumseh would not see them again. So resigned was he to his fate that he had painted himself black, in the Indian manner.[53] Unhappily there is nothing in the contemporary evidence with which this story may be checked, but if it took place it may have occurred at Moraviantown before the chief rejoined the main body for the battle that afternoon.

The family of Lemuel Sherman, who lived on the north bank of the Thames just downriver of the battlefield, was the source of another tradition about the Shawnee chief. David Sherman was a boy of fifteen at the time. By a story he gave to Benson Lossing and Miles Miller in October, 1860, he came across Tecumseh on the morning of the battle less than half a mile from the lines. The Indian was seated on a log with two pistols—Sherman thought of American manufacture—in his belt, and a white cow belonging to a neighbor was roasting nearby. After learning the boy's identity, Tecumseh is represented to have said, "Don't let the Americans know that your father is in the army, or they'll burn your house. Go back and stay home, for there will be a fight soon." Sherman died in 1865, but a descendant, William Sherman, elaborated the story when passing it to Katherine Coutts about the turn of the century. In his version, David and a youth called Ward were looking for cattle when they encountered Tecumseh on the afternoon of the fifth and were called over by him for interrogation. The boys were told to collect their stock and hurry home. There is, then, a certain consistency about this tale of David Sherman's, but like so many pieces of the Tecumseh saga, it can neither be proved nor invalidated.[54]

By about midday of the fifth both the American and the British-Indian armies were on the northern side of the Thames and poised for the decisive collision. The occasion was heralded by the first fatality of the day, which occurred during the morning when one of Colonel Richard Mentor Johnson's mounted volunteers, William Whitley, after fording the river at Arnold's, glimpsed an Indian lurking on the opposite shore. He shot the warrior dead, spurred his animal back into the water, swam across, and returned brandishing the victim's scalp. Reputedly he thrust the grisly trophy before the eyes of a friend, Young Ewing, and jeered, "See here Young this is [the] thirteenth Indian scalp I have taken and I'll have another before night or lose my own!" Whitley's triumph was vividly remembered in after years, for he cut a striking figure. An inveterate Indian fighter of more than sixty years, he attired himself in a cocked hat and hunting shirt, slung a wampum belt across his shoulder bearing a powder horn and bullet pouch, and carried a knife, tomahawk, and silver-mounted rifle. Yet the memories of the courageous old frontiersman's exploit were tainted with regret, for, as he had prophesied, he was not to survive the day.[55]

Two aspects of Procter's conduct of the retreat from Amherstburg, and those among the most rehearsed of many calumnies thrown at the general, have hitherto eluded analysis because of their general nature. They now demand attention before the scene is shifted to the battlefield of Moraviantown. During the court-martial in 1814–1815, charges were preferred against Procter that he had encumbered the division with unnecessary baggage and neglected to destroy bridges along the path of the retreat. Both allegations appear to have been exaggerated, and the small support they earned in the testimony led to Procter's acquittal. Not without reason, however, they have occasionally been resuscitated, although usually in an intemperate fashion. In one of the more extreme assertions, for example, a soldier of the Forty-first insisted that Procter's personal effects impeded the retreat and that "instead of using every effort to keep ahead of the enemy until we were reinforced [we] were detained in taking forward the general's baggage, etc."[56]

Warburton and Evans both believed that excessive baggage was taken from Amherstburg and Sandwich, but they were unable to say that it had obstructed the army's march. Most of it did not even travel with the division, which was escorted by only a few carts and wagons carrying light baggage and cooking utensils. Captain Hill alone was prepared to blame the excessive baggage for delaying the troops when he testified that it hampered the march "for a short period" on September 29 between the River Ruscom and Trudelle's.[57] Evans put his finger on a more important point in his statement that the retreat might have been expedited had the resources allocated to baggage been available to the army. There was a scarcity of wagons about the Thames, a fact that did not deter the British from burning some at Amherstburg and assigning others to the unnecessary baggage, much of which was private property. Some of the baggage was shipped upriver to Dolsen's and there transferred to wagons for removal to Bowles's, Sherman's, Moraviantown, and Delaware. It was natural that both soldiers and private citizens abandoning their homes in Amherstburg or Sandwich should want to take some of their personal possessions with them, but the army's retreat from Dolsen's and the forks was seriously inconvenienced by its lack of road transport. Only five spare wagons had left Sandwich with the division and two of them were abandoned, stranded on the south bank of the Thames on October 4. The same day valuable stores and ammunition had to be sent upriver from Bowles's by boat for the want of wagons, and the result was their capture early the following morning. In this respect, at least, the amount of baggage contributed to the British defeat.[58]

Procter's failure to destroy all the bridges was first made a public issue by Major General Harrison, whose dispatch of October 9 to the American secretary of war surmised that:

He [Procter] must have believed . . . that I had no disposition to follow him or that he had secured my continuance here. . . . As he neglected to commence the breaking up the bridges until the night of the second instant. On that night our army reached the river which is twenty five miles from Sandwich and is one of four streams crossing our route, over all of which are bridges, and being deep and muddy are unfordable for a considerable distance into the country. The bridge here was found entire. . . . At the second bridge over a branch of the River Thames we were fortunate enough to capture a lieut. of dragoons and eleven privates who had been sent . . . to destroy them. From the prisoners I learned that the third bridge was broken up. The bridge having been imperfectly destroyed, was soon repaired and the army encamped at Drake's farm four miles below Dalson's.[59]

A number of rivers emptied into Lake Saint Clair across the road from Sandwich to the Thames: the Petite River, Pike's Creek, the River aux Puces, the Belle River, the Carp River, the River Ruscom, and finally, Indian Creek, close to the mouth of the Thames. The first branches on the south bank of the Thames itself, just above the mouth, were Baptiste's Creek near Trudelle's and Jeannette's Creek. Most of the log bridges over these rivers could have easily been repaired, but a few of them, especially those spanning Pike's Creek, the River Ruscom, Baptiste's Creek, and Jeannette's Creek, might have given difficulties either because timber was not close at hand or because the streams were deep and wide. Nevertheless, the British left them intact because up to Trudelle's the Indians were well to the rear of the retreat and Procter, encouraged by Elliott, believed that the destruction of the bridges would have rekindled native suspicions that they were to be abandoned.[60]

Once the Indians and British had been consolidated on the Thames, these misgivings became inapplicable and indifferent efforts were made to destroy the bridges left behind. Dixon planned to undertake the task until interrupted by the retreat from Trudelle's to Dolsen's, and Hall was only marginally more successful when he broke one of the two bridges above the mouth of the Thames on October 1. The following day witnessed Ensign Holmes's ill-fated attempt to destroy the other that resulted in his capture.[61] Thereafter it was the Indians who retreated eastward along the south bank of the river, pursued by the American army, and Tecumseh rather than Procter was responsible for destroying any bridges in his wake. Those over McGregor's Creek duly received attention from the Indians, but it is uncertain if Arnold's Creek and the other small streams thereabout were endowed with bridges of any significance. Since the area was thickly wooded such bridges could have been replaced without much exertion.[62]

On the fifth Harrison's forces forded the Thames above Arnold's and on the march to Moraviantown encountered two more bridges across streams that fell into the north side of the river. One was the mill dam belonging to the family of John and Joshua Cornwall that supported the main road, but since the creek it spanned was fordable close by its destruction would have served little purpose. A party of British soldiers under Captain Chambers was detailed to burn the mill dam, but unaccountably they set fire to the mill only and retired leaving the dam unscathed. A happier job was made by the group at another bridge, which crossed a gorge, but their success simply demonstrated the futility of many of these exercises. When the Americans reached the obstacle, they "soon filled the ravine with fence rails and passed over. . . ."[63] Thus, while the performance of the British and Indians was, in respect of the bridges, ragged, it is by no means evident that greater energy in this direction would have produced significant military benefits.

THE BATTLE OF MORAVIANTOWN:
OCTOBER 5, 1813

Almost without a struggle . . .

AHEAD of the British and In-
dian allies that morning of October 5 lay Fairfield, a small village
of missionary Indians established on the north bank of the Thames
in 1792 and colloquially known to all as Moraviantown. Some four
to 4½ miles upstream from the Sherman farm, it possessed a chapel
and sixty to seventy houses on either side of a road that ran parallel
to the river, and about were scattered the few cornfields that gave
the Indians their frugal livelihood.[1] Every indication was that
Procter would make his stand there. He had examined the ground
on October 3 and informed his engineer that he intended moving
the troops to the place and desired works to be erected accordingly.
While Warburton was quartering the division at Sherman's on the
evening of the fourth, Procter had again been upriver, a trip that
did not change his opinion of Moraviantown as a suitable place for
battle. When the general rejoined his men after they had marched
from Sherman's on the morning of the fifth, he told Chambers that
it was a fine position.[2] About the same time Troughton was
ordered to send his field artillery forward to the village and to
arrange it "as I thought best calculated for the defence of the
Moravian Town," except for one 6-pounder that was placed in the
rear of the retreating division.[3]

The position at Moraviantown was certainly favored for defensive purposes. Behind the village lay a raised plain protected by a
deep, broad ravine that passed across its front from the river to a

wood marking the opposite flank. This height commanded the adjacent area, including the bank across the river; the bridge that permitted the road to transverse the gorge could have easily been destroyed and the brush on the approaches to it cleared. Situated on the height an army would have been difficult to dislodge. A cavalry charge against its front would have been broken by the ravine; the army's left flank would have rested above the river, while on the right the wood, occupied by the Indians, could have proven a formidable barrier to overcome.[4] The ground did exhibit some weaknesses, however. Although the river that guarded one flank was fast and perilous to any boats that might attempt to assault the height, there was a ford nearby the British would have had to cover with artillery. Morever, the woods on the other flank, extending from Moraviantown to Delaware, thirty-four miles away, were not very thick near the heights. Captain William Caldwell contemptuously referred to them as "all scrubby bushes." It was not ideal for the Indians, and there was doubt as to whether they would fight there. In addition, the height itself was too extensive to be effectively occupied by so small a force as Procter possessed, and Captain Hall believed that a "continuation of the high land at the head of the ravine" weakened protection at the right of the front.[5]

While preparations were under way at Moraviantown—to cook food, to care for the sick, and to erect works—the main body of the Right Division marched up from Sherman's. It did not reach its destination. En route it was intercepted by General Procter, back from Moraviantown, who in a short while was apprised of Chambers's report that the boats had been captured and Harrison was advancing. Apparently he formed an exaggerated impression of the proximity of his pursuers. Halting the division, Procter faced it right about and marched it back fifty or sixty paces to a position he had presumably noticed earlier to be defensible. Then he took some of his staff, including Hall and Elliott, and rode to the rear to investigate Chambers' information for himself. Several pieces of intelligence convinced Procter that the Americans were close by. Billy Caldwell reported that he had been told by scouts that the enemy was advancing; Cornet Pierre Lefevre of the Canadian Light Dragoons, while reconnoitering downriver below Cornwall's, encountered the Americans and was chased back; and Procter,

Elliott, and Hall also retraced part of the division's path. Satisfied that Harrison was upon him, Procter returned to his army and ordered them into battle formation, although Moraviantown was within two miles upstream.[6] In doing so he lengthened his already impressive list of errors. The formation was hurried, but the troops stood on the field some three hours before receiving the American attack, sufficient time to have completed their march and perhaps partaken of the provisions at Moraviantown before meeting the enemy assault.[7] The battle of Moraviantown was, therefore, actually fought a mile or so southwest of the village Procter was preparing for defense. Its site can be fairly precisely determined, for most of the bayonets, bullets, tomahawks, muskets, and the remains of men and horses have since been unearthed in lot four of the Gore of Zone, Kent County.[8]

An immediate product of the decision to fight before reaching Moraviantown was further diminution of the strength of the already emaciated division. By dividing his forces before a superior enemy, Procter was transgressing an elementary axiom of military strategy. The scale of his blunder is demonstrated by an examination of the British and Indian forces actually on the field during the engagement. Since Harrison's army was accompanied by only two 6-pound guns, Procter could have enjoyed an enormous superiority in artillery with his nineteen or twenty servicable guns—four or five 12-pound carronades, one 18-pound carronade, two 24-pound long guns, seven 6-pounders, three 3-pounders, one 8-inch and one 5½-inch howitzer.[9] But these he had split three ways. Most of the ordnance, with some ammunition, had been abandoned or destroyed at the forks of the Thames or at Bowles's when the British retreated from their positions on October 4. The spare ammunition for the remaining artillery—the six guns of the field train—was lost with the boats the following morning, and later in the day a 6-pounder, three 3-pounders, and a howitzer were sent ahead to Moraviantown. Thus, when the Right Division faced the American army southwest of the village in the afternoon, it was actually inferior in artillery, fielding only one 6-pound gun with little or no spare ammunition. Procter's later statement that the field train was "posted upon the heights [at Moraviantown] in our rear to protect a ford by which alone we might have been turned upon the left, and to support our retreat" does not mask the manifest squandering of one of his few advantages. [10]

As with guns, so with men. The Indian force, it has been shown, had lost more than a thousand warriors since the beginning of September. The natives had crossed the Thames by a ford at Moraviantown, where they expected to fight, and discovered a place of security two miles from Procter's new ground and 1½ miles from the ford where their families could be deposited in safety. Upon learning that Procter was forming for battle to the southwest, they made their way downriver and stragglers were still joining the lines moments before the action commenced. Probably some were too late. Minutes before firing began the Indians were counted. Each brave was given a stick and when the sticks were collected along the Indian line, they amounted to a mere five hundred. [11]

Precise figures for the strength of the Right Division on the field near Moraviantown are not available, but the army certainly betrayed a steady attrition; desertion, sickness, enemy action, and baggage, boat, cattle, and escort duty had all taken their toll. Taking the Forty-first Regiment of Foot first, a return for October 5 based upon a narrative of Captain Hill enumerates 379 men with Procter, 29 serving as additional gunners, 144 detailed to the boats, 63 with the baggage or sick at Moraviantown, and 101 men sick at the village. [12] A superficial examination would conclude that the first two of these categories, 408 men, were present on the battlefield and the balance, 308, absent, but the figures are misleading. It is possible, for example, that some of the 144 men assigned to boat duty, and in the third category, did in fact participate in the battle. Most of the boats and more than sixty men of the Forty-first were captured early on the fifth, but others escaped and their crews could have rejoined the division in time for action. Chambers reported taking men off surviving craft. On the other hand, Hall deposed that an additional 18 men were detailed to enable them to continue. [13]

Similar confusion obscures the additional gunners who had been drawn from the regular force to support the artillery. A return dated October 1 affirms that 29 men of the Royal Artillery and 8 of the Provincial Artillery accompanied the Forty-first, and Warburton believed that they were in the field on the fifth. In truth, most of them seem to have been with the siege train at Moraviantown, and only 5 regular gunners attended the single 6-pounder that saw action. Some, at least, and perhaps all, of the additional artillerymen were, however, with Procter and probably inspired Warburton's testimony.[14] It appears also that about thirty convalescents were marched from the sick quarters at Moraviantown to share in the engagement, but it was the opinion of Evans that some of his men were absent driving the cattle herd, which was situated five to six miles from the field.[15] All this leaves a murky picture indeed. Most of the 408 men given in the first two categories of the statement of the Forty-first for October 5 were likely to have served in the battle, excepting small parties delegated other and safer work, and some reported as sick or with the boats might also have participated.

Then there were auxiliaries to the Forty-first listed in the return of October 1 as Canadian Light Dragoons, 50; Royal Artillery, 29; Tenth Royal Veteran Battalion, 23; Royal Newfoundland Regiment, 15; and Provincial Artillery, 8. The artillery, as has been noted above, were for the most part at the Moravian village. According to Sergeant Philip Brooks, other auxiliaries had been lost with the boats, 4 or 5 of the Royal Newfoundland corps and 14 of the Tenth Royal Veteran Battalion, while Lieutenant Richard Bullock reported on December 6 that "the number of our dragoons did not exceed 20" on the field. This evidence suggests that about forty men—dragoons, Tenth Royal Veteran Battalion, and Royal Newfoundland Regiment—may have to be included in Procter's engaged force. Given such inexactitude in the data, Sir George Prevost's remark that the total number of regulars in the battle did not exceed 450 is probably as accurate an estimate as any.[16]

General Harrison's army outnumbered the forces of Procter and Tecumseh by about three to one, but once again the figures are disputed. Most of the fighting fell to the lot of Colonel Richard Mentor Johnson's regiment of mounted Kentucky militia, mustered in the spring and summer. They had been well drilled in Ohio, and maneuvers for flanking, charging in lines, and reforming in an enemy's rear were incorporated in their standard fighting instructions. At least a thousand of Johnson's men served in the battle, armed with muskets or rifles, tomahawks, and knives. Harrison's infantry (who confusingly were also often mounted) consisted of five brigades of Kentucky militia assembled at Newport on the Ohio in August under the command of the veteran Governor Isaac Shelby, a force the major general assessed in reporting the battle as under twenty-five hundred men. They were high-spirited, but many were merely inexperienced boys, and the brigades had only recently been efficiently armed. In addition, the Americans employed about 120 regulars (all those of the Twenty-seventh Regiment who had accompanied the march and obtained their baggage from the boats in time to join the volunteers) and about 260 Indians.[17]

Writing his dispatch of October 9, Harrison gave his militia and regulars a strength of "something above three thousand," a figure inconsistent with the known size of Johnson's regiment and with the statistics the general had given for his infantry. Some days later, upon the representations of Governor Shelby, Harrison reduced his estimate to under twenty-five hundred men on the battlefield, exclusive of Indians. It is not impossible that the pursuit left some men fatigued and sick along the road, as Harrison's aide, Charles Scott Todd, informed the *National Intelligencer*, and about 150 infantry remained near Dolsen's to protect the gunboats, the *Scorpian*, the *Tigress*, and the *Porcupine*, which proceeded no farther because of the danger of enemy fire from the high river banks. On balance, although a recent historian has calculated that Harrison fielded 3,440 men, in addition to his Indians, it seems that a figure of 3,000 would be a respectable guess at the total force beneath the American banner at Moraviantown.[18]

Procter, therefore, confronted an army much stronger than his own, with his command divided. Instead of using his time to consolidate behind a strong defensive position, he had been caught in disarray. Much of his strength lay behind him, abandoned, captured, or defecting; ahead, at Moraviantown, were other contingents unable to help. He had planned first to fight near Chatham and then at the village, and he finished making his stand at neither. The crushing consequence of opportunities squandered and situations mismanaged now bore upon the British commander with a remorseless finality. So much had been lost in men and

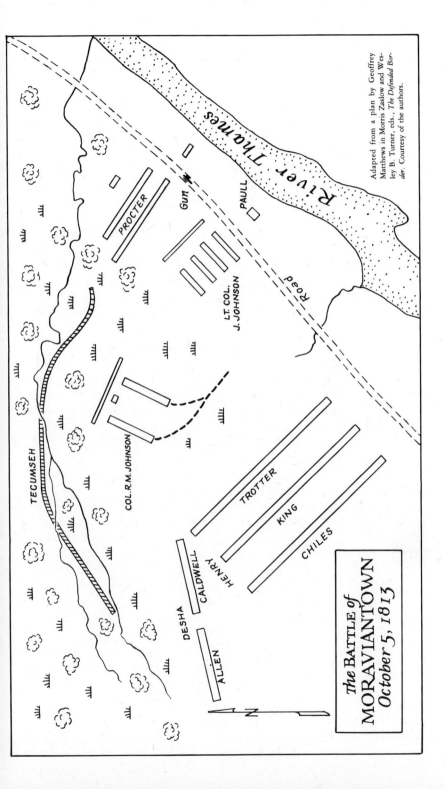

Adapted from a plan by Geoffrey Matthews in Morris Zaslow and Wesley B. Turner, eds., *The Defended Border.* Courtesy of the authors.

River Thames

PROCTER

Gun

PAULL

Road

LT. COL. J. JOHNSON

COL. R. M. JOHNSON

TECUMSEH

TROTTER

KING

CHILES

DESHA

CALDWELL

HENRY

ALLEN

N

The BATTLE *of* MORAVIANTOWN October 5, 1813

materiel after the retreat from the forks that the most judicious course remaining to the division would have been to fall back to the Centre Division without risking a general engagement. But Procter was no longer master of his fate; he was driven inexorably toward the final reckoning. Probably no one knew until shortly before firing that so many of the Indians had been lost, but with the enemy snapping at his heels, Procter may have realized that his credit in the service and Britain's prospects with the Indians then and later demanded as little ignominy as possible. Rather than be chased helplessly up the Thames, he turned like a stag at bay, hoping against hope that somehow he could achieve a victory.

The British-Indian army took up position after noon of the fifth in an area that possessed some natural advantages. The Thames guarded the left flank. About, the land was flat and studded with beech, oak, and sugartree, which thickened farther away from the river. On the left a few yards from the river and passing along its side through the wood was the main road. Perhaps 650 yards from the river, where the cover became dense, a large swamp ran along the foot of a ridge roughly parallel to the Thames but narrowing the distance between the two as it stretched upstream. A smaller swamp, lying between the main swamp and the river, was about 250 yards from the latter.[19]

The British occupied the wood from the river to the small swamp, while their Indian allies manned the thick cover between the two swamps, extending their line along the large swamp so that they could rake both vanguard and flank of an attacking force. Procter anticipated that the trees would inhibit the enemy cavalry and that the narrow front between the Thames and the big swamp would prevent Harrison from deploying his full strength against the British-Indian line. Entirely satisfied with the position, he later averred that "accident and misconduct deprived me of a victory which seemed certain."[20] His tactics, apart from repelling an assault, were outlined to de Rottenburg on November 16: "A plan of co'operation was cordially established with the Indians, who were to turn the left of the enemy; whilst the troops should resist the right. The Indians did turn the left of the enemy and execute their part faithfully and courageously."[21]

Tecumseh's dispositions were, indeed, excellent. In selecting ground suitable for Indian warfare, Procter had relied upon the sound counsel of Elliott, who had been with him for much of the day, but it appears that the Shawnee chief himself chose the actual battle position for his warriors when he reviewed the formation of the British troops. Lieutenant Allan McLean recollected the moment for the members of Procter's court-martial:

Q. Did Tecumseth appear in spirits or satisfied with the position taken up and the distribution of the force?
A. He did. I recollected the general asking Tecumseth which would be the best place for his young men to fight. His answer I think thro' Colonel Elliot was this place will be as good a place as any pointing to the right. [22]

Tecumseh secreted his men in the wood between the two swamps and along the arm of the larger swamp on his right so that the Americans would have to face his fire at front and at flank. The timber was thick enough to provide cover for the warriors and to check enemy cavalry, as Johnson's regiment was to discover ("finding it impractible on account of logs & the thickness of the woods to break through the Indian line & form in their rear I ordered the men to dismount & fight the Indians in their own way"), and it would afford a refuge if the day went badly. There was little need for improvising defenses on such ground, but Captain William Caldwell, who was on the Indian left, mentions a breastwork of two logs, and local tradition, probably transmitted by the Shermans, ventured that the Indians employed the only abatis used in the battle. Some scouts were sent to reconnoiter the enemy, and Captain Billy Caldwell acted loosely as an intermediary between Tecumseh and Procter. [23]

The representatives of many tribes waited grimly in Tecumseh's line: Shawnee, Ottawa, Ojibwa, Delaware, and Wyandot from the heartland of the Old Northwest; Sac, Fox, Kickapoo, Winnebago, and Potawatomi from the prairies of Illinois, the upper lakes, and the Mississippi; and even a band of Creeks from the South who had attached themselves to the Shawnee chief's star. [24] Sprinkled among them were also a few members of the British Indian Department. Captain William Caldwell occupied the position where the Right Division and the Indians met, next to the Shawnee on the extreme left of the Indian formation, while farther to the right among the Indians were other leaders, successively Tecumseh himself, a significant warrior called Winepegon or Brisbois, Naiwash, Lieutenant James Fraser, the Ojibwa Peckickee or Skivahee, and Lieutenant Jacob Graverot.[25]

There were two weaknesses in these dispositions. First, the five hundred warriors could not satisfactorily man the wood and the swamp and must have been spread thinly; second, Tecumseh's left was protected by the Right Division, which had been drawn up in a thoroughly inadequate fashion. Nevertheless, the Indians believed that man for man they were superior fighters to the Americans; and they seemed satisified by the prospect of battle, and Tecumseh was now in good spirits.[26] This is worth emphasizing because most historians have portrayed the chief in an abnormally pessimistic mood, haunted by a presentiment of his own death. The story first appeared in 1821 in the interviews conducted by a biographer, Benjamin Drake, with the half-blood Anthony Shane and his wife, Lamateshe, a relative of the famous chief. The Shanes informed Drake that before the final battle Tecumseh told his followers that his body would remain upon the field. He removed his sword, passing it to a chief with the remark that it was to be kept safely and given to Tecumseh's son when he had earned the reputation of a warrior, and then stripped off his British officers' uniform, except the plume, and attired himself as an ordinary Indian.[27]

The reference to a British uniform is an error easily explained. Shane was with the American army at Moraviantown and saw the body of Tecumseh upon the ground after the battle. His story attempts to reconcile the native costume in which the chief then appeared with a mistaken belief that Tecumseh generally adorned himself in regimentals.[28] But the balance of the Shane testimony might not be inaccurate, for it is partly supported by independent testimony. The author of *Lucubrations of Humphrey Ravelin*, of whom something has already been said, alleged that Tecumseh, on the eve of battle, "seemed to have a presentiment of what was to occur" and told the Indians not to elect his son as their chief, for "he is too fair and like a white man." As this source also declares that the boy was then merely fourteen or fifteen years of age, the words

Black Hawk, the Sac chief, by Charles Bird King, 1837. Although he joined the British and Indian forces on the Detroit River for the July campaign of 1813, his presence at Moraviantown is disputed. Subsequently he led the Sacs in victories over the Americans near the Mississippi, on July 21, 1814 and May 24, 1815. Lieutenant Colonel Robert McDouall described him as "perhaps the ablest and bravest [Indian] since the death of Tecumseh."

attributed to Tecumseh seem preposterous, but the story as a whole adds weight to Shane's information.[29]

An elaborate exposition of the legend was set forth in an account by "W" that purported to give Black Hawk's version of Tecumseh's death. "W" does not engender faith in his material by refusing to identify himself but assured his readers of its authenticity:

He [Black Hawk, a famous Sac chief] was fond of recounting his earlier exploits, and often boasted of his being at the right hand of Tecumseh, when the latter was killed at the battle of the Thames. His account of the death of this distinguished warrior was related to me by himself, during an evening that I spent in his lodge some winters ago.[30]

Before the battle, the Sac chief is reported to have said, Tecumseh, Shabbona (a Potawatomi), Billy Caldwell, Black Hawk, and two other Potawatomis were seated upon a log smoking their pipes when a message arrived summoning Tecumseh to Procter. "W" continued:

He went immediately, and after staying some time rejoined us, taking his seat without saying a word, when Caldwell, who was one of his favourites, observed to him—my father what are we to do? Shall we fight the Americans? "Yes, my son," replied Tecumseh, "We shall go into their very smoke: but you are now wanted by the general. Go, my son, I never expect to see you again."

"W" claimed that one of the Potawatomis to whom the chief referred corroborated his narrative, yet it disagrees with the celebrated autobiography that Black Hawk dictated through Antoine Le Clair, United States interpreter to the Sacs and Foxes. This work denies that Black Hawk was even at Moraviantown. After detailing his presence in Procter's abortive attack upon Fort Stephenson in the summer, the autobiography complains that: "The British army were making preparations to retreat. I was now tired of being with them—our success being bad, and having got no plunder. I determined on leaving them and returning to Rock River. . . . That night, I took about twenty of my braves, and left the British camp for home."[31] British records do attest, however, that many Sacs served in the Moraviantown campaign, and Black Hawk may have been one of them. "W" was not the only person to be regaled with the chief's reminiscences of Tecumseh's death. Charles A. Wickliffe was said to have received an account, and C. S. Todd was certainly informed by the old Sac that he had been on the Thames that day.[32] It is conceivable therefore that it is Le Clair rather than "W" who is in error.

Slight support for the Black Hawk anecdote is provided by the evidence that Billy Caldwell gave to Procter's court-martial on January 10, 1815: "I did not see General Procter with Tecumseh—I was too late. The orders I received from the Major General were that he wished I should be by him during the action, but I said that if the Indians engaged on the right I must be there. He told me to come as often as possible during the action."[33]

It is here confirmed, at least, that Procter conferred with Caldwell after he had seen Tecumseh, as the Sac narrative implies, but this far from substantiates the greater part of Black Hawk's story. Subsequent accounts of Tecumseh's foreboding were obtained by Lyman C. Draper, whose quest for materials for a biography of Tecumseh spanned several decades. In 1868, Joseph N. Bourassa, a nephew of Shabbona, one of the Indians mentioned in the Black Hawk story, told Draper that his uncle claimed that on October 4 the Indians held a council in which Tecumseh's opinion was that they would be defeated if they fought and that his own life would be lost in the battle. Nevertheless, he would lead them if they wished.[34]

Much the most important of the many versions on this theme was given Draper on August 6, 1863 by Captain William Caldwell, a member of the Indian Department who unquestionably participated in the battle alongside Tecumseh. He was, it must be said, nearly eighty when Draper met him, and had probably been influenced by earlier published material. A degree of suspicious self-congratulation also emerges from the Caldwell interview. According to his story, Tecumseh was contemptuous of the British lines, and remarked to Billy Caldwell: "See, these people are just like sheep, with their wool tangled and fastened in the bushes they are trying to push aside to effect an entrance. They can't fight—the Americans will brush them all away, like chaff before the wind."

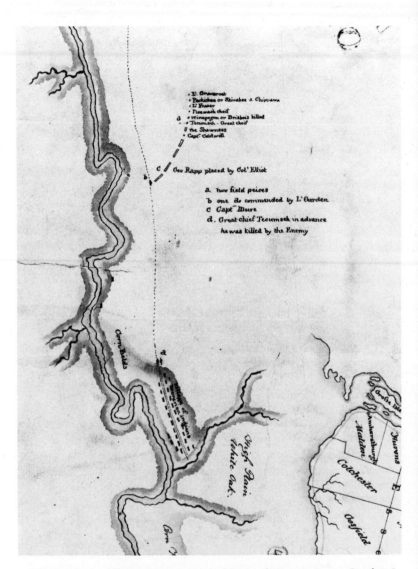

The British and Indian positions in the Battle of Moraviantown, October 5, 1813, by George Williams on a map of August 9, 1814. The map was probably prepared with the assistance of members of the Indian Department who were present in the action. *Courtesy National Map Collection, Public Archives of Canada.*

Between-the-Logs, a Wyandot of Lower Sandusky. He was firmly
attached to the American interest. After spending a year in the village of
Tecumseh and Tenskwatawa about 1807, he returned to his people repudiat-
ing the Prophet's pretensions. In August, 1813 he attempted to persuade the
British-allied Wyandots to defect, and the following month he accompanied
Harrison into Canada. *Courtesy British Library.*

Noticing the chief's pensive mood, Captain Caldwell tapped him on the shoulder.

"What's the matter?" he asked.

"No one will stand by me and fight today," Tecumseh replied.

"Yes, Tecumseh," volunteered the captain, "one man will—I am that man; I will stand by you till the last—I will pledge myself not to run till you set me the example."

Tecumseh raised three fingers. "Yes—you, I and Billy Caldwell I know will fight—but what can we do alone?"

Before firing began, Tecumseh, Thomas McKee, William Caldwell, Elliott, and a young Shawnee aide to Tecumseh, were seated on a log when they distinctly heard the noise of a flying bullet, although none had been fired. Tecumseh jumped, placing his hands before and behind his body as if shot, and Caldwell inquired if anything was wrong. Tecumseh said "he could not exactly tell, but it is an evil spirit which betokens no good." Elliott related that during the Revolution, Colonel William Caldwell, the father of both the captain and Billy Caldwell, had experienced the sensation of being shot in the legs a day before it actually occurred. Alarmed at this suggestion, Caldwell recommended that Tecumseh be prevented from fighting, but Elliott insisted that if the chief was absent he would be blamed for any disaster. Tecumseh himself would not hear of it. "No," he said, "I can't think of such an act."[35]

It is well to remember that such stories are frequently encountered in reminiscences of celebrated men and women. The biographies of Nelson, for example, are replete with them. With the advantage of hindsight it is easy to abstract events from their context and to misconstrue their meaning. Tecumseh was killed, and chance remarks that seemed to augur the event were remembered and exaggerated. Not unlikely, most men steeling themselves for battle reflect upon the possibility of death, but usually they are mistaken and their pessimism, lacking significance, passes unrecorded. In this instance, Tecumseh, wearied by the misfortunes of the retreat and the evident duplicity of his British allies, may have weighed the matter more deeply. He may even have resolved to conquer or die. But while Tecumseh's prescience has been repeatedly alluded to by his biographers, the better evidence of Baby, McLean, Cochran, and Richardson establishes that the chief exhibited no lack of confidence as he prepared for his final encounter.

Linked with this legend is Tecumseh's reputed dissatisfaction with Procter's plan of action. Perhaps this story owed something to the delight many writers have taken in exploiting the differences that must have arisen between Tecumseh and Procter over the conduct of the retreat. It, too, borrowed from the wisdom of hindsight. Billy Caldwell and Shabbona are represented to have said many years after the battle that Tecumseh had been so displeased with Procter's plan that he submitted an alternative that Caldwell claimed would have been successful. Caldwell is further reported to have stated that Procter was twice lobbied on the subject by Tecumseh and himself and that Caldwell was with the general when the first shots were fired.[36] In refutation of this particular anecdote, which epitomizes the manner in which larger-than-life legends are constructed, it suffices to say that Caldwell specifically testified at the court-martial that he had heard no Indians express dissatisfaction with the disposition of the forces awaiting attack.[37] The Indians were undeniably displeased with their allies, and on the day of the battle a Sac leveled his piece at Colonel Elliott and threatened him, but this related to the failure of the British to fortify the forks and the pusillanimity that the warriors presumed lay behind it.[38]

While the Indians dribbled into battle formation on the right, the remains of the Right Division had been hastily assembled shortly after noon. Between the river and the small swamp the troops formed a line nearly 250 yards long in an open wood. A little to the front, on the main road, was placed the solitary gun, loaded with spherical and common case shot, and supported by the artillerymen, four marksmen from the Forty-first, and ten dragoons under Cornet Pierre Lefevre. The other dragoons were assigned to the rear. "The men appeared to be in good spirits," recalled Adjutant Lewis Fitzgerald, "but at the same time complained for want of food. I heard them express a wish when they were halted to meet the enemy." A similar esprit de corps was detected by Lieutenant Richard Bullock. The soldiers had grumbled about being halted the second time, immediately previous to formation, and remarked "that they were ready and willing to fight for their knapsacks: wished to meet the enemy, but did not like to be knocked about in that manner, doing neither one thing nor the other."[39]

Tecumseh reviewed the British troops after they had been formed into line and attempted to raise morale. Richardson recalled:

Only a few minutes before the clang of the American bugles was heard ringing through the forest . . . the haughty chieftain had passed along our line, pleased with the manner in which his left was supported, and seemingly sanguine of success. He was dressed in his usual deer skin dress, which admirably displayed his light yet sinewy figure, and in his handkerchief, rolled as a turban over his brow, was placed a handsome white ostrich feather, which had been given to him by a near relation of the writer . . . and on which he was ever fond of decorating himself, either for the Hall of Council or the battle field. He pressed the hand of each officer as he passed, made some remark in Shawnee, appropriate to the occasion, which was sufficiently understood by the expressive signs accompanying them, and then passed away forever from our view.[40]

The chief had words for Procter. An article in the *London Quarterly Review* alleged that he concluded with remarks of encouragement: "Father, tell your young men to be firm, and all will be well." Coffin, who resorted to the reminiscences of McLean, Procter's aide-de-camp, states that Tecumseh's last words to the general were, "Father! Have a big heart!"[41] The most insightful account of Tecumseh's inspection was given by Captain Hall at the court-martial:

After the line was formed I first me[t] General Proctor riding down from the right of the line towards the left with Colonel Elliot and Tecumseth. After they had passed the line and returned again, Colonel Elliot interpreted some observations that had passed between him and Tecumseth intended for the general. The first was that our men were too thickly posted—that they would be exposed to the enemy's riflemen, and thrown away to no advantage. The second was to desire his young men to be stout hearted as the enemy would make a push at the gun; Tecumseth then left the general apparently in very high spirits.[42]

Tecumseh's observations were acute. Skilled marksmen would have made short work of Procter's line; even when he had thinned it down it suffered heavily from snipers.[43] Furthermore, as the chief prophesied, the British 6-pounder was an early target for attack. Procter tried to obviate one of the dangers by thinning out his line, but he thereby increased its vulnerability to other perils, and Tecumseh did not see the final dispositions. The general withdrew about eighty men from the first line, commanded by Evans (Warburton acting in a general supervisory capacity), and formed them into a reserve line under Muir and Bullock. The two lines were irregular, the men seeking such cover as they could find in a sparse wood of recent growth. In more open places they presented considerable gaps, and single boles sheltered several soldiers, and Procter, as one officer remembered, lost "the advantages of close order without acquiring those of the extended, the most proper for such a situation."[44] Nor were the lines parallel, the distance between them varying from a hundred yards or more to a few paces. In the rear were the dragoons, about forty to fifty yards behind the second line.[45]

Procter should have realized that if his men had been invested with greater security from enemy gunfire, the open lines—which in Chambers's opinion "covered ground that six times the number would not have occupied in close order"—invited cavalry attack.[46] Only tight formations of infantry were proof against a mounted onslaught. Given these circumstances, Procter ought to have constructed an abatis, for which there was no shortage of timber, much of it in fallen trees, or at least placed his reserve line in a position where it could rapidly move forward to support the main line if it became necessary. In the event, the wood obstructed cooperation between the different components of the army, reducing general visibility to some forty yards. The British could not see their Indian allies, enveloped in the thick wood to the right; the first line was only intermittently within sight of the second; and when the enemy eventually appeared, they were visible only "here and there" at a distance of 150 yards.[47] The idea of an abatis seems to have escaped Procter, or he may have mistakenly believed that there was not time to construct one, but he had his scouts, some of them Indians, both downstream and across the river and ought to have received sufficient notice of an American advance.[48] If he had set men to work upon a breastwork, even the mere dragging of fallen trees and logs in front of the British position, they should have found ample time to reform upon the approach of the enemy and been the better protected against cavalry attack.

As it was, the Right Division waited nearly three hours before receiving Harrison's attack about three or four o'clock in the afternoon.[49] The American commander drew his infantry up in three lines, George Trotter's brigade of five hundred men in the vanguard, John E. King's brigade about 150 yards behind, and David Chiles's brigade in the rear acting as "a corps de reserve." These forces, their right toward the road and their left upon the larger swamp, were commanded by General William Henry. To protect their left flank from the Indians, Harrison's remaining two brigades of infantry, commanded by James Allen and Samuel Caldwell and under the direction of General Joseph Desha, were formed "en potence" upon Trotter's left, facing the long swamp. Governor Shelby, who stood at the head of the whole of the infantry, stationed himself at the angle (the crotchet) formed by Desha's division and Trotter's brigade. Harrison placed his few regulars, under Colonel George Paull, on the extreme right of his army, in the small space between the main road and the Thames, and gave them instructions to seize the enemy artillery. Ten to twelve Indians were "directed to move under the bank."[50]

Originally, the major general considered using Colonel Richard Mentor Johnson's mounted regiment on the left to attempt to turn Tecumseh's right, but the swamp made this tactic hardly feasible. In addition, Major Eleazor D. Wood reported that the British were waiting in open lines. Harrison wrote:

A moments reflection . . . convinced me that from the thickness of the woods and the swampiness of the ground, they [the mounted volunteers] would be unable to do anything on horseback and there was no time to dismount them and place their horses in security. I therefore determined to refuse my left to the Indians and to break the British lines at once by a charge of the Mounted Infantry. . . . Conformably to this idea I directed the regiment to be drawn up in close column with its right at the distance of fifty yards from the road (that it might be in some measure protected by the trees from the artillery) its left upon the swamp and to charge at full speed as soon as the enemy delivered their fire.[51]

The choice of Johnson's regiment to spearhead the attack was so amply vindicated during the engagement that its commander exuberantly and extravagantly claimed later that Moraviantown was "fought solely by the M. Regt. at least so much so that not fifty men from any other corps assisted."[52] As the troops steadily approached the British lines, one of Johnson's companies discovered that the small swamp on Procter's right and the Indians' left could be crossed. Immediately Colonel Johnson redeployed his regiment. The First Battalion, about five hundred strong and arranged in four charging columns of double files, was assigned to the colonel's brother, Lieutenant Colonel James Johnson, and to Major DeVall Payne with instructions to break the British lines. To precede it an advance guard on foot acted as skirmishers. Colonel Johnson himself led the Second Battalion, about equal in strength to the first, across the small swamp to attack the Indians. In the lead marched the hundred men of Captain Jacob Stucker's company, in line and on foot, while behind them massed the balance of the battalion, deployed in two columns approximately four hundred yards apart, the right under Johnson and the left commanded by Major David Thompson. A bold tactic designed to draw the enemy fire was the formation of a "forlorn hope" of twenty or so riders led by the veteran William Whitley, which was to charge ahead of the two columns, and with memorable dash Johnson himself chose to eschew safety and accompany these horsemen.[53] Once the men were in position, the two battalions of mounted volunteers advanced, resolutely determined to avenge the blood spilled by the sons of Kentucky at the River Raisin and Fort Meigs.

For the British the battle was over quickly. Shortly after the American bugles shrilled through the air, Lieutenant Colonel James Johnson's skirmishers, creeping forward, opened fire on the British front line, causing a number of casualties. But the principal onslaught was made by the four columns of cavalry at full gallop. Simultaneously, Harrison's regulars rushed forward to secure the

British 6-pounder. The weapon was limited to a range of about fifty yards, but even when the Americans appeared on the road before it the gun remained silent. Startled by the first crackle of musket and rifle fire, the horses of the gun-team bolted, and as panic spread the artillerymen and Lefevre's dragoons were soon in flight to the British reserve line, abandoning the piece behind them. Their conduct was unfortunate, if not disgraceful. Although Lefevre claimed that the gun was discharged at the enemy, Bombardier James Lamb (the senior noncommissioned officer in attendance) and Joseph Benac, a dragoon, disagreed, and admitted that the 6-pounder was forsaken without being fired, an opinion held by most of the other British officers.[54]

The front line of the Right Division fired upon the oncoming cavalry, but almost immediately—and about the same time that confusion occurred about the gun—they broke, flanked on the right and pierced on the left. The troops withdrew from the left of the line, some reloading, some throwing down their muskets, some reforming behind the reserve line, and others scattering into the woods. Warburton was blunt enough about the matter. "I do not think the troops made the resistance they should have done," he reflected. "They fired immediately after the enemy's riflemen commenced, and I do not think a man of the first line loaded a second time. They immediately dispersed . . . ."[55] The reserve discharged their guns as best they could, firing obliquely to the flanks, and the Americans were momentarily checked on the left. Probably only a few of the British soldiers fired a second round. They were quickly outflanked, and the line took flight from the left. Within a few minutes the Right Division had been hopelessly routed.

When the first line crumbled, Procter rode in front of the reserve calling futilely to the retreating soldiers to rally. "For shame men!" he shouted. "For shame 41st! What are you running away for? Why do you not form?"[56] But none could stop the stampede, and Hall cried out, "This way General, this way!" Procter then moved quickly to the main road as the second line fired and fled with his guard, evidently while some of his troops were still on the field.[57] Warburton, Evans, and Muir were taken prisoner. The former alleged that his commander quitted the army before the second line had broken, but Hall testified that Procter not only fled after the collapse of the reserve but also briefly considered joining Tecumseh. "In a very short time after that," Hall said of the flight, "the general said do you not think we can join the Indians—on looking round I replied look there Sir there are the mounted men betwixt you and them. We continued our retreat."[58] Within minutes Procter and his staff sped into Moraviantown, where the general ordered Troughton to rearrange his artillery, drank something without dismounting, and then galloped away leaving no further instructions. Hall, as if the presence of the guns had suddenly been remembered, shortly returned, calling from horseback at a distance that Troughton should "do the best I could, or to that effect." The lieutenant had no other option than to spike the pieces and abandon them to the enemy. Procter's carriage and papers were also captured by the Americans, but not the regimental colors, which had been sent on with the baggage to the head of Lake Ontario.[59]

The success of the First Battalion of mounted Kentucky volunteers had indeed been spectacular. Outflanking their British adversaries, the cavalrymen encircled the Right Division and most of it surrendered, and during the pursuit on the fifth and the sixth others were brought in. Accurate figures for the British casualties are not available. Bullock reported twelve killed and thirty-six wounded; Harrison, twelve killed and twenty-two wounded; and Warburton and Evans, more than a year later, eighteen killed and twenty-five wounded.[60] By contrast the American casualties had been negligible, as Harrison informed his Secretary of War:

our column at length getting in motion broke through the enemy with irresistible force. In one minute the contest in front was over. The British officers seeing no hopes of reducing their disordered ranks to order, and our mounted men wheeling upon them and pouring in a destructive fire immediately surrendered. It is certain that three only of our troops were wounded in this charge. . . .[61]

Richard Mentor Johnson was not even prepared to go that far. Many years later he wrote that the First Battalion's only casualty in the charge upon the British was one horse killed. McAfee, who commanded a company under Lieutenant Colonel James Johnson, was more generous to his foes and credited them with killing two or three Americans, a figure that is ill sustained by surviving muster rolls of the mounted regiment.[62] Harrison's allegation that the British was routed "in one minute" was almost certainly an exaggeration, but the division could find little solace in its own assessments. Hall, McLean, Captain William Caldwell, and Adjutant Fitzgerald all contended that the engagement was contained within four minutes, and Bullock believed that it lasted for twice that time. Both estimates are plausible, but the view of Evans, Warburton, Muir, and Chambers that the second line held its position some ten minutes after the first had been broken is consistent neither with the casualties inflicted upon the Americans nor the circumstances of the action.[63]

Why had the British done so badly? Recriminations flurried fast in the following months. In his dispatches Procter blamed the disaster on the soldiers, whose champion, Lieutenant Bullock, cautioned that "from the well-known character of the regiment, any observations emanating from those whose interest it is to cast a direct or indirect reflection upon its conduct, cannot be received with too much distrust."[64] The wounds were reopened in the court-martial at the close of the war, in which Warburton, Evans, Muir, Chambers, and Bullock appeared as witnesses for the prosecution. This umbrage had existed long before the battle, for Procter was an unpopular commander reliant upon a coterie of confederates such as Hall, but staying aloof from his leading subordinates and refusing to supply them with essential information. The division was scarcely a model of harmony and cooperation when it engaged Harrison's forces at Moraviantown. Then, too, Procter's dispositions were far from satisfactory. He failed to concentrate his strength behind a well-prepared position. Many of his men and nearly all of his artillery were elsewhere when he gave battle, and in an open wood where the timber and undergrowth gave little protection from cavalry, he constructed no defensive works. The inability of the commissariat to maintain provisions must also have impaired the vigor of the British soldiers, and on the field the trees impeded marksmanship and enchanced the suddenness of the American attack by permitting their cavalry to approach partly unseen.

In such sharp onslaughts the weaponry for the period was not shown to the best advantage because of its slow action. The Forty-first was probably armed with the East India pattern "Brown Bess" smooth-bore flintlock musket, employing a 39-inch barrel to project a .75-caliber ball. The piece was serviceable for hitting an individual man-sized target at ranges of up to sixty yards or more but the priming was slow. Paper cartridges containing ball and powder were used. The soldier bit open the end of the cartridge, placed some of the powder into the pan of the musket and the main charge into the muzzle, and then rammed down the bullet and paper. Although trained men might be able to fire as many as four rounds a minute, this laborious process was not conducive to the maintenance of a steady fire rate in circumstances such as those in which the Forty-first found itself at Moraviantown.[65] But having said all of this, a 6-pounder and hundreds of muskets had left the enemy almost unscathed. The British were thrown into consternation by the Kentuckians; they lacked steadiness and evinced neither morale, discipline, nor efficiency.

The only real opposition was made by the Indians in the woods and swamps to the right of Procter's army. Afterwards, the dismal performance of the Redcoats occasioned bitter comments among the warriors and their leaders, who not unnaturally felt that they had been abandoned on the field by their British comrades. Elliott complained to William Claus that the conduct of the Right Division was "shameful in the highest degree," an opinion endorsed by Major General Edward Baynes, adjutant-general, in his public statement of November 24. On behalf of Prevost, he censured the troops for falling "almost without a struggle" and regretted that the division's "well earned laurels" had been "tarnished" by conduct that called "loudly for reproach and censure . . . ."

On the other hand, the Indians had "gallantly maintained the conflict under their brave chief Tecumseth . . . ." Before the court-martial was convened in 1814 some of the British witnesses were on the defensive and endeavored to minimize the Indian stand. "I do not think," Evans explained, "there was any material opposition made to the enemy on our right, after the 1st line gave way we had not the means of supporting the Indians. I believe Tecumseth was killed early." Nonetheless, Billy Caldwell, who fought beside the Indians, was unable to disguise his feelings about the respective contributions. Asked if there had been sufficient warriors to contest the enemy, he replied, "Yes. We drove those that opposed us, and we would have driven the whole if the troops had done their duty." Cochran, for one, was prepared to make a clean breast ot it. "Two other columns had attacked the Indians," he wrote, "who having properly tree'd themselves, withstood them so gallantly that the enemy were obliged to retire . . . ."[66]

The most expansive of the scanty contemporary British accounts of the Indian battle is that by James Fraser, a member of the Indian Department:

> The firing commenced the regulars fired one volley, that was all I heard. The enemy then attacked the Indians who were on the right, and the action continued with them upwards of an hour. When the action first commenced with the Indians the Americans retreated, until they came to an open place in the wood, when the Indians retreated in their turn, until they came to a swamp, where the Americans tried to get round our flank, but were prevented by the swamp. The distance that we drove the Americans was about a mile & a half. We then returned to the ground were the action commenced and some of the Americans were killed by the Indians. We then retreated to the Moravian Village, and the American mounted men pursuing us; we were obliged to take to the woods again & night came on, and that was the last we saw of them . . . ."[67]

From this and other evidence, an acceptable outline of the engagement can be reconstructed. After the British lines had fired and presumably broken, the Americans advanced on the Indian position.[68] The left of Tecumseh's force, posted between the two swamps, received the charge of Colonel Johnson's second battalion of mounted volunteers, first a line of skirmishers a hundred or more strong, and then an assault by cavalry in two columns preceded by the "forlorn hope." Biding their time, the warriors duly delivered what Harrison terms "a most galling fire . . . ."[69] One survivor of the "forlorn hope" remembered that "we were suddenly checked and separated," and another that "the fighting became very severe,

each party mingling with the other. Colonel R. M. Johnson and
Dr. Samuel Theobald . . . were all that remained on horseback.
The remainder of the forlorn hope were all, in a few minutes, either
killed, wounded, or had their horses shot from under them."
William Whitley, John Mansfield, John McGunnigal, and
Samuel Logan were killed or fatally wounded, and among the
others injured was Johnson himself, who was eventually hit five
times and forced to retire crippled from the field.[70] As the charging
columns joined the melee, striking the Indian line obliquely, the
action intensified, and Captain James Davidson, whose company
headed Thompson's column, was wounded in the thigh, abdomen,
and breast.[71] Unable to make immediate headway, Johnson instructed his men to dismount and fight on foot.[72] John Richardson
witnessed part of this action:

> An American rifleman who had been dismounted within a few paces of
> the spot where I stood was fired at by three warriors of the Delaware tribe.
> The unfortunate man received the several balls in his body, yet, though
> faint and tottering . . . made every exertion to save himself. The foremost
> of his pursuers . . .within fifteen paces of his victim . . . threw his
> tomahawk, and with such force and precision, that it . . . opened the skull
> and extended him motionless on the earth. Laying down his rifle, he [the
> Indian] drew . . . his knife, and after having removed the hatchet . . .
> proceeded to make a circular incision throughout the scalp. This done, he
> grasped the bloody instrument between his teeth, and placing his knees
> on the back of his victim, while at the same time he fastened his hands in
> the hair, the scalp was torn off without much apparent difficulty, and
> thrust still bleeding into his bosom . . . . All this was the work of a
> minute.[73]

Confronted with superior numbers and their left flank exposed
by the dispiriting retreat of the British, the Indians gradually gave
way. As Captain William Caldwell, who accompanied them,
reported, they "retired by degrees as the Americans advanced."[74]
Farther to the right, the firing lasted longer. The Indians there
engaged the American infantry at the junction of Trotter's front
line and Desha's flank division, and probably created a panic
among Shelby's inexperienced recruits for they drove the leading
militia back a considerable distance—Elliott and Fraser said about
a mile and a half—with surprising ease. Unfortunately, this prog-

ress was not sustainable. Captain James Mason's company, on the left of Henry's division, pressed up from behind, stood firm under fire, and with some men from Desha's division charged the thickets sheltering the Indian snipers. Shelby, anticipating the orders of his commander in chief, deployed some of James Simrall's regiment from the rear to support the wavering troops in the van, and Harrison himself rode to the crotchet to help restore order. As the infantry and Johnson's men intermingled, the Indian right fell back to its original position, where the warriors, said Elliott, "were much surprized to find we [the British] had not been equally successful . . . ." They nevertheless resisted for some time before retiring into the outer swamp toward Moraviantown, exchanging a spasmodic fire with the pursuit. Although Thompson's men attempted to chase the retreating warriors for a short distance, they failed to bring them to significant action and the Battle of Moraviantown was over.[75]

Estimates of the time during which the Indians were engaged vary. Some British officers, feeling uncomfortable under criticism, gave minimum figures. Muir absurdly stated that while the Indian firing lasted but "a few minutes" after the defeat of the British front line, the reserve line that he commanded maintained station ten minutes after the commencement of the action. More munificently, Chambers acknowledged "some firing on our right from the Indians which I do not suppose continued more than two minutes after the 2d line was broke." Evans remembered hearing "some straggling shots for twenty minutes perhaps—after the 1st line gave way." Warburton remembered a skirmishing from the Indians that lasted about a quarter of an hour after the British lines had collapsed.[76] The truth seems to be that the Indians engaged the Americans only after their allies had been defeated. Captain William Caldwell, who was on the Indian left, specifically reported that he heard two volleys from the Right Division, "which I supposed to be the one from the front line & the other from the reserve," and that "it was after the troops gave way that the action commenced between us and the Americans."[77]

On the other hand, Richard Mentor Johnson's claim that the battle lasted for one hour and twenty minutes must surely be discounted. Probably the sharp fighting was over quickly, especially on the Indian left, and estimates of the duration of the action depend upon how much of the scattered fire in the outer swamp the witnesses had heard. Charles A. Wickliffe, then a private in his brother's company but later a state governor, was the only participant who left on record a claim to have timed the affair. "The battle," he said, "from the first gun to the time of the Indian shout for retreat lasted fifty five minutes by my watch."[78]

The Americans were left to consolidate their position, tally the cost, and squabble over the glory. At least fifteen of their men were killed or fatally wounded, all of them in action with the Indians, and another fourteen were injured.[79] The Indians lost a comparable number of braves, a minimum of six chiefs, nine warriors, and a white Indian interpreter named Andrew Clark, sixteen in all killed or fatally wounded. Among the chiefs who died were Tecumseh and the Shawnee Wassakekabows or Wahsikegaboe (Firm Fellow), both of whom left widows, that of the latter being Tecumapeace, Tecumseh's beloved sister. The other leaders lost were Skipukinaka and Waabicaba, both Kickapoos; Civil Man Son, a Seneca; and Winepegon. The fatalities among the warriors were Wasinwa, a Shawnee; Taponta, Sigaya, and Myata, Sacs; Kabish, an Ottawa; Wanoyantinna and Moquommis, Ojibwas; and Snake and Olinkpas, Delawares.[80]

Three principal reasons can be assigned for the defeat of the Indians. Most obviously, they had been significantly outnumbered, probably far more than they realized, especially after the rout of the British released some of Johnson's First Battalion for further action on the American left.[81] Second, the British flight must have undermined Indian morale and it exposed their left flank to enemy attack. Third, the warriors were shaken by the death of Tecumseh, perhaps the only leader capable of keeping them in an unequal contest. One of the soldiers of the Forty-first who remembered retreating through the dark forest after the battle and meeting some of the Indian refugees on the way was told the news of the chief's death. Byfield wrote: "I . . . made my escape farther into the wood where I met with some of the Indians, who said that they had beaten back the enemy on the right, but that their prophet [Tecumseh] was killed, and they then retreated."[82]

Several references to Tecumseh's death have been found that are contemporaneous with the campaign. Captain Robert B. McAfee provided the first under an entry in his diary dated October 5. During the Indian battle, he wrote: "repeated charges and repulses took place on each side. Col. Johnson was wounded in the first fire & Genl. Tecumseh it is said fell by the hands of our Col."[83] More generous detail was furnished by Peter Trisler to his father in a letter written three days after the action:

> In this charge Col. Johnson was badly wounded. As soon as I saw him fall I immediately called out to several of our men to save Col. Johnson. I saw an Indian rushing on him when he was down, but he managed with the bravery and strength he had left to shoot the Indian before he was in striking distance of Col. Johnson. Tecumsey was shot directly in the left side of the breast. He bled to death immediately. I looked at him after his death. He was a fine looking man. His British friends took his body to Sandwich for burial.[84]

It should be noted that while Trisler claims to have witnessed Johnson's duel with an Indian and to have observed Tecumseh's body on the field, he does not specifically link the two events. The style of this letter, which moves abruptly from one subject to another, prevents any such connection from being established, and the possibility that its writer was swanking to his father and depicting himself as an actor in a scene he had merely heard of secondhand cannot also be discounted.

The Trisler letter remained unpublished in private hands, and the press was slow to learn of the great chief's death. There was doubt about the fact among the American high command, and the public, accustomed to reading bogus reports about Tecumseh, may have been wary. As recently as September 28 "brig. gen. Tecumseh" had been reported killed in a skirmish, and on the very day of the battle he had been resuscitated for another account that explained that he had turned upon his British allies and was harassing their retreat from Fort Malden.[85] Not until October 28 did any of the generals risk a pronouncement. "There is little reason to doubt," Cass then ventured, "but that the celebrated Tecumseh was killed in the battle. His body was seen by us all, and recognized . . . and subsequent information confirms the identity."[86] What this "subsequent information" was did not appear, but the first official British admission that Tecumseh was dead surfaced in a single sentence of Procter's dispatch of October 23, which simply recorded that: "With deep concern I mention the death of the chief Tecumtheé, who was shot on the 5th instant."[87]

From November 2, American newspapers carried the story that the Shawnee's body had been found on the field of Moraviantown. A letter from someone with Harrison's army dated at Detroit, October 11, informed the *Chillicothe* (Ohio) *Fredonian* that "Tecumseh has fallen . . . no Indians were captured; but a great many were slain."[88] And an account in *The Weekly Register* of November 13 maintained that: "I have conversed with several officers who were in the army when Procter's army was captured. . . . It is certain that Tecumseh was killed in the action; his body was viewed by many of the British officers, who all acknowledged it"[89] By far the fullest narrative was penned by an American officer at Arnold's mill on October 9 and transmitted to a friend in New Lisbon, Ohio. Major Thomas Rowland wrote:

> The Indian force in the late action amounted to 1000. Tecumseh is certainly killed—I saw him with my own eyes—it was the first time I had seen this celebrated chief. There was something so majestic, so dignified, and yet so mild in his countenance, as he lay stretched on his back on the ground where a few minutes before, he had rallied his men to the fight, that while gazing on him with admiration and pity, I forgot he was a savage. He had received a wound in the arm and had it bound up before he received the mortal wound. He had such a countenance as I shall never forget. He did not appear to me so large a man as he was represented—I did not suppose his height exceeded 5 feet 10 or 11 inches, but exceedingly well proportioned. The British say he compelled them to fight.[90]

It took rather more time to recognize the implications of the death of this Shawnee leader for the continued vitality of the British and Indian alliance and the nativist cause generally, but within a few years the assiduous if patriotic British historian William James was assessing the incident as the paramount consequence of the Battle of Moraviantown. It was an opinion to which John Richardson unreservedly subscribed. "The severest loss we sustained," he reflected in 1827, "was that of the gallant and unfortunate Tecumseh."[91]

6

WHO KILLED TECUMSEH?

Rumpsey, Dumpsey, Who killed Tecumseh?

WITH exaggeration one historian has written that "from 1813 to the Civil War the interminable question agitating the Republic and in campaign years provoking acrimony and fisticuffs was:

> *Rumpsey, dumpsey*
> *Who killed Tecumseh?*"[1]

More accurately, another has referred to the affair as "one of the most controversial shots in frontier history."[2] Both statements suggest the zealous debate that took place about Tecumseh's death for generations after the Battle of Moraviantown, in the press and around private firesides. Undoubtedly the great chief's fall was a matter of contemporary importance, pregnant as it was with implications for the survival of British-Indian cooperation on a large scale, but the actual manner of it can hardly be deemed a significant question. Yet no other event of the retreat provoked so much conjecture or such intense argument. In part the controversy reflected nothing more than a natural curiosity about the celebrated, but it was the lure of public office that sharpened the discussion.

For decades veterans of the battle claimed votes in local and national elections on account of their contributions to the defeat of the arch Indian enemy. The foremost recipients were Richard Mentor Johnson, whose continually troublesome wounds and shattered left hand bore mute testimony to his gallantry on the field, and William Henry Harrison, the commander in chief of the American army. Johnson pressed his claims on behalf of the Democrats for more than thirty years. He represented Kentucky in the Senate from 1820, served as vice president of the United States from 1837 to 1841, and was even mooted for the presidency as late as 1848. Of the burly Kentuckian's claims to attention, none was more relentlessly advertised than his reputed shooting of Tecumseh at Moraviantown. He was styled "Old Tecumseh" and "Tecumseh Johnson," and though John Catron might reject the view that a "lucky random shot, even if it did hit Tecumseh, qualifies a man for Vice-president," political plays and ballads volubly depicted the desperate encounter between the Shawnee chief and the American colonel.[3] Harrison fared even better than Johnson. "Old Tippecanoe" was elected to Congress in 1816 and became the short-lived ninth president of the United States in 1841. When his grandson was elected to the same office in 1889, one Texas newspaper took the opportunity to recall the days when the death of Tecumseh had been a bone of political contention.[4]

Initially, there were few indications that Tecumseh's fate would become the most controversial incident of the campaign. Neither Harrison, Shelby, nor Johnson mentioned it in their letters, and when Samuel R. Brown produced an account of the battle in which he was a participant he expressed no uncertainty about the matter:

On the left, the contest was more serious . . . . The Colonel [Johnson] most gallantly led the head of his column into the . . . enemy's fire, and was personally opposed to Tecumseh. . . . He rode a white horse, and was known to be an officer of rank; a shower of balls was discharged at him . . . his horse was shot under him—his clothes, his saddle, his person was pierced with bullets. At the moment his horse fell, Tecumseh rushed towards him with an uplifted tomahawk, to give the fatal stroke, but . . . he drew a pistol from his holster and laid his opponent dead at his feet. He was unable to do more, the loss of blood deprived him of strength to stand. Fortunately, at the moment of Tecumseh's fall the enemy gave way . . . he [Johnson] was wounded in five places; he received three shots in the right thigh and two in the left arm. Six Americans and twenty-two Indians fell within twenty yards of the spot where Tecumseh was killed . . . .

Brown added that many viewed the body of the chief and discovered the features "majestic even in death," but that some of the soldiers scalped and disfigured it.[5] Then, leaving the plagiarists busy with this account, he provided a more comprehensive version that was published the following year. Some of his amendments are interesting. Johnson had now been hit four times before turning his horse toward Tecumseh and was shot by the Shawnee in the hand as he approached. Taking a tomahawk or sword, Tecumseh then advanced and was killed by the colonel. Johnson rode his wounded animal to the rear and was assisted to dismount before the animal died.[6]

Few of Brown's immediate successors were able to improve upon his information. It was *The Weekly Register*'s claim that Tecumseh received a musket ball in his left arm moments before his death; the *Impartial . . . History of the War* said that he was already severely injured when he was killed aiming at Johnson; Thomson had it that Tecumseh was shot through the head as he leaped toward Johnson's wounded and staggering horse, and the *London Times* of August 11, 1814 said that the Kentuckian "War Hawk" Henry Clay had exhibited in Washington the previous winter a razor strop made for him from the skin of the Shawnee chief. British accounts of 1815 said that the body had been partly flayed.[7] It took another Kentuckian to challenge Johnson's hitherto undisputed claim to have slain Tecumseh. Robert B. McAfee, whose history of 1816 remarked that:

"Tecumseh was found among the dead, at the spot where colonel Johnson had charged upon the enemy . . . and it is generally believed, that this celebrated chief fell by the hand of the colonel. It is certain that the latter killed the Indian with his pistol, who shot him through his hand, at the very spot where Tecumseh lay: but another dead body lay at the same place, and Mr. King . . . had the honor of killing one of them."[8]

This salvo opened the first stage of the controversy about Tecumseh's death, emphasizing both the manner of the chief's fate and the author of it. Primarily the contestants vied to prove that Johnson did or did not merit the distinction of having killed the famous warrior.

In approaching this question, the idiosyncrasies of the evidence must firmly be borne in mind. Most of the accounts of Tecumseh's death were written long after 1813, when partisan writing—personal, patriotic, and political—multiplied the inaccuracies produced by the postwar rationalization of events, failing memory, and occasional senility. Fabrications of the most ostentatious kind were unloaded upon a gullible and hungry public. So tangled has the issue become that it is now impossible to provide a satisfactory reconstruction of Tecumseh's last moments, but a close analysis can at least clarify the contradictions in the evidence and expose the more extravagant untruths.

Necessarily, the claims made on behalf of Johnson demand attention first. That Tecumseh's death was attributed to Colonel Johnson shortly after the battle is satisfactorily established by McAfee's diary, already quoted. Equally certain is the fact that Johnson had killed an Indian during the engagement. Harrison and Charles Wickliffe, a private, heard of it after the action, and Trisler chronicled it for his father on October 8.[9] The colonel himself was always reticent about the pretensions that helped him to the vice-presidency, admitting that he had shot an Indian but avoiding declaring that his victim was Tecumseh.[10] Indeed, only three accounts of the contest by Johnson have been found, two in campaign speeches of 1840 and one supplied the Indian agent, Thomas L. McKenney.

The colonel said that he had been hit four times during the early firing, in the left leg, thigh, and arm, and that his gray mare had sustained seven wounds and was barely able to stand. It is not surprising, therefore, that his story becomes confused. Two of the accounts described how his mount ran into difficulties at the head of a fallen tree, in one stumbling to its knees and struggling to its feet, in the other becoming embroiled in the branches. Extricating the animal, Johnson began to walk it alongside the tree toward "a large but likely-looking Indian" who approached him from its foot and who shot him with a bullet striking near the upper joint of his left forefinger, crippling his hand. Resolutely, the colonel threw his bridle reins over his left arm, and used his right to draw a pistol charged with three buckshot and a ball. As the Indian raised a tomahawk Johnson shot at him: "his heels flew up and he came down like a tobacco hogshead. I never saw a man fall so heavy in my life." Johnson told McKenney that he then lost consciousness, but subsequently he learned that his horse wheeled and carried him back to the American lines before falling. In a third account, however, the colonel maintained that the animal died on the field as he attempted to bring it over a log. "A tall, good-looking Indian approached me with his tomahawk ready for a throw. My horse lay in a position that did not permit me to be entirely dismounted. I pulled out a loaded pistol from my holsters and shot him." Thus Johnson perpetuated the same confusion Brown had introduced in his early published accounts. [11]

Johnson's campaign managers were left to provide the more graphic version of the famous victory in a biography expressly designed to enhance his political aspirations. William Emmons told how Johnson rode to a large fallen tree before him, passed around its head to his right, and advanced upon an Indian "arrayed in the habiliments of war, clad in the richest savage attire, and his face painted with alternate circular lines of black and red, from the eye downward . . . ." The horse stumbled, drawing the attention of the Indian, who shot Johnson with his rifle and then raised his tomahawk "with a fierce look of malicious pleasure." The colonel held a pistol, loaded with a ball and three buckshot, against his thigh and discharged it into the Indian's breast, killing him instantly. "The battle at that point was ended" because the natives, "filled with consternation" at the loss of the warrior, "raised a horrid yell and instantly fled." Johnson, on his part, "was taken from the battle ground faint, and almost lifeless," but before he could be revived sufficiently as to enable him to speak "the tidings ran through the camp that he had killed Tecumseh . . . ." [12]

The weakness in the Emmons account was less the fanciful detail it embodied than its failure to identify Johnson's victim as Tecumseh. It seems to be true, as Emmons continued to explain, that the Shawnee's body was recognized on the battlefield by Anthony Shane and that a British medal "known to have been presented to Tecumseh" by his allies was taken from it, but the reasoning that led the author to deduce that this was the body of the Indian whom

Johnson had slain was inconclusive. Tecumseh, he said, was found "upon the very spot" where Johnson's encounter took place, but was he the only Indian who lay at the scene? McAfee did not think so. Emmons also recorded, upon the authority of Shane, that Tecumseh had apparently been shot by a horseman because his wounds, a ball and three buckshot—the charge said to have been used by Johnson—ranged downward from the breast to the back. But again, Indians were not incapable of stooping and where was the proof that Johnson's pistol had been loaded as described? Certainly Johnson wrote McKenney to that effect, but he probably had no clear recollection of it and was merely repeating the popular report. As Garrett Wall of the "forlorn hope" remarked: "It was the common talk, and generally understood, that Col. Johnson's pistol had been loaded a few days previous by Capt. Elijah Craig with a ball and three buckshot."[13] Unfortunately, Craig, who died nine days after the battle, was not in a position to confirm such rumors, and one of the regulars with the army later said that the American muskets employed cartridges containing a ball and three buckshot. It would seem then that Tecumseh could have received his wounds from any one of the muskets carried by his enemies as well as by Johnson's pistol.[14]

These accounts from the Johnson camp fail to establish that Tecumseh was killed by the colonel; neither do they provide a clear picture of the duel from the viewpoint of either contestant.[15] As the controversy intensified, many witnesses came forward with contributions that shared the fundamental disagreement about the basic facts already noticed. Some informants insisted that Johnson withdrew from the fray on horseback, while others depicted a gripping contest in which the colonel struggled beside his fallen mount to shoot an advancing antagonist. This discrepancy is interesting because it stretches credibility to believe that genuine spectators could have been mistaken as to whether the colonel was rescued from his dead horse or rode it to safety. Admittedly, Johnson's own accounts betray precisely this confusion, but he of all, upon the verge of insensibility, had excuses for inaccuracy. The inference must be that one of the versions is incorrect and that those who promoted it were either unreliable or fraudulent.

Dr. Samuel Theobald, Garrett Wall, James Davidson, and Ambrose Dudley were positive that Johnson's horse brought him from the battle. Theobald, a member of the "forlorn hope," wrote: "I know the period was a very brief one from the firing of the first guns which indeed was tremendously heavy, 'til Col. Johnson approached me, covered with wounds, but still mounted." Johnson begged Theobald to stay by him and to reserve his fire for an emergency. The ground was so miry that the two rode their horses at a walk to the surgeon's stand at the rear, close by the river. There the colonel was assisted from his white pony, which shortly expired of seven wounds. Theobald fetched some water from the Thames for his commander, and then returned to the field with Garrett Wall, noticing that as they crossed the smaller swamp firing was still going on "some distance off on our left."[16]

The doctor's principal points, that Johnson retired on horseback while the battle was still raging, are corroborated by Wall, who remembered carrying a mortally wounded soldier from the field toward the close of the firing and observing Johnson "passing by me on horseback into the lines, very bloody, apparently weak and exhausted: one of the volunteers was leading his horse by the bridle." Captain Davidson recalled that: "A short time after the charge commenced, and in the heat of battle, I saw Johnson pass, supported on his horse, badly wounded. He was immediately borne from the field. It was so short a time from the commencement of the action, that it would hve been a most fortunate chance if the first Indian he met was Tecumseh . . . ." The colonel, he added, was escorted from the front by Theobald and others, and he heard later that Johnson's white horse died after its rider had been removed.[17]

Ambrose Dudley served as paymaster to Trotter's brigade. In 1840 he wrote unequivocally that:

As I passed the left, near the crochet, after the firing had ceased on the right, I met Colonel R. M. Johnson passing diagonally from the swamp towards the line of infantry, and spoke with him; he said he was badly wounded—his grey mare bleeding profusely in several places. The battle continued with the Indians on the left. The infantry, with some of Col. R. M. Johnson's troops mixed up promiscuously with them, continued the battle for half an hour after Colonel Johnson was disabled, and had ceased to command his men. [18]

But while these accounts are convergent, James Knaggs, a private, remembered Johnson's achievement differently in 1853:

During the battle we charged into the swamp, where several of our horses mired down, and an order was given to retire to the hard ground in our rear, which we did. The Indians in front, believing that we were retreating, immediately advanced upon us, with Tecumseh at their head. I distinctly heard his voice, with which I was perfectly familiar. He yelled like a tiger, and urged on his braves to the attack. We were then but a few yards apart. We halted on the hard ground, and continued our fire. After a few minutes of very severe firing, I discovered Col. Johnson lying near, on the ground, with one leg confined by the body of his white mare, which had been killed, and had fallen upon him. My friend Medard Labadie was with me. We went up to the colonel . . . and found him badly wounded, lying on his side, with one of his pistols lying in his hand. I saw Tecumseh at the same time, lying on his face, dead, and about fifteen or twenty feet from the colonel. He was stretched at full length, and was shot through the body, I think near the heart. The ball went out through his back. He held his tomahawk in his right hand, (it had a brass pipe on the head of it;) his arm was extended as if striking, and the edge of the tomahawk was stuck in the ground. Tecumseh was dressed in red speckled leggings, and a fringed hunting shirt; he lay stretched directly towards Col. Johnson. When we went up to the colonel, we offered to help him. He replied with great animation, "Knaggs, let me lay here, and push on and take Proctor." However, we liberated him from his dead horse, took his blanket from his saddle, placed him in it, and bore him off the field. I had known Tecumseh from my boyhood; we were boys together. There was no other Indian killed immediately around where Col. Johnson or Tecumseh lay, though there were many near the creek, a few rods back of where Tecumseh fell. [19]

Despite the aura of propaganda exuded by Knagg's affidavit, it finds desultory support elsewhere. Labadie is said to have witnessed Johnson's shooting of Tecumseh and to have confirmed that he assisted Knaggs and another soldier to carry the colonel to safety; Pierre Navarre named Joseph Nadeau, Knaggs, Labadie, and himself as the men who disengaged Johnson from his fallen mount, but he was "positive" that the colonel had not slain

Tecumseh "from the relative position of the parties." An aide to Shelby, Major W. T. Barry, reportedly said he saw some soldiers taking Johnson in a blanket to the rear. Johnson himself, speechifying in Detroit in September, 1840, complimented Knaggs upon his courage and declared that Labadie "bore me bleeding in his arms from the field of battle . . . ."[20]

In 1859 an account of Isaac Hamblin, who claimed to be standing only a few feet from Johnson when he shot Tecumseh, was published:

He [Hamblin] was well acquainted with Tecumseh, having seen him before the war, and having been a prisoner seventeen days, and received many a cursing from him. He thinks that Tecumseh thought Johnson was Harrison, as he often heard the chief swear he would have Harrison's scalp, and seemed to have a special hatred towards him. Johnson's horse fell under him, he himself being also deeply wounded; in the fall he lost his sword, his large pistols were empty, and he was entangled with his horse on the ground. Tecumseh had fired his rifle at him, and when he saw him fall, he threw down his gun and bounded forward like a tiger, sure of his prey. Johnson had only a side pistol ready for use. He aimed at the chief, over the head of his horse, and shot near the centre of his forehead. When the ball struck, it seemed to him that the Indian jumped with his head full fifteen feet into the air; as soon as he struck the ground, a little Frenchman ran his bayonet into him, and pinned him fast to the ground.[21]

Hamblin and Knaggs tendered the most memorable picture of Johnson at the Thames, wounded beside his dying horse, shooting his charging adversary. Others endorsed this popular story.[22] Among many veterans who entertained friends with reminiscences of Moraviantown, Samuel Baker was prepared to offer a variation. The way he remembered it, Tecumseh was molesting another soldier with his axe when the colonel dashed forward to shoot him, putting the Indians to flight. Baker's accounts, given sixty or more years after the event, hardly warrant priority, but they were generally consistent. He was adamant, for example, that the troops gathered around the dead chief within minutes of the shooting and while he was still warm and bleeding.[23]

The circumstances surrounding Johnson's fight will probably remain forever obscure, but Theobald, Wall, and Dudley carry more conviction than Knaggs, Hamblin, and Navarre, all of whom advanced doubtful pretensions to have known Tecumseh and interspersed their anecdotes with manifestly fictitious elements. Suffice it to say here that the words attributed by Knaggs to Johnson were inappropriate to the engagement betwen the Second Battalion of mounted volunteers and the Indians; that Tecumseh's body does not seem to have been bayoneted; that Navarre's reminiscences once extended to the claim that he himself had shot Tecumseh to save Johnson; and that Johnson's remarks about Knaggs and Labadie were made after the veterans had been presented to him during a political campaign in Michigan when the colonel was more interesting in courting the local voters than in demystifying the Battle of the Thames.[24]

Wanting the dubious testimony of Knaggs and Hamblin, the essential evidence to prove that it was Tecumseh who fell by Johnson's hand is missing. The most valuable material bearing upon the subject is still Trisler's letter of October 8, 1813, of which something has already been said in the previous chapter. Johnson certainly killed one of the Indians about the place where Tecumseh was discovered, and he might have been the chief.[25] The only major point against its plausibility was made by Benjamin Drake, who argued that if Tecumseh's death precipitated the retreat of the Indians, as is generally believed, he could not have been killed by Johnson, who retired early and while the battle was still being fought. Few have doubted that the fall of Tecumseh demoralized his warriors. Wickliffe has written:

I am satisfied that the Indians did not retreat until after Tecumsie was killed. I can remember that preceding each Indian yell which accompanied their fire to have heard the sound of an Indian voice loud and distinct as tho it was a command to the charge or to fire. I heard this when the heavy and last charge was made on the angle formed by Chiles and Trotters of Kings brigade. After that struggle I heard that voice no more. And the body of Tecumsie was found near that point according to my recollections.[26]

Equally, despite Wall's dissenting voice, there has been general unanimity that Johnson's presence on the ground was brief. In 1859 a Captain Ferguson wrote that the colonel "was wounded in the very commencement of the charge, before the two lines had come in close contact, and was immediately borne from the field."[27] The discrepancy, however, is capable of reconciliation because the Indians' left gave way while the right was actually repulsing the American infantry. If, as will shortly be demonstrated, Tecumseh was stationed with the left of his line, between the two swamps, his death could have prompted the retreat in this section and permitted the action to continue for some time upon the right.

Johnson was not the only soldier paraded as the slayer of Tecumseh. As early as 1816 the claim of David King, a private in Captain Davidson's company of mounted volunteers, had been placed before the public. It is unfortunate that the only comprehensive statements about King emanate from his commanding officer, or from Michael Davidson, the latter's twin brother who led an infantry company at Moraviantown. According to one informant, James Davidson was a brother-in-law to King's father, and it is possible that the special pleading that marks these accounts is not unrelated to a desire for familial prestige.[28]

Stationed to the left of the "forlorn hope," Davidson's company charged in platoons of four and received from the enemy a volley followed by a furious charge. Whitley was killed, and an Indian who tried to scalp him was fended off by Davidson with his sword until one Massey slew the warrior by firing under the belly of the captain's horse. David King, a youth of eighteen or so, then retrieved Whitley's gun, still loaded with two balls, and carried it with him when he later accompanied about six other soldiers to the right to frustrate Indian flanking maneuvers. Davidson feared that King and his comrades were pressing forward too eagerly and that they would be cut off, and he started toward them. About half way there he heard one of the men, Clark, warn King that an Indian was aiming at him. The warrior then turned his weapon upon Clark, but exposed the left of his breast to King, who shot him with Whitley's piece and shouted, "Whoop! By God! I have killed one

A British medal of the kind issued to Indians during the American Revolution, front, *left*, and back, *right*. This one is preserved in the National Numismatic Collection of the National Museum of American History, and is presumably the medal that in the last century was exhibited in the Museum of the Mint and credited with having been taken from Tecumseh's body after the battle of Moraviantown. There is nothing to substantiate this claim, although Tecumseh is known to have worn a medal of the Revolutionary period. During the War of 1812 similar medals were issued to Indians, but they were inscribed "1812." *Courtesy Smithsonian Institution.* (Photo. Nos. 80–19602 and 80–19603).

damned yellow bugger!" Several witnessed the incident, including Clark, Jacob von Preece, and a soldier named Giles. The voice of the Indian commander was alleged to have ceased about the time King shot his warrior, and the natives began to retreat.

That same evening King led a party, which included Davidson, to find the Indian's corpse that he might plunder it. The spot was recognized by a nearby tree and log, and when the body was discovered and rolled onto its back it revealed two bullet wounds, about an inch apart, just below the left nipple. King stripped the body, but Davidson heard that the next day his brother, Michael Davidson, and Charles Wickliffe troubled to visit it. Harrison and two British officers also came, and the Indian was identified as

The "Battle of the Thames," a highly inaccurate lithograph of 1833 by John Dorival. It was registered by William Emmons and issued to promote Richard Mentor Johnson's campaign for the vice-presidency by depicting him as the slayer of Tecumseh. *Courtesy Library of Congress.*

Tecumseh by a scar on the left cheek and notice that one leg was more than an inch shorter than the other. Subsequently souvenir hunters peeled strips of skin from the cadaver to take home.

Not the least interesting features of this story are the differences between Davidson's two accounts. In 1831, King sought out his victim to obtain the fine leggings:

The Indian from his dress was evidently a chief. His fanciful leggings, (King's main object in hunting out the body,) his party-colored worsted sash, his pistols, his two dirks, all his dress and equipments were the undisputed spoils of King. He kept one of the dirks, the sash and moccasins for himself; the rest he distributed as presents among his messmates.

It was upon this statement that Drake pounced in his biography of Tecumseh, published in 1841. One of the few facts that was established, he said, was that Tecumseh entered the battle "in his usual plain deer-skin dress," confirmed, among others, by Francis Baby in a statement made on October 6 to one of Harrison's aides. The distinct dress of the Indian killed by King, therefore, proved conclusively that he was not Tecumseh.[29] It is surely no coincidence that Davidson's next account of 1859 contradicts his earlier narrative on this very matter of the Indian's costume. The warrior was no longer attired like a chief, but "plainly but more comfortably dressed than the rest of the Indians," wearing a fine wampum belt and carrying superior knives and arms, and King's expedition to find the body was motivated by a desire to sequester the knives rather than the leggings. These amendments admit of but one interpretation that strips Davidson of credibility: he had altered his story in an effort to prove that King had killed Tecumseh.[30]

No one verified Davidson's statements, and King himself was believed to have died in Tennessee about 1847. The remarks about the identification of Tecumseh's body were certainly confused, for both Harrison and Wickliffe have left their own accounts and neither mention the British officers who Davidson said inspected the body with them. Harrison could not recognize the Indian, while Wickliffe satisfied himself that it was Tecumseh from a description he had earlier obtained from a British prisoner. But

King's claim is open to an objection more serious than these inaccuracies. As in the case of Johnson, nothing convincing actually establishes that the Indian killed and stripped by King on the fifth was Tecumseh. None of those party to despoiling King's Indian on the evening of the battle are described as witnesses to the identification of Tecumseh's body the following day; indeed, when Wickliffe saw Tecumseh on the sixth he was still wearing his hunting shirt and leggings.

King's claim need not be rejected summarily. Possibly he deserved an abler advocate than Captain Davidson. The third man commonly credited with having slain Tecumseh, William Whitley, has not even that much support, for, inspiring as the old man must have been, he cannot be said to have shot anyone in the battle. The material in his favor is both vague and circumstantial. Abraham Scribner, a private in James Coleman's company, reported that Whitley "was seen to take aim at the Indian said to be Tecumtha" and that his rifle was found empty. Dudley remembered viewing three Indian bodies and picking up some gossip from another spectator who claimed to have witnessed the shootings. Whitley had ridden to a tree, behind which one of the warriors—the man later identified as Tecumseh—had been trying to shoot, and killed him before losing his own life to a second Indian.[31] A member of the "forlorn hope," Richard Spurr, claimed to have seen Tecumseh and Whitley fatally wound each other simultaneously, but his account lacks any authentic ring. In addition, an infantryman, James S. Whitaker, maintained that Tecumseh was found ten or fifteen steps from Whitley, and that he had received two bullets in his left side. It was known, Whitaker persisted, that Whitley generally charged his gun with two balls and that the weapon was found empty in its owner's right hand.[32] Apart from this hearsay, the only evidence incriminating Whitley is the assertion that his body lay close to that of Tecumseh, a point which in itself establishes little.[33]

Over the years various "witnesses" appeared to champion less famous candidates for the dubious distinction of having shot Tecumseh, but under scrutiny they fall short of corroborative detail. Medard Labadie, who has already been introduced, was said

to have killed the chief in defense of Johnson. Jacob Harrod
Hollman, a private in Stucker's company, has also been named. It
was alleged that he shot Tecumseh as the warrior was scalping
Whitley, and that he obtained two pistols as trophies.[34] One of the
more extravagant legends identified Tecumseh's assailant as 86-
year-old James Mason, an Irishman from County Wexford, and
others in the queue included a teenager called Adair, C. H.
Grooms, Alford Pennington, and a man called Thompson.[35]

In the light of the evidence currently to hand, it may fairly be
concluded that Johnson and King are the only applicants who
matter, and that the former's claim is surely the stronger. It alone
appears in the contemporary documentation, and three years
passed before anyone publicly disputed it. Nonetheless, no one was
able to clinch the argument, and more qualified informants were
rooted out in an effort to uncover the truth. Gradually "inside"
Indian accounts appeared in print, the words of Tecumseh's closest
friends, of men who had fought beside their chief in his last battle.
It is to their statements, to which many looked for definitive
answers about the question of Tecumseh's death, that the analysis
must now turn.

Unfortunately, the Indian materials on Moraviantown were
submitted long after the battle, when time or senility had taken its
toll. Some were distorted by the legend of Tecumseh, and almost
all were served up through white intermediaries whose motives for
misrepresentation need to be examined. The confusion endemic to
this kind of testimony is exemplified by that of Chief Sha-wah-
wan-noo, an Ojibwa veteran of the campaign who lived in retirement on Walpole Island, in Lake St. Clair, until his death in
August, 1870. The old man knew nothing of value about Tecumseh's final stand, and all that Andrew Jamieson could squeeze out
of him was that the Indians had fled in a panic from the
battlefield.[36] John Richardson visited him in 1848 and also solicited an account. Unable to answer the major's inquiries directly,
Sha-wah-wan-noo consulted another survivor of Moraviantown,
Shawanabb, and eventually produced an unlikely tale more consistent with the dime-novel fiction than with reality. Claiming to

have been "aide-de-camp" to Tecumseh, Sha-wah-wan-noo told how the Shawnee hero had been shot while on horseback under his fifth rib. Realizing that he was dying, he dismounted and discharged three pistols at his enemies before taking a sword and cutting at them until he fell exhausted. An American then dispatched him with an axe and sliced a piece of his thigh away to bear to his superiors. The Indians buried their chief under a large tree stump six feet high, hewn on four sides, and adorned with characters that proclaimed the number of men Tecumseh had killed with his tomahawk.[37]

The first "Indian" account was received by the Americans the morning after the battle from Andrew Clark, a white man who had been raised among the natives and become a follower of Tecumseh. Sadly, only one contemporary reference to Clark has been found—Bond's statement that an Indian interpreter was killed in the battle—and nothing further was said about him until 1834, when William Henry Harrison recalled that a mortally wounded French Canadian was discovered on the battlefield the following morning. Harrison visited him and was informed by the dying man that he had seen Tecumseh killed, "& I think that he was taken off by the Indians."[38] Captain Benjamin Warfield, whose company was responsible for finding the Canadian, told C. S. Todd that he had been ordered to scour the ground with his men and that a wounded British Indian interpreter named Clark was dragged from concealment in the root of a tree and taken to the major general. En route he conversed with Warfield and "distinctly informed me . . . that he [Tecumseh] had been shot down by his side & I think killed, but that the Indians had taken him off the ground." Clark repeated this information to Harrison, but the following day ("as well as I recollect") he died.[39]

Harrison and Warfield offer the best information available on the subject of Clark. Both officers spoke with him in pursuit of their official duties and may have remembered accurately what he had said. Other accounts, written even later, appear more contrived. The fullest is by Alfred Brunson, who recalled that on the morning of the sixth he noticed a severely wounded half-blood lying by the root of a tree and attended by British and American surgeons. He was heavily bandaged, but claimed to have served Tecumseh as aide and interpreter. The chief, he said, had entered the battle determined to kill Harrison or die, and when he saw a mounted American officer he took him to be the general and made toward him. "As he moved out," Brunson quoted Clark, "the Indians as well as myself drew out after him, in the form of a triangle, with Tecumseh at the point." The American and Tecumseh leveled their pieces simultaneously, but the Shawnee fired first and rushed forward to obtain the scalp of his fallen antagonist. A fusillade of bullets then cut Tecumseh, Clark, and other Indians down, and although the Shawnee chief rose to try again, he was finally killed by a young rider who pulled a pistol from his belt because he had discharged his musket. Shortly after providing this information, the half-blood died.[40]

Brunson believed that the officer shot down by Tecumseh was Whitley, and in 1872 went so far as to claim that Clark had actually described the chief's victim as a man in a cocked hat and a wide wampum belt that carried his powder horn and bullet bag. This clearly identified him as Whitley. Then and later, Brunson was also prepared to elaborate about Clark himself, depicting him as a small, rather slim man under thirty, possibly the son of a French fur trader, and versed in English, French, and several Indian languages.[41] The opinion that Tecumseh met his fate while endeavoring to scalp Whitley recalls the testimony of others on this point. Massey and Hollman have been credited with avenging the old frontiersman's death, while Dudley's information suggested that it was neither of these survivors, since the soldier who shot Whitley's killer was himself slain immediately afterward. The possibility that several Americans fired at once enhances this confusion.[42]

Whatever Clark said about Tecumseh has been lost in conjecture, and the one safe conclusion is that he gave the Americans a firm indication that the chief had been killed. In succeeding decades a number of alternative Indian accounts were channeled into print that merely accentuated the mystification. Caleb Atwater, appointed by the United States as a commissioner to negotiate with the Indians of the Upper Mississippi at Prairie du Chien in

1829, took the opportunity to renew some old acquaintances, Nawkaw (Wood) or Caraymaunee (Walking Turtle) and Hoot-shoopkaw (Four Legs), Winnebago chiefs who had been close confidantes of Tecumseh. "Carrymauny, the elder," wrote Atwater, "three times repeated to me his history, and requested me to write it in a book. He complained to me that in all our accounts of Tecumseh, we had only said of him that, 'Winnebago who always accompanies Tecumseh,' without calling the Winnebago by his name . . . ."[43] According to the two chiefs, Tecumseh was killed in "the very first fire of the Kentucky dragoons, pierced by thirty bullets, and was carried four or five miles into the thick woods, and there buried by the warriors . . . ." Atwater was convinced of the truth of the story. "This account," he said, "was repeated to me three several times, word for word, and neither of the relaters ever knew the fictions to which Tecumseh's death has given rise."[44]

The Winnebago chiefs, like Clark, raised the possibility that the Indians removed Tecumseh's body as they retreated. In 1838 the *Baltimore American* published a contribution from Black Hawk, the famous Sac chief, that bore upon the same point. The article, written by "W," has already been discussed. It told how Black Hawk, with a party of Sacs, was situated to Tecumseh's right at Moraviantown. The Americans advanced, and the Indians fired upon them from the undergrowth. It was said that: "They faltered a little, but very soon we perceived a large body of horse—Col. Johnson's regiment of mounted Kentuckians—preparing to charge upon us in the swamp. They came bravely on, yet we never stirred until they were so close that we could see the flints in their guns, when Tecumseh, springing to his feet, gave the Shawnee war-cry, and discharged his rifle."

But "at the first discharge" the chief fell forward over a fallen tree, dropping his rifle; "a sudden fear came over" his followers and they fled. That night, however, they returned and discovered Tecumseh where he had fallen, a bullet wound above the hip, his skull broken by the butt of a gun, a blow probably struck to extinguish life, but otherwise untouched. Nearby lay the body of "a large fine-looking Pottawattomi . . . decked off in his plumes and war-paint . . . scalped, and every particle of skin flayed from his body." Tecumseh's only ornamentation, Black Hawk said, was a British medal about his neck.[45]

There is some support for this perplexing account in C. S. Todd's testimony that Black Hawk once told him that he had been present when Tecumseh fell and that the chief "was certainly carried off by his followers."[46] But the story of the Indians spiriting away Tecumseh's body in the night and the exaggerated allusion to the flayed Potawatomi are obvious errors. Brunson declared that bodies could not have been removed by the Indians overnight because the field was enclosed by the American camp. This is unlikely and Brunson was senile and confused when he made the statement, but Gaines, who was on duty some fifty yards from the battleground throughout the night, more correctly implies that the task would have been difficult.[47] Furthermore, it was not until the sixth, the day after the action, that any bodies were mutilated; Indians returning to the field during the previous night would not have seen such an outrage. Black Hawk's Potawatomi was probably a fiction designed either to torpedo the exaltation of those Kentuckians who had exhibited portions of Tecumseh's skin or to exonerate the Indians from the odium of permitting their leader to suffer the indignities of desecration.

While Black Hawk's very presence at Moraviantown is open to question, Billy and William Caldwell, Tenskwatawa, and Shabbona were certainly with Tecumseh that day. The paucity of the Tenskwatawa materials suggest that the prophet possessed little information about his brother's death. This, at least, was the substance of remarks he made to C. C. Trowbridge in the 1820s. The most anyone claimed to have gotten from him was a statement he was represented to have made to Lewis Cass, Abraham Edwards, George Croghan, and others that Tecumseh and his opponent had fatally wounded each other in the battle, a tidbit preserved by Edwards's son.[48]

By contrast, the Caldwells may have been better informed and it is regrettable that they were not invited to speak about Tecumseh's death when they appeared at Procter's court-martial. By the time Draper interviewed William Caldwell in 1863, when the old man was nearly eighty, his imagination was as wild as a prairie fire.

Tecumseh, he said, wore a dirty linsey hunting shirt, belted at the middle, a cap and buckskin leggings, and was armed with a small silver-mounted rifle of good quality, a tomahawk, a knife, a pouch, and a powder horn. About the time the Right Division was broken the chief suddenly put his hands to his body, contriving at the same time to hold fast to his rifle, and cried "Waugh!" Caldwell inquired if he was wounded.

"Yes," replied Tecumseh, pointing to the British and indicating that they had shot him in the back and that the ball had emerged from his chest. Nevertheless, he said that he could walk and began to retreat, but after a few yards became so weak that he found it difficult to step over a large fallen oak. In attempting to sit down, he fell with his back upon the tree and then rolled partly on his left side, dead. Caldwell took the chief's firearm, which lay still primed in Tecumseh's open right hand, but fearing that someone might accuse him of stealing it, propped it against a tree. He left Tecumseh where he had fallen, about three hundred yards from the road, and fled, meeting along the way Elliott and Tecumseh's son, a youth of only some seventeen years. When they were told of the Shawnee's death, Caldwell noticed that the boy's hands trembled as he loaded his piece.[49]

It is improbable that Tecumseh was killed by his allies without firing a shot at the Americans, and surprising that if Caldwell had been with the chief in his last moments that he omitted to mention it when giving an account of his role in the battle to the court-martial. Billy Caldwell was said to have parted with a more credible story in which he encountered Tecumseh retreating after the engagement. The Shawnee was using his rifle as a staff and had plainly been hit in the chest.

"I am shot," he told Caldwell in English. Later, Tecumseh's friends found the body, unmutilated, close to the battlefield at a spot where he had lain down to die. A contradictory statement was supposed to have been furnished an acquaintance by Billy Caldwell in the 1830s. Here, Caldwell and Tecumseh were sheltering behind a fallen tree when the latter commanded his followers to retreat. Terrified, Caldwell ran, but Tecumseh's body was subsequently discovered at the same place by the returning Indians.[50]

Billy Caldwell died in Iowa on September 27, 1841, without troubling to leave a definitive narrative of Tecumseh's last battle. One of his closest friends was Shabbona, or Chambly (Burly Shoulders), a Potawatomi chief whose credentials for reporting the truth about Tecumseh's death seem to be impeccable. His intimacy with the chief had been longstanding. According to a testimonial issued by Billy Caldwell at Amherstburg on August 1, 1816, "Chamblee" joined Tecumseh on the Wabash in 1807 and remained with him from the commencement of hostilities in 1812 until the battle of Moraviantown. Moreover, Shabbona's life was not a short one. He lived near Chicago until his death in 1859 and afforded many investigators an opportunity to interview him. Evidently he enjoyed discussing his lost leader. John Wentworth "was told . . . that the only way I could interest him was to make inquiries about Tecumseh, for whom he, in common with all others of our western Indians, had the utmost adoration to the end of his life."[51] Perhaps for these reasons more has been written about Shabbona's recollections than about those of any other eyewitness. Perhaps rather too many people questioned the chief, because his voluminous testimony is disappointing. An honest but naive man, Shabbona became increasingly confused the more he pondered those last few moments of Tecumseh's life.

The first reminiscence that can positively be attributed to Shabbona was contributed to the *Blairsville* (Pennsylvania) *Record* in 1837 by Robert A. McCabe, the director of the Potawatomi emigration to the West. Sometime in October, 1836, while the tribe was moving to new lands across the Mississippi, McCabe was told by Shabbona that he had been to Washington that spring and instantly recognized there the man who had killed Tecumseh, Richard Mentor Johnson. McCabe reported that Shabbona told him:

I never saw the man who killed Tecumseh, before nor since the battle, till last spring, at Washington. I cannot be mistaken in the man. I was very near him when he shot my friend. And the instant I saw him at Washington, I recognized him. On the day of the battle I was one of Tecumseh's aids, and on his right. There was another chief on his left. Tecumseh remarked to us: "That man on the white horse, or the white faced horse, (I cannot be certain which he said,) is the head chief of the men opposed to us. If we can kill him we may do well yet. Come with me." We all then started. But before we arrived at the place where the white chief was, the chief on Tecumseh's left, turned his horse and fled. I should have liked to have done so too, for the bullets were too plenty there. As we arrived where the white chief was, his horse fell to his knees, and Tecumseh raised his hatchet to finish him. He disengaged a pistol from his saddle and shot Tecumseh through the breast. On seeing Tecumseh fall, I went off as fast as I could, and have been a good American ever since that day."[52]

The more quoted account was given by Shabbona in the United States Hotel, Chicago, a year or so later and published in the *Chicago Democrat*. According to it, Tecumseh was wounded in the neck and believed that he was dying. Having nothing to lose, he rushed upon Johnson and was raising his tomahawk to strike when he was shot dead. Shabbona "described the colonel's horse very minutely," the paper reported. "He was very large, and white, with occasionally a jet black spot. Another Indian in company, whom Shaw-ben-eh said was but a boy at the time of the battle, interrupted him to say that his mane and tail were black." On the following morning Shabbona, the boy, and "many others" found Tecumseh's body on the field, unmolested, and beside it that of another warrior whose skin had been removed. When asked about what became of Tecumseh afterward, Shabbona became agitated. Warriors, he said, died on the battlefield, and so Tecumseh, the bravest man there ever was, was left unburied. His faith in the hero was undiminished, and he believed that the Potawatomi Tribe would not have been forced to emigrate west of the Mississippi if Tecumseh had survived.[53]

Most of the accounts given by Shabbona exhibited only minor modifications to detail. He was heard to have described how Johnson rode around the root of a fallen tree behind which some Indians were taking cover. Tecumseh quickly rose to his feet and shot down Johnson's horse, but as he leaped forward the colonel killed him, exclaiming, "you damned Indian!" The natives then fled.[54] Another witness was told that the incident occurred after Tecumseh had led a successful charge against the American center, presumably the infantry, but had been thrown onto the defensive by a counterattack of the American horsemen.[55] William Hickling, who knew Shabbona fairly well, wrote:

> With reference to the vexed and probably ever to be unsettled question of "who killed Tecumthe?" I like so many others who have troubled their heads with this subject have never arrived at any satisfactory conclusion . . . . . I knew Shab-bone for a number of years, he often being a visitor at my former home in Ottawa, & I have often conversed with him on the subject, and pointed out to him the discrepancies that existed between his version of the affair, and that given by Black Hawk . . . however, to the day of his death, Shab-bo-ne was in the firm belief that a bullet from the pistol of Col. Johnson was the cause of Tecumseh's death. Shabbone said that he was only a few yards distant from Tecumseh, at the time the colonel dashed forward on his "white horse" several yards in advance of his men towards a number of Indians who were clustered around Tecumseh, that the colonel's horse stumbled & nearly fell, seeing which Tecumseh advanced towards Johnson with his tomahawk raised ready to strike, that then Johnson drew his pistol & fired the fatal shot, at the same time in a loud voice, heard distinctly by Shabbone uttering the soldierly words of "God dam," upon receiving his death wound Shabbone states that Tecumseh leaped up from the ground some two feet & then fell down apparently dead . . . that when Tecumseh fell, that the action had been going on for some little time, and that Black Hawk's assertion that Tecumseh fell at the first discharge from Col. Johnson's men was incorrect. I believe that all the Indian accounts of the battle agree in relation to the hasty retreat of the Indians . . . after the fall of their great chief. Both Shabboneh & Caldwell state that the body of Tecumseh when found after the battle was partially skinned & mutilated by the Kentuckians . . . .[56]

At superficial glance, Shabbona would seem to have settled the whole question in favor of Richard Mentor Johnson, but deeper consideration raises disturbing reservations about these accounts. Maybe they conform rather too snugly to the stories then being ardently circulated by Johnson's propagandists. Sure it is that every one of them was set down during or after the colonel's campaign for the vice-presidency, and if Shabbona himself had no interest in the outcome of that struggle, he had small control over the words the less impartial might place in his mouth. The

ridiculous tale of Shabbona's recognition of Johnson in Washington in 1836 is the most suspicious of all the details. How could the
chief have been so sure about a face he had seen only once before, for
but a few minutes, at a distance in the heat of a battle twenty years
gone? More likely Shabbona was introduced to Johnson in Washington and told of his reputed shooting of Tecumseh. It is impossible not to believe that the old warrior in some way allowed it to
influence his memory of what had occurred.

Although an anecdote of General John Hunt was written at too
late a date to guarantee precision, it suggests something of the
transformation that might have developed in Shabbona's mind.
Hunt met Shabbona at Columbus while the chief was traveling to
Washington and received from his favorite story: Tecumseh fired
from behind a tree at a rider on a white horse and was killed as he
went forward with his tomahawk. Subsequently Hunt saw the
Indians again, as they made their return journey, and was told that
they had spoken with Richard Mentor Johnson, and "from the fact
that Johnson rode a white horse and other incidents of the fight,"
they believed him to have been the slayer of Tecumseh.[57] It would
have been an easy matter for Shabbona, in the many years left to
him, to have integrated his memory of Johnson and the popular
report about him with his own recollections of Tecumseh's death
until the two became inseparable. An eminent settler of Illinois,
Gordon Hubbard, sensed that this was the case. He "often talked"
with Shabbona

on this subject & am strong in conviction that I am not mistaken . . . he
was no doubt convinced of the truth of the current story that Johnson shot
Tecumseh, as he was in the habit of taking for granted reports of that fact
to him. To my questions often repeated How could you tell that the man
riding the white horse did fire the shot that killed [Tecumseh] when so
many were firing? & was there not more than one white horse rode by the
Americans, his replies were always that no one could so say & no doubt
more than one white horse. You Americans say Johnson killed him & he
Johnson should be beleaved—somebody killed him & I saw a man on a
white horse fire and Tecumseh fell. Some one else may have shot him . . . .
He has always told me that he was close by him when he fell. I never
understood him to say that Tecumthe advanced on seeing the horse

stumble. I have heard Mr. [Billy] Caldwell say that the body of Tecumthe
was mutilated by cutting strips of skin . . . .[58]

Hickling was in friendly disagreement with Hubbard about
Shabbona's recollections, but admitted that the latter "had a much
larger and more intimate acquaintance than myself, with both
Caldwell and Shab-o-nee . . . ."[59] Eventually he acknowledged
that "upon an examination and comparison of the different statements made by the old chief [Shabbona], I have come to the
conclusion that his ideas and memories of the battle, particularly in
relation to the killing of Tecumseh, 'are much mixed,' and not of a
character sufficiently accurate to be placed on record as correct
history."[60] Nonetheless, Shabbona cannot easily be dismissed. He
remained firm on some points, particularly that Tecumseh died in
combat with the rider of a white horse and that the Indians fled
upon the chief's death, and his stories embody convincing detail,
such as the oath uttered by the American as he shot Tecumseh. It is
regrettable that Shabbona cannot unequivocally be credited with
any of the Indian statements obtained before his visit to Washington in 1836, for they might have offered his reminiscences un-
polluted by the interpolations of the Johnson saga.

Hope may yet flicker upon this count, however, because an early
version of the death of Tecumseh could have originated with
Shabbona. The informant is not named, but Thomas Forsyth, the
Indian agent who collected the story in 1816, describes him first as
a Potawatomi visiting Fort Clark and later as an Ottawa. It is worth
noting that while Shabbona became a Potawatomi by marriage, he
had been born an Ottawa. Forsyth also mentions that his witness
had lived with an uncle at Tippecanoe, Tecumseh's town on the
Wabash, for three years, and that this same uncle had been
captured serving with Barclay's squadron. Now Shabbona did live
at Tippecanoe for a time, and he may have referred to the Indians
taken in the Battle of Lake Erie, for in his only known letter, in
which he styles himself Tecumseh's aide, he alludes to "two of
Tecumseh's young men" who were captured with Barclay.[61]

The Indian told Forsyth that he had been with Tecumseh and
two other chiefs at Moraviantown. The Shawnee, armed with a

saber and two pistols, stood on the left of the gathering, while successively upon his right were Nesscottinnemeg, the narrator, and Kichekemit, a Potawatomi. They planned to fire upon the enemy horsemen and then to rush forward, seize the bridles of the animals, and unseat their riders. But the cavalry charged too quickly and were too many. The informant admitted firing unsuccessfully before hiding behind a bush. Kichekemit fell, Nesscottinnemeg fled, and Tecumseh "engaged with a foot soldier: the soldier having run his bayonet through Tecumseh's leather coat near the hips, and the latter trying to disengage himself from the bayonet with his sabre in his hand when a horseman rode up and shot him through the head . . . ." The Potawatomi chief then ran, but about three days later revisited the field and found that Kichekemit and Tecumseh had been scalped, and that a strip of skin about a foot long and the width of three fingers had been taken from the latter's right thigh.[62]

This seems a far cry from the accounts Shabbona gave after 1836, but it is convergent with evidence gathered from him at an uncertain date by Captain Robert Anderson. In this interview, Shabbona reported that Tecumseh had been fighting a foot soldier armed with a musket. Catching his adversary's bayonet under his arm, Tecumseh raised his tomahawk to strike him when he was killed by a man on a spotted or red-roan horse with a red plume in his hat who shot him with a pistol. A day or more later Shabbona saw Tecumseh's body but it was not mutilated.[63] The possibility exists that Shabbona propagated two distinct versions of the death of Tecumseh, and that the metamorphosis occurred after a conversation between the Potawatomi and Johnson in Washington in 1836.[64] If this hypothesis is correct, the earlier story had a mounted man killing Tecumseh while the chief engaged a foot soldier, and the successor supported the classic encounter of Colonel Johnson.

Shabbona's two mixed-blood nephews, David K. Foster and Joseph N. Bourassa, reinforced both alternatives. Foster drew generously for his information upon the old Black Hawk yarn, which he had no doubt inextricably confounded with whatever Shabbona might have told him. Before the battle, Foster explained, Tecumseh was smoking with his chiefs and informed them with a melancholy earthward look that he had been nicked on the ear in the previous engagment and would not survive the day. The prediction had already been made to his family about three months before. During the ensuing action, the Shawnee killed a soldier and was stooping to scalp him when he was shot and bayoneted by an American private who rode up with a musket. The Indians soon avenged their chief, and hid his body in the brush until the following morning, when it was carried away for burial. Another warrior was seen nearby who had been skinned by the Americans.[65]

Foster's account had little in common with the familiar tale of the white horse, which Bourassa, who was nearly fifty when his uncle died, was willing to uphold. This version bears all the hallmarks of a contrivance. Tecumseh was foolish enough to instruct his warriors to attack with tomahawks since the Americans would fire too high, in pursuit of which luckless policy he advanced upon Johnson, here described as mounted upon a cream or white colored mare with spots. Shot in the temple, Tecumseh fell backward as Johnson collapsed of his wounds, and the Indians retired, except for a Potawatomi, O-ketch-gum-mee (The-Fish-Who-Upholds-the-Earth), who recklessly ran among his enemies with his hatchet until brought down. After three days Shabbona and Tecumseh's son recovered the great Shawnee's body. It was lying on its back in a leafy hollow, still clenching a tomahawk, not far from the remains of Tecumseh's nephew, a man of similar age and stature whose thighs had been skinned. Tecumseh himself wore nothing distinctive, merely a buckskin suit with fringe along the seams of the upper sleeve and down the back, but his medal, inscribed "General Tecumseh," had been used by his nephew in the battle and drawn the Americans to the wrong body.[66]

Bourassa must not be taken too seriously. Educated in the 1830s at an Indian academy sponsored by Richard Mentor Johnson, he must have been thoroughly conversant with the colonel's claims, which he unreservedly affirmed. The introduction of the nephew, an artless device designed to spare Tecumseh mutilation, was exposed by the conspicuous fiction of the British medal. References to such a medal are scattered throughout the literature, but even if it had displayed Tecumseh's name, which it did not, it could hardly have advertised a rank which, popular rumor notwithstanding, the chief never possessed.[67]

In closing Shabbona's conflicting testimony, Foster and Bourassa's blending of original material with the products of imagination and hearsay, serves a caution about the rampant plagiarism that infests this subject.[68] Another scribbler was D. B. Cook, the editor of the *Niles Weekly Mirror*, who presented what may have been a bogus rehash of the Shabbona stories. Cook claimed that in 1838 he had interviewed an Ottawa Christian called Noon-day, who dwelt in Barry County, Michigan, using the Reverend Leonard Slater as interpreter. Purportedly taken from Cook's contemporary diary, the material was not published until 1885 and its substance will not be unfamiliar. Noon-day said that Tecumseh addressed his men before the fight, inspiring them with loyalty. During the battle Noon-day stood on the chief's right and saw the contest with Johnson that left the Shawnee dead on his face, shot through the breast in the commonly recounted manner. He was dragged away by Noon-day and Saginaw and borne from the field as the braves retreated. "We laid him down on a blanket in a wigwam, and we all wept, we loved him so much. I took his hat and tomahawk." Cook inquired as to how Noon-day knew the identity of Tecumseh's killer, and the old warrior replied that Lewis Cass had once taken him to see President Martin Van Buren in Washington, where he met and recognized Colonel Johnson ("I had never seen him since, but I knew it was him.") Perhaps to inject some authority into an account that mirrored so closely its predecessors, Cook informed Draper that Noon-day, a tall, broad-shouldered, and muscular man, wept while discussing Tecumseh and that he died about 1858.[69]

Shabbona was the most celebrated of several Indians who are supposed to have established that Tecumseh was killed by Johnson. The earliest of these reports was sent from Illinois in 1824 by an anonymous contributor, who wrote that an Ottawa chief who had been at the Thames "was at my house a few days ago" and identified Johnson as the man who shot Tecumseh.[70] Much the

best material tending to the same conclusion was provided in a
vivid interview of a Potawatomi conducted by William Clark,
sometime governor of Missouri Territory and superintendent of
Indian Affairs at Saint Louis. Drake gave it in 1841:

A Potawatamie chief was thus questioned: Were you at the battle of the
Thames? Yes. Did you know Tecumseh? Yes. Were you near him in the
fight? Yes. Did you see him fall? Yes. Who shot him? Don't know. Did
you see the man that shot him? Yes. What sort of looking man was he?
Short, thick man. What color was the horse he rode? Most white. How do
you know this man shot Tecumseh? I saw the man ride up—saw his horse
get tangled in some bushes—when the horse was most still, I saw
Tecumseh level his rifle at the man and shoot—the man shook on his
horse—soon the horse got out of the bushes, and the man spurred him
up—horse came slow—Tecumseh right before him—man's left hand
hung down—just as he got near, Tecumseh lifted his tomahawk and was
going to throw it, when the man shot him with a short gun—Tecumseh
fell dead and we all ran.

Thomas L. McKenney, who passed the statement to Drake, gave
a fuller version five years later. In describing how the American
officer shuddered when wounded by Tecumseh while extricating
his horse from the top of a fallen tree, the Potawatomi moved his
body from side to side. Tecumseh, he said, was hit in the forehead,
near the eyes.[71]

For the greater part of the nineteenth century "true" accounts of
Tecumseh's death filtered through one Indian source or another. A
relative of Tecumseh, the wife of Anthony Shane, was informed by
two of her brothers that the Shawnee chief was killed by a Kentucky private. The son of Tecumseh's friend, Stephen Ruddell,
maintained that some Shawnees had reported the chief mortally
wounded attacking a mounted officer, and that he had been carried
away to die the same evening.[72] The last narrative to come to light
was written by John Norton, an educated Mohawk who met
Tecumseh's brother, son, and sister, and other of his followers in
1814. In his journal Norton declared that "the intrepid Tecumthi"
was last "seen rushing boldly forward upon the hostile ranks, when
victory seemed to incline to their side" and that his body was
"barbarously" flayed after the action.[73]

These Indian statements on the death of Tecumseh are among the most treacherous primary sources relating to the War of 1812, transmitted not only years after the event but almost always through intermediaries. Lapses of memory on the part of both informant and recorder were multiplied by the difficulties of translating from the Indian tongues and the opportunities the circumstances afforded for charlatanism. Consequently, the material runs its full course without resolving the controversies about Tecumseh's fall. Credible accounts variously represent him to have died during the first volleys (the Winnebago chiefs), embattled with Johnson (Shabbona and the Potawatomi at St. Louis), and fighting a foot soldier (the Potawatomi narrative of 1816). These contradictions preclude the presentation of firm conclusions, but—as with the American accounts—the case for Johnson emerges more strongly than any single alternative. The possibility is therefore preserved that legend and reality finally became one as the two foremost heroes of the campaign met in a decisive combat.

From the farrago of Indian evidence only two facts emerge with consistency: Tecumseh was killed in action against the mounted men, and his death signaled the native retreat in that quarter. Some of the witnesses mentioned infantrymen, but never to the exclusion of cavalry, and they may have referred to those in Johnson's regiment who dismounted in accordance with their commander's instructions. The inference must be that Tecumseh fought on the left of the Indian line and that his death in the early part of the fight undermined the Indians' resistance and terminated the engagement at that point.

Indeed, the Indian stories raise more problems than they solve. Many of them said that the warriors either retreated with Tecumseh's body or retrieved it later unmutilated, information that called into question the American identification of Tecumseh after the battle (and the substantial amount of pleading dependent upon it) and unleashed a new phase of the Tecumseh controversy. Tracing the tenuous lead of the Indian testimony, recent historians have tended to insist that Tecumseh's body never fell into the possession of the Americans, as if the point was beyond dispute. To determine the propriety of these remarks, it is time to test the degree of certainty with which the Shawnee was identified once the powder smoke had cleared.

When rumor proclaimed the death of the arch foe, victorious soldiers spent part of October 6, 1813 satisfying a morbid if understandable curiosity by gathering about the body of a warrior accorded the distinction of being Tecumseh, and not a few bore home mementoes of the occasion, clothing, hair, and even a few strips of the Indian's skin. It was not until the 1830s that the owners of these trophies, some of which had been exhibited in Kentucky, were confronted with the distressing news that Tecumseh's old warriors were repudiating the relics. Tecumseh's body had not been identified at the Thames, and it was another who the Kentuckians had so diligently abused. Statements such as these, which surface late, can never be taken at their face value, but they were credible and persistent enough to demand deeper invesigation.

Private Wickliffe had endeavored at the time to confirm that the Shawnee chief had been killed. He found the body on the morning of the sixth sprawled upon its back, clad in leggings and a hunting shirt but already despoiled of moccasins. Wickliffe numbered among his acquaintances one Christopher Miller, for many years a prisoner among the Indians, and had been informed by him that Tecumseh was slightly pockmarked and that one of his legs was shorter than the other because of an old injury. He examined the dead Indian and found that one limb, bearing a distinct scar, was about an inch short. Wickliffe next consulted a British prisoner and learned that Tecumseh, unlike his braves, had painted his face half black and half red, that he was pockmarked and that a bandage about his arm covered a wound sustained at Chatham. These details were confirmed upon Wickliffe's second visit to the body, when he washed the paint from the face with a shaving brush to detect a small number of pockmarks. The Indian had been shot below the nipple ("I think there were three holes. I know there was more than one."). The last of five or six times that Wickliffe saw the corpse that day it was badly mutilated. About forty yards from it lay another Indian of similar height and dress, whose eyebrows and hair were burned by gunpowder. He had been shot at close range in the forehead, above the eye, and Wickliffe believed him to have been the warrior felled by Johnson.[74]

Captain James S. Whitaker of Simrall's regiment was less satisfied that the body was Tecumseh's when he inspected it. He went further than Wickliffe, declaring that he had seen Tecumseh at Vincennes, but the utility of this experience was questionable inasmuch as it left Whitaker with an exaggerated impression of Tecumseh's size. He measured the body and found it five feet ten inches in height, "shorter & smaller in every way" than the Shawnee chief, although it generally resembled him. Unfortunately, independent testimony establishes that Tecumseh, contrary to Whitaker's belief, was about five foot ten. Whitaker also found that the Indian and been shot in the left side by two balls less than two inches apart, and that his thighs had been skinned by the soldiers. Dried blood on a bandage over his arm proclaimed that he had received an earlier wound, but Whitaker, unlike Wickliffe, stated that the British denied that Tecumseh had so been injured.[75]

Only five of the Americans at Moraviantown can positively be said to have known Tecumseh—Harrison himself, Anthony Shane, Simon Kenton, and the Conner brothers. Four examined the body. Harrison was so undecided that he refrained from announcing Tecumseh's death in his offical dispatch of October 9. Called upon later to justify this decision, he explained that he had set out with a party to examine the Indian toward the evening of the sixth, discovering the corpse naked and mutilated, strips of skin having been removed from the back. The face was "much swollen & it appeared to have had a stroke with a tomahawk or something else over the top of the head." The general "was certain that I had seen the person before, but I could not determine whether it was T-e or a Potawatami chief who had always been with him when ever I had seen him." As far as he could remember, the body lay close to where the infantry had engaged the Indians. Reinforced by the statements of his aides, Colonels O'Fallon and Todd, and —allowing for alterations to be expected over a lapse of time—of his son, Harrison's observations refute the stories that he identified Tecumseh. The significance of his testimony, however, can easily be exaggerated, for his acquaintance with Tecumseh was slight; he had not seen the chief for two years, and the body was in poor condition when he made his inspection.[76]

A more important witness was Anthony Shane, a half-blood Shawnee serving with the friendly Indians among the American army. He had known Tecumseh since childhood and was related to him by marriage. In 1834, Garrett Wall remarked that after the battle it was said that

the great Indian commander, Tecumseh, was slain. I asked by what authority? I was told that Anthony Shane, who had known him from a small boy, said so, and had seen him among the slain. In a short time I saw Shane with a small group of men, walking towards a dead Indian; as he approached the body I asked him if he knew that Indian. He said it was, in his opinion, Tecumseh; but he could tell better, if the blood was taken from his face. I examined the Indian. He was shot in the left side of the breast with several balls or buckshot, and entering near and above the left nipple. There was also a wound in his head too small for a rifle ball to make. The ball in his breast inclined from the left side towards the centre and downwards. I have no doubt the shot was from an elevated position. The Indian was afterwards recognized to be Tecumseh. He was at a small distance in advance of the ground on which lay the dead horses of the forlorn hope. His wounds were bleeding when I first saw him. On returning, Col. Johnson's pistols were examined, one was empty, the other loaded.[77]

This information parallels what Shane told Drake in 1821. Shane said that Tecumseh's brother-in-law lay dead ten or fifteen steps from his chief, the top of his head shot away. Tecumseh had been killed by a ball and three buckshot that entered the breast near the center and passed out close to the backbone between the hips. He had received no other wounds and lay on his back, but the skin of his left thigh was missing a strip about one inch in breadth and seven or eight inches in length. William Emmons was treated to the same story, but adds that the body was identified by a scar on the thigh, which had once been broken, and that it was inspected "immediately after the battle . . . was ended" at "the spot where several of the men had seen Col. Johnson kill an Indian commander . . . ."[78]

Drake's notes establish that, in 1821, Shane was positive that he had seen Tecumseh's body on the field, but Samuel Theobald endowed his inspection with a different complexion when he wrote of it in 1861. Twenty years before, Theobald had informed Todd that toward the end of the firing he and Garrett Wall returned to the battleground and observed the bodies of three Americans in close proximity, those of Mansfield, Scott and, a little in advance, Whitley. Close to the latter lay an Indian, and twenty to thirty steps beyond another, the man later presumed to be Tecumseh. Elaborating in 1861, Theobald added:

On the morning after the battle, which as I have stated closed late in the evening, a rumor was current through the camp that Tecumseh was killed & his body found & recognized. It was said that Genl. Harrison had seen & identified it. Still there seemed to be doubt . . . .Like every one else I felt a strong desire & curiosity to see the remains of the great warrior, & cast about . . . how I could satisfy myself that it was really the body of Tecumseh, and it occurred to me . . . that through Anthony Shane, a half blood Indian of the Shawnee tribe who had accompanied us thro' the campaign as Indian interpreter—being one of a company of about 40 Indians of that tribe, who Col. J. had procured . . . . I felt assured that Shane, who had informed me of his life long & intimate acquaintance with Tecumseh, belonging to the same tribe & raised together, would at once satisfy me fully on the subject. I accordingly went directly to him, & proposed to him to go with me to examine the body—he readily assented & conducted by one or more persons who had just been to see the body—we soon had it under our inspection. I found it to be one of the Indians I had noticed the preceding evening, lying near to Col. Whitley. The one farthest removed from him, but now stripped entirely of clothing & shocking to say, several strips of skin taken from his thighs & back. I expected of course, as the features were perfect, Shane would decide without hesitancy as to its being the body of Tecumseh, & felt no little disappointment when I observed him hesitating. He said, at length, after deliberately inspecting the body—"It is about Tecumseh's size & some like him, but he did not recognize it as the body of Tecumseh." . . . I must say however that notwithstanding the failure of Shane to recognize the body . . . that he did, after our return from the campaigns, furnish the friends of Col. Johnson a statement sustaining the impression that his body was found on the ground . . . .[79]

There are important discrepancies between Wall and Theobald about the intervention of Shane. Wall asserts that Tecumseh was identified immediately after the battle had ended, Theobald that Shane examined the body the next day, and Wall gave out that Shane's indecision was only temporary. Both Wall and Theobald saw the corpse more than once, on the evening of the fifth and on the sixth, and it is possible that one of them became confused as to when Shane's examination took place. That Drake obtained details of the mutilation of the body does not necessarily show that Theobald has the better of the argument because Shane most likely also visited the body several times.

Whether Shane had initial doubts or not, he was eventually satisfied that he had seen Tecumseh's body. It was an opinion Simon Kenton may not have shared. Kenton and Tecumseh were not strangers to each other, although they had not met for some six years. They had been rivals since 1792 when the Shawnee had routed Kenton's party in one of the innumerable skirmishes of the Northwestern Indian War, and they had frequently crossed paths afterward. The day after the battle on the Thames, Kenton looked at the "Tecumseh" body but was apparently unable to settle the riddle of its identity. Again, the picture is murky. A participant, Isaac Thomas, recalled that Kenton considered that the Indian might have been Tenskwatawa, Tecumseh's brother, and Mason Arrowsmith, a relative of the frontiersman, said that Kenton had doubted that the Indian was Tecumseh because the Shawnee chief possessed a "fine" set of teeth. The commonest impression of Kenton's acquaintances was that the old borderer was reluctant to concede that the body had been Tecumseh's.[80]

The last Americans whose qualifications for identifying Tecumseh were satisfactory were William and John Conner, who headed some of the Indian allies of the United States at Moraviantown. As a trader with the Delawares on the White River, Indiana Territory, before the war, William had mixed with both Tecumseh and The Prophet. His brother-in-law said that Conner considered Tecumseh "a very superior man; but not equal to the prophet in craft and eloquence," while his son remembered that his father often spoke of the brothers and had been befriended by Tenskwatawa, with whom he was the closer. Tecumseh he described as a magnetic, persuasive man, humane, temperate, and frank and possessing a finer presence than did his brother. Before the war he had discussed his intentions openly with Conner. Because of the usefulness of the Conners in Indian country, John had been employed by Harrison as an interpreter and emissary, in which capacity he had often visited Tecumseh's village of Tippecanoe.[81]

No firsthand accounts of William Conner's inspection of the body at Moraviantown survive, but secondhand sources of independent origin leave little doubt about his broader conclusions. An anonymous donor to the *National Intelligencer* supplied the first report while Conner was serving as a member of the Indiana legislature ("If I err in any particular, I hope he will correct it."), and additional material was provided after the trader's death by friends and relations. Conner saw the dead warrior at least twice. Among the first to discover it, he refreshed his memory after a soldier had peeled a strip of the Indian's skin from the "outer part of a thigh just below the upper joint."[82] In later years Conner never doubted that the body was Tecumseh's, although his son indicated that some preliminary confusion as to whether the chief or his brother had been killed was only dispelled when one of Conner's Indians lifted one of the eyelids. The Prophet, it was well known, was blind in one eye. Conner credited Whitley with the shooting because Tecumseh lay close by him and had been slain by a ball from a small-bore rifle similar to that owned by Whitley. As Conner's brother-in-law remembered the story, the body also bore a wound on the top of the head that may have been the work of a saber.[83]

The evidence of the principal American witnesses has now been reviewed with the equivocal results that so tenaciously haunt this subject. Shane and Conner, despite suggestions of inital uncertainty, affected to have identified the Indian as Tecumseh; Harrison simply did not know; and Kenton doubted that the chief had been left on the ground. Fortunately, the British material is so positive that it satisfactorily solves this particular mystery. James, whose contacts included British officers who had fought at Moraviantown, declared himself astonished that Harrison had censored reference to Tecumseh's death in his dispatch when members of Procter's army had identified the chief's body on the field.[84] Circulated by scurrilous American hacks, the statement stung the general to deny in 1834 that any British regulars had seen Tecumseh's body. It was so swollen and mutilated when he saw it on the sixth that "I would not suffer any person who had been attached to the British army to be called to examine it . . ."; indeed, "early in the morning . . . I sent them [the British prisoners] down the river to a farm house & only two of them were permitted to return again to our camp in charge of an officer to search for some baggage which had been plundered from them by the women of their army."[85] But this was closing the stable door after the horse had bolted, for the testimony shows that British personnel viewed Tecumseh on the evening of the fifth before they were dispatched downriver.

On the night of the battle Colonel John O'Fallon took a Canadian interpreter over the field, and the body of Tecumseh— O'Fallon said dressed plainly in a dark fringed cotton hunting shirt—was identified. The interpreter also mistakenly named another of the dead Indians as The Prophet. Lieutenant Colonel Francis Baby, escorted by another of Harrison's aides, Major John Chambers, also saw the body, although on the following day when it was in a mutilated state.[86] Then Richardson recalled that members of the Forty-first accompanied some of Harrison's staff to the scene late on the fifth and returned satisfied that they had seen Tecumseh, sadly making "it the subject of conversation, in presence of General Harrison." Captain Chambers was said by an American witness to have been one of the British officers concerned.[87] Ensign Cochran attributed the initial discovery of Tecumseh to Captain Edward McCoy of the Forty-first, who was captured in the battle but permitted "to search the forest on our right for the missing officers of his own corps; and the flaying [of Tecumseh] only occurred after McCoy recognised the chief, who till then had lost but as usual the scalp which all Kentuckians invariably stript off a dead Indian."[88] That some sort of identification took place is confirmed by the evidence Warburton gave at Procter's court-martial in 1814:

Q. Do you know any thing of the death of the chief Tecumseth who fell in the action of the 5th October?
A. I know he was killed, there are officers who saw him when he was dead.[89]

Afterwards, when the subject of Tecumseh's death was regularly aired in American newspapers, appeals were frequently made to British officers. They were recruited in the cause of both Hollman and King, but the fullest statement along these lines was written by William Gaines:

There were not only one but a number of dead Indians lying around, but I am positive about Tecumseh as he was pointed out to me by a Quarter Master Sergeant of the British Army whom we had as a prisoner, & who said he had been acquainted with him for two years. That he had been in the habit of visiting Fort Malden and associating with the officers more or less every week, attending their balls & parties, and that he received the pay of a brigadier general from the British Government. I am satisfied that this sergeant was well acquainted with him.

Gaines may have been telling the truth, although he was not always consistent. On November 25, 1881, he admitted that the body had been so disfigured and bloody as to defy adequate description, but a week later his story was that Tecumseh had not been mutilated when Gaines saw him, but that the subsequent report was that he had been skinned.[90]

The meager record of the British involvement in the identification of Tecumseh, and Trisler's interesting remark that they recovered the body for eventual burial, satisfactorily cuts through much of the apocryphal mythology that has enshrouded the end of the Shawnee chief. It was indeed his body that was found and mutilated by the Americans. This conclusion sharpens the focus upon Tecumseh during his last battle. He chose to command from the left of his line, somewhere between the two swamps, attended by the more fervent of his supporters, but to the right of the Shawnee contingent. His strong, athletic figure was attired in fringed buckskin leggings, a hunting shirt (probably drawn about the waist with a sash), breechcloth, moccasins, and a turban. Gaines believed that his fine deerskin was decorated with beads and three silver half moons and bound by a red sash, while James Bentley remembered the chief's body in a plain blue shirt and leggings, he felt, of a similar color. Distinguishing features of Tecumseh's appearance were a bandage about his left arm and a British medal, his solitary ornament, suspended from around his neck.[91]

The Shawnee was near enough the advancing infantry to have directed the first attack upon Harrison's "crotchet," but he was killed in the fierce fighting that opened the engagement between the Indians and Johnson's mounted regiment. A squally discussion failed to determine whether his body was found closer to the spot where Johnson was wounded or to that on which Whitley died, but the two cannot have been far apart because both officers rode together into the fray. Captain Mason said that Tecumseh lay about a hundred yards from where one of his infantrymen had been killed, but merely a few steps from what he took to be Johnson's fallen horse.[92]

One or two Indians were killed about Tecumseh, including his brother-in-law, and Clark was mortally wounded. The manner of the chief's death remains a mystery, but a remarkable British plan of the field prepared a few months after the battle with the help of the Indian Department affords a vital clue by designating the spot on which he was killed. It was slightly forward of his station in the line, and the accompanying annotation, "Great chief Tecumseh in advance . . . killed by the enemy," suggests that the Shawnee might have fallen leading a charge or running upon the Americans, a point that recalls the testimony of John Norton, quoted above.[93] Whatever happened, Tecumseh received a fatal charge in the left of his breast. His body also revealed damage to the head, by a blow or a bullet, but these wounds could have been administered after death.[94] The fighting spirit of the Indians melted like frost in sunlight when their leader died, and the line receded into the dark woods. Farther to the right, the Americans had been repulsed, but dismay must have spread with the tidings of Tecumseh's death,

The "Death of Tecumseh," a patriotic American lithograph of 1845 by N. Currier, idealizing Johnson and grossly misrepresenting his arch Indian foe. *Courtesy Library of Congress.*

"Battle of the Thames—Death of Tecumseh," a painting by Alonzo
Chappel, engraved by W. Wellstood, and published by Johnson, Fry and
Company of New York in 1857. *Courtesy Library of Congress.*

and the collapse of the left permitted Johnson's men to increase their pressure upon the remaining pockets of Indian resistance. Overpowered, the warriors were forced into the sanctuary of the swamp and then retreated toward Lake Ontario.

Most witnesses remembered Tecumseh's body on its back, although Gaines said that the limbs were drawn up. Identified by British prisoners, it was also examined by some Americans acquainted with Tecumseh, and who referred to injuries the chief was known to have suffered to his legs, one a broken thigh and the other a bullet wound received at Monguagon the previous year.[95] Then on October 6 the souvenir hunters got to work, and when the warrior had been stripped of clothing, disappointed Kentuckians tore skin from his back and thigh. Brunson said that the rapacious soldiery so thoroughly scalped the corpse that some of them came away with fragments of skin the size of a cent piece and endowed with a mere tuft of hair.[96] When Samuel Baker was interviewed in 1886 he was still able to display a piece of Tecumseh's skin, "old and used up but . . . genuine."

This regrettable barbarity has given rise to many tales, but the most exaggerated of them was given to Alfred T. Goodman on April 16, 1870 by George Sanderson, who had been a captain of the regulars at Moraviantown. He claimed that the soldiers had peeled skin from Tecumseh in a patch that measured six inches in length and one and a half inches in width. By noon of the sixth the body was unrecognizable, and it was left covered with brush and logs while the troops inspected their trophies. The skin, said Sanderson, stretched like gum elastic, one two-inch piece, when dried, extending to nearly a foot in length![97] Base and inexcusable as this behavior was, it exemplified the peculiar ferocity with which the border wars were prosecuted by both red and white. Tecumseh heads a line of distinguished Indian leaders who were similarly abused after death, a company that includes King Philip, Osceola, Black Hawk, Kamiakin, Mangas Coloradas, and Sitting Bull.

As the nineteenth century faded, so the excitement over the death of Tecumseh blew itself out. The men of Moraviantown were all dead, and those who remembered the heady political strife of the thirties were aged and feeble. Their legacy was a mass of testimony that inextricably fused myth and reality, the most pertinent of it presented in the preceding pages. One fact, however, remains beyond contention. Tecumseh had promised at Amherstburg that he would leave his bones upon the land rather than surrender it to his enemies, and on the field of Moraviantown he made good that vow. While Procter fled, the Shawnee chief resisted the American onslaught, outnumbered but unflinching. He died as a warrior, with his foes before him, leaving behind a void that none of his successors could fill.

7

AN EPILOGUE: 1813–1815

_____

The disaster . . . has not influenced . . . our Indian allies
nor given to the enemy any advantage.

AFTER their defeat the remnants
of the broken British-Indian army doggedly continued their retreat
over the thirty-four miles of difficult road from Moraviantown to
Delaware, and thereafter to Oxford, Burford, Dundas, Ancaster,
and Burlington, on Lake Ontario, where they joined the Centre
Division and some assessment of the disaster was possible.[1] The
Right Division had been destroyed. Harrison recorded its losses as
12 killed and 601 prisoners, taken before, during, and after the
action.[2] A British muster made at Burlington on November 10
lists 250 men present and 613 missing. Although it was admittedly incomplete because some of the returns had not then been
presented, it corresponds exactly to Harrison's figures.[3] Two
weeks later a printed return published with Baynes's General
Orders of November 24 acknowledged a loss of 634 soldiers on the
retreat.[4] Most of them faced a miserable captivity in the United
States, at Chillicothe, Ohio, or Frankfort, Kentucky, until a
convention signed on July 16, 1814 granted the disease-ridden
prisoners a merciful release.[5]

The Indians suffered lightly in the battle and may have recruited
a few warriors from the Delaware villages of Moraviantown and
Muncey Town farther up the Thames. Moraviantown was occupied
by the Americans on the night of the battle and ransacked and
burned between then and the seventh when Harrison retired to
Sandwich, and it is possible that some of the refugees may have

joined Tecumseh's warriors streaming upriver to Delaware.[6] About two thousand Indians had reached Dundas by October 24.[7] When allowance is made for the Moravian Indians and some of the Munsies, it is clear that few more than three hundred braves from Tecumseh's proud army had managed to regroup. The loss of the Shawnee chief and Roundhead deprived them of their principal proponents of intertribal unity, and Procter's vacillation and ultimate defeat scattered many of the warriors and induced others to abandon the British flag. The Wyandots and Shawnees in particular seem to have become badly dispersed, as a return of October 26, which is summarized below, demonstrates:

Ottawas and Ojibwas	117 men and	234 women and children
Munsies, Delawares and Nanticokes	143 men and	266 women and children
Moravian Indians	29 men and	47 women and children
Sacs and Musquakes	60 men and	105 women and children
Shawnees	17 men and	30 women and children
Wyandots	8 men and	6 women and children[8]
	374	688

Procter was, of course, held accountable for the disaster. Two dispatches, dated October 23 and November 16, were asked of him, the first being considered deficient in detail, and Lieutenant Bullock, the most senior of the other surviving officers of the Forty-first, was solicited to the same purpose. Despite these, the adjutant-general's orders of November 24 censured the division and criticized its commander for encumbering the army with baggage, inadequately transporting ammunition and provisions, and neglecting to retard the enemy advance.[9] The inevitable court-martial, however, had to wait less troubled times. It was not until the end of 1814, when the war was almost spent and most of the important witnesses to Procter's conduct had been released from captivity in the United States, that the trial was convened in Montreal, sitting intermittently from Wednesday, December 21 to Saturday, January 28, 1815, under the supervision of Major General de Rottenburg. Four other major generals, six colonels, and six lieutenant colonels comprised the court. Deputy Judge

Advocate Andrew William Cochran undertook an uncompromising prosecution, while Procter conducted his own defense. A total of thirty-four witnesses came forward to give evidence. [10]

The terms of reference finally adopted by the inquiry excluded a charge that Procter had prematurely encouraged Barclay to fight on Lake Erie when additional seamen were on their way to Amherstburg, but it embraced five indictments framed by Sir George Prevost. [11] In brief, they were:

(1) that Procter did not immediately make "the military arrangements best calculated for promptly effecting such retreat and unnecessarily delayed to commence the same until the evening of the 27th of the said month [September] . . . ";

(2) that he "did not use due expedition or take the proper measures for conducting the said retreat . . . ," encumbering the Right Division with baggage and neglecting to destroy the bridges along the way;

(3) that he failed to provide sufficient security to the boats, wagons, carts, stores, and provisions, most of which were captured on October 4–5, or to ensure adequate victuals for the troops the day previous to battle;

(4) that he promised to fortify the forks of the Thames near Chatham but did not do so, neglected to occupy the heights at Moraviantown, and adopted an unfavorable position to offer battle; and

(5) that his dispositions on the field on October 5 were not to the best advantage, that his attempts to rally the men and support the Indians were insufficient, and that he prematurely quit the field. [12]

On the first count, Procter was acquitted, but the verdict on the second was ambivalent. The court exonerated the general of the charges concerning baggage and bridges, but it declared that he had not taken the correct measures in directing the retreat. He was judged free of blame on the matter of victualing mentioned in the third indictment, but was censured for affording inadequate protection to stores, provisions, boats, and wagons. On the fourth and fifth charges, Procter was convicted of making his stand on unsuitable ground within two miles of the Moraviantown heights and of stationing the army to its disadvantage on the battlefield. "Upon the whole," it was added, "the court is of opinion that the prisoner . . . has in many instances during the retreat and in the disposition of the force under his command been erroneous in judgment, and in some, deficient in those energetic and active exertions which the extraordinary difficulties of his situation so particularly required." Procter was sentenced to be reprimanded in public and to have his rank and pay suspended for six months. [13]

The general had indeed met obstacles that would have taxed a far abler commander. At the extremity of a long and precarious supply line, opposing an enemy with superior resources, and dependent upon a volatile Indian force, he could have been forgiven an honorable failure. His strategy, indeed, was respectable. It was the direction of the retreat and the tactical disposition of the troops under his command that pronounced Procter's failings. The possibility of a retreat had been with him throughout the summer, and he had committed himself to it as early as September 12, time enough to have reconnoitered the Thames, chosen and fortified a defensible position, and consolidated the whole of his guns and men behind it before the Americans came up. There, if he could have kept open his supply chain to the Centre Division, he had prospects of repelling the enemy or of holding them until the winter, when the scarcity of provisions or sickness could have forced one of the belligerents to retire.

Many of the Indians accompanied him as far as Dolsen's, and had Procter dealt frankly with them and proven himself a more inspiring leader, he might have been able to prevail upon the whole, through Tecumseh and Elliott, to have backed a plan for joint British-Indian action. Instead, he systematically destroyed the confidence of the natives, first by preparing to quit Amherstburg without consulting them, and then by neglecting to fortify and defend the forks of the Thames at Chatham. Thereafter, all his endeavors drew him deeper into the mire. To appease the warriors he promised to stand at a place of which he was largely ignorant, a decision that contributed to the fiasco at Chatham. By the latter he effectively gave the game to the Americans. His army was caught unprepared by an enemy advance which in itself was hardly an energetic performance, and confused and alarmed he retreated upriver, sacrificing stores, guns, and provisions. On October 5 the weary catalog of errors was consummated by a display of thoroughly bad field tactics on the part of the general. He misjudged the proximity of the enemy, fought within two miles of the second site he had chosen for his battle, and again divided his depleted forces. Formed for action, his troops were denied the most elementary defenses against cavalry.

The few years remaining to Procter were overcast by the shadow of Moraviantown. Reviewing the verdict of the court-martial, the Prince Regent—that most inconsiderable of British monarchs— rescinded the suspension of Procter's pay and rank, but confirmed the public humiliation that formed the more serious portion of the sentence. Thus, the general's incompetence came to be broadcast throughout the army; the findings of the court were read, at the direction of a general order, before the muster of every regiment. Procter was never again employed and died late in 1822 in Bath, England, at the age of fifty-nine.

While Procter languished beneath a cloud, his conquerors disputed the glory of a victory from which much had been expected at the time. Isaac Shelby hoped that the British would be driven from the western district of Upper Canada and their influence with the Indians destroyed. Armstrong, the American secretary of war, anticipated that Harrison might sail down Lake Erie and annoy the rear of the British Centre Division. Fleeting hopes were raised among the politicos in Washington that Canada might become a permanent possession of the United States; and McArthur, who had been left in command of Detroit when Harrison was campaigning up the Thames, saw the annexation of British and Indian territory as a means of breaking Indian resistance to the settlement of the Old Northwest. Wrote McArthur in defense of an armistice he had concluded with some of the Indians who had left Tecumseh:

It is certain that I have as little respect for those wretched beings as any other person can have, yet I was of opinon that we might save the lives of many women and children on our frontier, and the expense of hunting down those savages over a vast wilderness, which cannot at present be useful to any human being but themselves, and that, by puting an end to the Indian war, it would facilitate the sale & settlement of our wild land. And knowing that if we kept possession of the lakes and Upper Canada (which I trust will never be relinquished) there never could be another Indian war. [14]

The American success had certainly been a striking one, the annihilation of Barclay's squadron on Lake Erie acting as a curtain raiser to the destruction of the British-Indian army in the West. The battles were a tremendous moral uplift to a nation that had seen little success along the Canadian border during eighteen months of fighting, but they realized far less than the American commanders hoped. Within a few months of Moraviantown, Earl Bathurst, the British secretary of state for war and colonies, was able to confide in Prevost that: "On the subject of the disaster which appears to have befallen the force under the command of Genl. Proctor . . . it is at least satisfactory to observe that it has not influenced the conduct of our Indian allies nor given to the enemy any advantage beyond that of which they were already in possession."[15] The statement would be a surprising one to many who have written of the War of 1812 because it has become conventional to claim that the Battle of the Thames and the death of Tecumseh destroyed the Indian confederacy. But there is much truth in Bathurst's opinion. If Perry's victory gained for the United States the command of the Detroit frontier, Moraviantown supplied little more. It neither brought western Upper Canada under the control of the Americans nor extinguished the British-Indian alliance.

Major General Harrison did not exploit his victory on the Thames by entrenching American arms west of Lake Ontario. His invasion force was composed chiefly of short-term enlisted militia, troops unsuitable for protracted campaigning or occupation, and in October the fierce Canadian winter was closing in. Plans to press the campaign were shelved, and after burning the village of Moraviantown, the Americans withdrew down the Thames on October 7. Most of the men were sent home for discharge, and Harrison himself left the West at the end of the month, having established garrisons at Detroit, Amherstburg, and Sandwich that were responsible to the governments of Michigan Territory and the state of Ohio. This tenuous grip upon the Detroit never looked safe. Although the Americans continued to control Lake Erie, Governor Lewis Cass of Michigan Territory, who administered the three American outposts, had but a few hundred regulars to man them, provisions were scarce, and before the end of 1813 most of his soldiers were sick.[16]

Although Cass claimed to command Upper Canada as far as Moraviantown and exercised executive authority over the region, in reality he clung to the Detroit frontier for want of a challenge and gazed upon a no-man's land beyond, over which both British and American patrols ranged for supplies or to raid enemy positions.[17] Even the naval supremacy of the United States on the lake failed to secure a firm control of the area. In December, 1813 an American patrol was captured on the lower Thames, but less than two months later it was the turn of the British to lose a detail, at Delaware. The following spring an American force advanced up the Thames and crossed to Pointe Aux Pins on Lake Erie to destroy it, and in March the severest skirmishing since the Battle of Moraviantown took place. On the fourth a band of regulars and militia under Captains James Lewis Basden and William Caldwell probed downriver from an advanced British base at Delaware and ran into an inferior enemy patrol of 160 men under Captain Andrew H. Holmes. Holmes occupied an icy hill, which the British bravely but vainly attempted to storm in what became known as the Battle of the Long Woods before they retired with losses of twenty killed or fatally wounded and forty-six injured. The American navy entered the fray two months later and ferried men from Presque Isle to Port Dover, which was burned. Oxford and Port Talbot were raided several times by the Americans in 1814, but the pièce de résistance came at the very end of the season when Duncan McArthur fielded a force that reached as far as the Grand River on November 6 before retreating along the Thames, ravaging the mills on the way.[18]

These hit-and-run tactics favored by the Americans were no substitute for the occupation of western Upper Canada, but they inhibited British efforts to recover the region without the application of greater resources than were available and bled the Thames of the means to support permanent garrisons. This was precisely what the American secretary of war, John Armstrong, had planned. To retain the initiative in the West, he argued that the United States must reduce the settlements of the Thames to "a desart" and conciliate the Indians by supplying their wants and resisting the temptation to impose upon them punitive land cessions.[19] As early as March, 1814, the new commander of the British army in Upper Canada, Lieutenant General Sir Gordon Drummond recognized that troops could not be quartered on the Thames and was drawn to suggest that Long Point could furnish flour and cattle for a garrison near Turkey Point instead. From there he proposed to detach small details to Oxford, Port Dover, and other places.[20] After McArthur's expedition Captain Chambers bemoaned that "not a single barrel of flour is to be purchased in the district," a situation that imperiled the ability of the British to hold even their position at the head of Lake Ontario during the ensuing winter.[21]

Although the Americans sustained their superiority on the Detroit for the remainder of the war, none doubted the fragility of that control. On December 22, 1813, Drummond was fully aware "that Detroit and the whole of the western country might be reoccupied by us at any moment without difficulty provided we had it in our power to detach a force for that purpose."[22] In less than a month he had formulated a plan to use nearly two thousand men, including four hundred western Indians, in a winter expedition across the ice against Detroit, Amherstburg, and Sandwich so that Britain's influence with the Indian tribes might be resuscitated. The number and state of Cass's troops suggest that Drummond would have made an easy conquest, but the mild weather and late winter forced him to abandon the project.[23] No greater progress was made on rebuilding the Lake Erie squadron. This matter was the subject of a report in May, 1814 by the quartermaster general of militia, in which it was pointed out that until navigation closed for the winter a naval dockyard on Lake Erie would be vulnerable to American attack. Building should commence at that time, when stores might also be assembled and Turkey Point—the site best suited for an establishment—

fortified. Drummond accepted these proposals, but the operation was postponed because of a deficiency in guns and stores, and the new year opened with little more than a start made to Turkey Point's defenses.[24]

In truth, although the war in the West lapsed in 1813–1814 it was less a consequence of the Battle of Moraviantown than that neither side was willing to invest the resources necessary to contend it. With the Northwest secure from Indian incursions, the United States rightly gave priority to campaigns farther east. A decisive victory on the Saint Lawrence or at Niagara would have cut the British communication lines and asphyxiated all enemy positions above. Accordingly, the West was tapped for ships and regulars required in the East and left reliant upon the militia, who were inexpedient for long campaigns and apt to refuse to cross the Canadian line because their primary function was home defense. After Drummond's plans against Detroit had been abandoned, the British too channeled most of their energies toward the front along the Niagara, Lake Ontario, and the Saint Lawrence.

In the absence of intensive American activity across the Detroit, Britain retained credibility in the West. Indeed, she even extended her influence about the Upper Lakes and the Mississippi, where the Indian alliance and Canada's fur trade alike dictated the Crown's interest. On Lake Huron the British ensign still fluttered boldly over the posts of Michillimackinac and Saint Joseph's, untroubled by Harrison and Perry who declined to challenge them in 1813 because of the inclement weather. The King's supremacy over these vast areas, like that of the United States on the Detroit, was precarious. It had depended for its supplies upon Amherstburg and was consequently seriously inconvenienced by Procter's retreat. Moreover, the demands upon Michillimackinac expanded as it strove to provide not only the Indians of the Upper Lakes and the Mississippi with presents but now also those previously assisted at Fort Malden. Its difficulties multiplied after Lieutenant Colonel George Croghan, sometimes commanding the American garrison at Detroit, built a fort at the head of the Saint Clair River, straggling the communications between lakes Saint Clair and Huron.

The victualing situation peppered the reports of the commanders at Michillimackinac, Captain Richard Bullock and his successor, Lieutenant Colonel Robert McDouall, who arrived on May 18 with provisions and reinforcements. On July 20 the latter reported that the demands from the Indians upon him had been "so much beyond our present means, that I have been obliged to refuse men suffering greatly from hunger, thereby tending to lessen their zeal and attachment, and subjecting me to the imputation of being a harsh and severe Father that had no compassion . . . for their starving condition . . . an ill-timed penury now would . . . render of little use what has already been done and expended on them . . . ."

Pessimism apart, the communications were kept open, however indifferently. A new artery ran overland from York to Lake Simcoe and there connected with waterways to Matchadash Bay, Nottawasaga Bay, or Penetanguishene Bay on Lake Huron, where a commercial schooner, the *Nancy*, plied back and forth to Michillimackinac on Mackinac Island. There was talk of using Matchadash or Penetanguishene Harbor to outfit additional vessels for the lake, but nothing seems to have come of the plan even though it won ministerial approval.[25]

Ironically, it was the one serious American attempt to root the British out of the Far West that firmly established Britain's naval supremacy on the Upper Lakes. In the summer of 1814, Croghan led a flotilla of five vessels containing several hundred men into Lake Huron to capture Michillimackinac. McDouall was ready for him, and though he had to evacuate Saint Joseph's, he repulsed the assault on Michillimackinac on August 4, costing Croghan eighteen men killed or captured and nearly fifty wounded. Withdrawing, the Americans found brief solace in their destruction of a blockhouse at Nottawasaga, in compelling the British to blow up the *Nancy* to save her from capture, and in leaving behind two schooners to stifle enemy traffic on the lake. But Lieutenant Miller Worsley, in the finest tradition of the Royal Navy, captured both of the American vessels and reestablished British naval command of Lake Huron for the duration of the war.[26]

Far from receding in this remote territory, the Crown extended its influence by establishing forward bases on Lake Michigan and the Mississippi. The "Red Head," Robert Dickson, whose controversial skills in managing supplies for the Indians did not entirely dispel his profound prestige among the Sioux, the Menominee, the Sac and Fox, the Kickapoo, and the Winnebago, arrived at Michillimackinac in October, 1813 to distribute the annual shipment of Indian presents. He then wintered on the west side of Lake Michigan and in the spring of 1814 had available hundreds of warriors for the King's service.[27] Some of them helped to defend Michillimackinac in August; others joined a skeleton force of British under Major William McKay for an expedition to Prairie du Chien, a fur post on the Mississippi in Illinois Territory, which has just been occupied by the Americans. On July 20, McKay compelled Fort Shelby, which protected Prairie du Chien with a scant garrison of sixty-six men, to surrender, and when the United States made subsequent efforts to recapture the position, the troops were frustrated by probably a thousand or more Indians who rallied to the British interest. The Americans still held Fort Clark, a newly constructed post at Peoria, but never succeeded in driving the British from the upper Mississippi.[28]

Since the Battle of Moraviantown did not extinguish Britain's influence in the West, no more did it prevent her interference with the natives. There can be no doubt that had the Redcoats returned to the Detroit they would have regained the active support of most of their old adherents among the disaffected tribesmen. There was a predisposition among them to favor Britain because of the many difficulties with the United States in the Northwest: "the Americans in war or peace they detest," wrote Judge Benjamin Parke.[29] But while American arms were ascendant in that quarter, the Indians remained sullen and silent. Even so recent an arrival in the West as McDouall was not slow to appreciate "the wily character of the Indian, & his propensity to change sides as the events of the war proves adverse or prosperous . . . ." Consequently, about Lake Huron, the Mississippi, and part of Illinois Territory, where Britain controlled the key posts of Michillimackinac and Prairie du Chien, the Indians gathered noisily to her support, but on the

Detroit frontier, now in American hands, a simmering resentment among the tribes was shrouded by an ostensible peace.[30]

Because so many historians have alleged that Moraviantown destroyed the Indian confederacy, as if Tecumseh alone held it together, it now remains to examine the British-Indian alliance during the last years of the war, with a view to demonstrating that although it remained a latently dangerous combination, it failed to realize its potential.

In the summer of 1813 the Indian alliance had been at its fullest. A new theater of the border war was then opened to the south by the Creeks, and on the Detroit the largest native army the Northwest had yet seen was assembled under Tecumseh. It was inevitable that such a concourse of warriors would disperse, and the process was already under way when it was accelerated by the retreat from Amherstburg, the ensuing battle on the Thames, and the death of Tecumseh. After Moraviantown many of Britain's allies returned to their homes in Ohio and the territories of Michigan, Indiana, and Illinois, restless under the regenerated suzerainty of the United States, while others about the Upper Lakes and the Mississippi more openly adhered to the British flag. A rump contingent of Tecumseh's followers remained in the King's service throughout the rest of the war, generally at the head of Lake Ontario. All of these bands continued to harbor British sympathies but so ineffectively translated them into deeds that the impression that Moraviantown and Tecumseh's death had terminated both the Indian war and the intertribal confederacy gained currency.

The Indians at the head of Lake Ontario, survivors of the retreat, were never more than a foundation upon which nothing was built, although their numbers were not inconsiderable. In January, 1814, Elliott reported that the Sacs and Foxes were due to return to their homes on the Mississippi, but six hundred other warriors were at Burlington and recruiting was progressing slowly.[31] Successive returns of this force provide a clear picture of its composition during the remainder of the conflict. The Ottawas and Ojibwas, interspersed by a few Potawatomis, increased their strength to about fourteen hundred and became the most populous component, able to furnish more than two hundred fit warriors from nearly twice that number of males. Next, with a population of about seven hundred and capable of fielding almost a hundred and fifty fighting men, were the Munsies, the Moravian Indians, and the Delawares. By contrast the Wyandots and a handful of Iroquois who camped with the western Indians remained pitifully diminutive bands, about one hundred fifty in all. The Sac and Fox, contrary to Elliott's expectations, stabilized at a little over a hundred persons, while the Shawnees and Kickapoos both developed respectable proportions. The latter numbered more than two hundred by the middle of 1814, and the former 244 in three musters, up to a third of them men. Thus, the British preserved a substantial number of Indian auxiliaries immediately to hand. When they called upon the western Indians to defend the Niagara frontier in July, 1814, 582 braves marched to the lines—239 Ottawa, Potawatomi, and Ojibwa; 138 Munsey, Delaware, and Moravian Indians; 62 Shawnee and 45 Kickapoo; 44 Sac and Fox; 38 Wyandot and 16 Iroquois.[32]

The view that the Indians collapsed as a military force after their defeat on the Thames was due less to the dispersal of the warriors than to their persistent incompetence in the field and consequent inability to affect the war. Charged with this, they would certainly have blamed the deficiencies of the British supply system, and with considerable justification. The concentration of soldiers and Indians at the head of the lake tortured the British commissariat, and at times the men survived on quarter rations. When the annual shipment of Indian presents arrived at Burlington in November, 1813, it clothed less than a third of the natives, while even at the end of the war Tenskwatawa protested that his warriors marched to and fro but never received the moccasins they had been promised, nor even an awl or needle. More to the point was the Shawnee chief who informed his allies that: "You made many promises to your children . . . which have not been fulfilled, but we bear it with patience because we make allowances, and we know for instance how difficult it is for you to get up the presents which we are so much in want of but Father when we hear our women & children crying for something to eat our hearts melt . . . ."[33]

The poor performance of the Indians was also a matter of leadership. In this respect the retreat of 1813 did prove decisive, for without Roundhead and Tecumseh to curb the factions and bind them to a single purpose the Indians fell to trivial but continuous bickering and became unmanageable. The loss of the Shawnee chief in particular proved to be an irretrievable blow, for his remarkable qualities had tempered the weaknesses inherent in the Indians as a military corps. His belief that without the British the Indians were incapable of checking the territorial ambitions of the United States lent him a fidelity to the Crown that was unusual. He was endowed with the intelligence to appreciate strategical situations and with the energy, eloquence, and influence to recruit and harness warriors to appropriate objectives. His talents in managing these undisciplined forces in the field had kept a British-Indian army of two thousand men waiting for his arrival before invading Ohio in April, 1813, and his tenacity and courage in battle preserved Indian equanimity under fire and rendered them capable of resistance even in adverse circumstances.

Not many weeks had elapsed after Moraviantown before these difficulties rose forebodingly to the surface. Lieutenant General Sir Gordon Drummond employed seventy western Indians in his successful campaign across the Niagara in December, 1813, suffering them to witness the British captures of Fort Geoge, Lewiston, Black Rock, and Buffalo. Matthew Elliott had them under control at Black Rock and Buffalo, but despite promises of forbearance the Indians ran amok in Lewiston, and drunken warriors looted and burned buildings, murdered a civilian, and even turned upon each other.[34] At the opening of the third year of the war, the British wrestled with the problems of rejuvenating the Indian alliance, expunging any notions that Moraviantown had weakened Britain's resolve, and finding a successor to Tecumseh. Initially, the high command suggested that Paukeesaa, Tecumseh's son, might be acceptable to the Indians as their new principal chief, but Elliott reminded his superiors that the boy had yet to prove himself a warrior.[35]

It was perhaps to test this proposition as well as to encourage the natives generally that Prevost invited Paukeesaa and Tecumseh's sister, Tecumapeace, with other leading western chiefs to Quebec on an elaborate diplomatic junket. Escorted by members of the Indian Department, the delegation arrived in York about February 14, 1814. In the party were Tecumseh's relatives, twelve chiefs representing the Ojibwa, the Ottawa, the Sac and Fox, the Kickapoo, the Delaware, the Muncey, the Iroquois, and the Winnebago tribes, and about twenty-six warriors. They were hosted for two days at the home of the deputy superintendent of Indian Affairs, William Claus, before most of them transferred to Jordan Post's inn where they were treated to three meals a day, bread, cheese, beef, liquor, and cider. Perhaps because of overindulgence, one of the party fell sick at Kingston and was left behind at Thebode's lodgings, attended by Jacob Graverot of the Indian Department, but twenty-five of the Indians reached Quebec in the middle of March.[36]

Sir George Prevost entertained them lavishly, receiving them on the fifteenth with the Mohawk John Norton and his wife in the great room of the Old Castle to military airs played by the band of the Seventieth Regiment. Naiwash and Mitass, the Indian spokesmen, were so overcome that they begged that the serious business be reserved for another day, and after partaking of refreshments in an adjoining room the warriors wound up the proceedings with the calumet dance. Two days later the council was reconvened at the same venue, and Naiwash, again seconded by Mitass, explained that the Indians intended to fight for their "old boundary lines" but were short of clothing and ammunition. Prevost was presented with black wampum and a war belt and rose to reply. He had been grieved, he said, to hear of the death of "a great warrior" (at which words Tecumseh's sister "was seen very unaffectedly to shed tears") but reminded the Indians that their cause and that of the British were one. He told them:

Our Great Father considers you as his children and will not forget you or your interests at a peace, but to preserve what we hold and recover from the enemy what belongs to us we must make great exertions and I rely on your undaunted courage with the assistance of my chiefs & warriors to drive the Big Knives from off all our lands the ensuing summer. My children, our Great Father will give us more warriors from the other side of the Great Water who will join in attacking the enemy and will open the great road to your country by which you used to receive your supplies and which the enemy having stopped has caused the distress and scarsity of goods you complain of . . . .

Prevost then returned the chiefs their war belt as a symbol of the continued alliance. Taking it up, Naiwash paced and chanted his determination to confront the enemy, followed by the other warriors:

> Under the clouds I stand,
> With this belt I go;
> By this, my heart is strong;
> I shall have courage to die by the foe.

When the ceremony had ended, Tecumapeace was presented to Lady Prevost and after shaking hands received a basket containing mourning ornaments and other gifts. Mrs. Norton was also given presents and the Indians again retired for refreshments, fortified by the promises Prevost had made, promises they would expect him to keep.[37]

Used to the frugal supplies at Burlington, the party was drowned in gifts. They received wampum, and from Sir John Johnson, superintendent of Indian Affairs, silverware. When they left their Montreal lodgings at the Cedars and Ebenezer Winters's on April 4, they had horses, bridles, and saddles to carry them home. Tecumseh's relations also received two shawls, a coat with an epaulet, buckles and earrings. Yet typically the whole exercise backfired upon the British, for hardly had the delegates reached home before the Shawnees took umbrage that the copy of Prevost's speech had been lodged with Naiwash, and two members of the embassy, the Shawnee Labathka and a Mohawk, Isaac Peters, accused the Ottawa chief and others of appropriating all the silverware.[38]

The Quebec exercise had not alleviated the problem of leadership among the tribesmen. While their representatives were being courted by Prevost, the warriors had been asked to carry ammunition down the Thames to their brethren about the Detroit, but the Shawnees flatly refused to cooperate. Although they ought to have known better, they evidently credited a rumor that Elliott was planning to ingratiate himself with the Americans and intended leading the Indians into a trap. So agitated did the natives become that Ironside feared for Elliott's life. It was nevertheless character-istic of this brave old Loyalist that, sick and in his final illness, he dismissed the dangers and persuaded two hundred of the other western Indians to accompany the British effort. But he could not make them advance beyond Delaware, and scarcely forty joined Captains Basden and Caldwell for their skirmish with Holmes on March 4. Most of the Indians scuttled back to the head of Lake Ontario, leaving one British officer to lament "the want of Indian chiefs."[39]

Some improvement seemed to have been effected the next month when the Shawnees accepted Paukeesaa as their village chief and his uncle, Tenskwatawa, the prophet, as their war chief. About the same time the latter was presented with a sword and pistols as gifts from the Prince Regent and was nominated princi-pal chief of the western nations. He promised his allies that even his "smallest boys, capable of bearing arms, shall be ready to march at a moment's notice."[40] Still, this betokened no greater energy on the part of the Indians. Before long Tenskwatawa and others were demanding large supplies of rum on which to besot themselves, and a rift had opened between the Shawnees, Kickapoos, Wyan-dots, and Delawares on the one side, and the Ottawas, Sacs and Ojibwas on the other, which led them to camp separately.

"We must again express our sorrow that the Shawanoes have parted with us," Naiwash complained. "Our Elder Brothers have made me ashamed."[41]

To this confusion the death of Matthew Elliott on May 7 and subsequent discord in the Indian Department further contributed. Elliott's successor, Colonel Caldwell, found difficulty controlling the western Indians because John Norton, newly commissioned as captain of the Iroquois of Grand River with independent authority to dispense presents, enticed some of them away with generous allocations of goods that the warriors, in acute want, were unable to resist. Some of the Ojibwas and Ottawas, the Munsies, Moravians, Shawnees, Kickapoos, and Wyandots were soon lured—

"debauched" Caldwell said—to the Grand River, and Naiwash abjectly admitted his inability to "keep our young men in our hands" because Norton "speaks loud, and has strong milk, and big breasts, which yield plentifully."[42]

Any who doubted that the Indians, torn in petty dispute and bandied between competing British agents, would contribute to the summer's campaign prophesied truly. In May the British requested three hundred Indians to help raid Sackets Harbor and despite some misgivings the chiefs agreed to turn out. When the Americans crossed the Niagara, seized Fort Erie, and marched into Upper Canada, it became necessary to transfer available forces to that front, and the Indians were directed to join Major General Sir Phineas Riall, who attempted to intercept the enemy advance. One war party, supervised by Colonel Caldwell, arrived in time to participate on July 5, 1814 in the Battle of Chippewa, in which Riall was thrown back by his adversaries. The Indians, Drummond remarked, were "as usual . . . of little service" in the engagement. Penetrating too far into the woods on the British right, they were almost surrounded by enemy riflemen and Indians and had to be rescued by a company of light infantry.[43] Soon afterward a second contingent, mainly Shawnees and Kickapoos under Tenskwatawa, arrived from the Grand River, but almost immediately quit the camp and withdrew to Burlington, leaving the British dumbfounded. Had Riall breached Indian etiquette by failing to return wampum The Prophet had sent him? Or were the Indians annoyed that a party of warriors who had raided over the Niagara and burned barracks at Hardscrabble, near Lewiston, had been prevented by the British from bringing back captured livestock? Norton's explanation was that the Indians had seen their British allies jettison an obsolete cannon on the evening of the seventh and noticed some of the Redcoats moving to the rear. Augmenting their imaginations by drinking, they fancied that the British were retreating, and the next day only twenty braves—Iroquois as well as western Indians—remained at the lines. Whatever may have been the cause of the Indian behavior, Drummond denounced it in the terms once employed by Elliott of the troops at Moraviantown.[44]

At Burlington, Caldwell managed to reform the Indians and 582 of them set off for the lines on July 14 with Colonel Hercules Scott's detachment. They rejoined Riall, and some of them participated in the famous Battle of Lundy's Lane, north of Chippewa, which halted the American advance into Canada and threw the enemy back into Fort Erie. It was Drummond's unsuccessful siege of Fort Erie, however, which at last permitted the Indians to distinguish themselves by repulsing an American sortie and inflicting heavy losses upon it on August 21. It is uncertain whether this success, which resulted from what Drummond sarcastically termed "uncommon spirit" on the part of the tribesmen, can be more justly ascribed to the western Indians or to the Iroquois.[45]

The operations of 1814 baldly demonstrated the incohesion and indecision that wracked the Indian forces during the last year of the war. Back at the head of the lake, on October 6, Naiwash, perhaps the ablest of the suviving leaders, appealed to the chiefs for unity in words that perfectly encapsulated the problem:

We Indians who are from the westward, perhaps the Master of Life would give us more luck if we would stick together as we formerly did . . . and we probably might go back & tread again upon our own lands. Chiefs and warriors since our great chief Tecumtha has been killed, we do not listen to one another, we do not rise together, we hurt ourselves by it, it is our own fault . . . we do not when we go to war rise together, but we go one or two and the rest say they will go tomorrow . . . .[46]

The Indians were sufficiently inspired by Naiwash's plea to agree once more to camp together at Dundas, but they were incapable of acting in concert for long. Norton circulated unfounded stories that Caldwell could not supply them because the Indian presents allocated his department had been captured by the Americans, and Tenskwatawa and some of his Shawnee and Kickapoo followers quickly returned to the Iroquois cantonment on the Grand River. Upon this occasion, 98 of the 225 Shawnees with the British and 184 of the 213 Kickapoos refused to follow The Prophet and stayed at Dundas, but Norton's machinations had again exposed the fragmentary character of the western Indian army. They also pointed to one of the underlying causes, the deprivation in the Indian camps. In October the British again tried to raise war parties for service on the Niagara, but Captain William Elliott wrote from Dundas on the fourteenth that "after such flattering promises I am sorry to say we have met with more delay in moving them [the Indians] to the lines than I had the least idea of—yet their excuse had some truth they being all barefooted . . . another reason of their delay is that they are so much dispersed trying to get provisions to feed their wives & children."[47] These circumstances nullified such spasmodic efforts as the Indians were willing to make. When McArthur brought the war to their doorstep by reaching the Grand River on November 6, those tribesmen who endeavored to help the British repel the invaders were unable to keep up with their allies because they lacked moccasins. Drummond was compelled to absolve the Indians from further service so that they could scatter across the country and hunt for the winter.[48]

The steadiest of Britain's "sable" allies, those who had retreated with Tecumseh and Procter and settled at the head of Lake Ontario, thus proved themselves an inconsiderable asset to Canada in the months after Moraviantown. They were ill equipped and possessed no effective leaders. Many of Tecumseh's old warriors from Ohio, Indiana, Michigan, and Illinois had drifted back to their camps, hostile to the United States but disenchanted with the British. Once the protecting arm of Great Britain had been removed by Perry's victory on the lake, they sensed their insecurity, and they missed the British commissariat because their war-torn economy was hardly proof against the approaching winter. The condition of the Indians who tarried about the Detroit after Procter's retreat was truly deplorable, as Samuel Brown, who was in Detroit soon after the battle of Moraviantown, remembered:

A few days after Proctor's defeat, the town was so full of famished savages, that the issue of rations to them did not keep pace with their hunger. I have seen the women and children searching the ground for bones and rinds of pork, which had been thrown away by the soldiers; meat, in a high state of putrifaction, which had been thrown into the river, was carefully picked up and devoured; the feet, head and entrails of the cattle slaughtered by the public butchers, were collected and sent off to the neighbouring villages.[49]

Scarcely had the British left before the tribesmen—Ottawas, Ojibwas, Potawatomis, Miamis, and Kickapoos—began to approach their late enemies with extended hands and professions of friendship. McArthur, who commanded the regulars at Detroit while Harrison was chasing Procter and Tecumseh up the Thames, was not blind to their duplicity, but with few soldiers to protect the local settlers he found it prudent to promise the applicants an armistice and rations, provided they supplied hostages and declared fealty to the United States.[50] Harrison sanctioned these actions when he returned to Detroit, aware that the Indians could still be driven upon the British by hunger, and concluded an armistice with the principal penitents on October 14. The signatories included Potawatomi, Miami, Ottawa, Ojibwa, and Wyandot chiefs. In treating with them Harrison knew that many, particularly the Potawatomi leader Main Poc, put their names to his document without any intrinsic commitment to the United States.[51]

Although, as it transpired, these Indians were out of the war for good, large numbers of them remained disaffected and would have risen for the British had the latter returned to the Detroit. In this sense Perry's battle, by driving the British into the interior, successfully dismantled part of Tecumseh's confederacy without destroying its potential as a threat to the United States. Lewis Cass, who succeeded to the responsibility of dealing with the Indians, continued to placate them with the issue of such rations and annuities as he could assemble, in accordance with the policy of the secretary of war, who believed that the tribes would only be conciliated "by supplying their wants and by assuring them that their present boundaries shall continue . . . ." The shortages of ammunition and of clothing fueled native restlessness, however, and Cass was soon reporting that in contravention of the armistice of October 14 the Potawatomis were committing minor depredations.[52] By December he had concluded that the Indians' pretensions of peace were "hollow." "It is a fact not now to be questioned," he wrote, "that the attachment of most of them to the enemy, is much more sincere, than to us," a point about which the British were far from ignorant.[53]

In December, 1813, Drummond, revolving his plans to capture Detroit, instructed Matthew Elliott, then near the head of Lake Ontario, to send tidings of Britain's winter successes over the Niagara to the tribes of the Old Northwest with the word "that we shall shortly revisit them in power." The Indians replied that their armistice with the United States had not affected their relationship to the British; the warriors "have only taken the Big Knife by the finger end and have spoken to them from the lip outwards and that they are always ready to obey their Father's order as soon as given."[54]

In the spring of 1814 hundreds of Indians, according to one report twelve hundred, hearing nothing of the cancellation of Drummond's plan, gathered in the vicinity of the Detroit ready to assist the British. When the Redcoats did not come, the disappointed tribesmen tried to encourage their late allies. In March, Main Poc relayed to them the information that his men were "sitting on their war club waiting to take it up when an opportunity may offer." The Ojibwas of the River Saint Clair said that although they were being closely watched by the Americans, they had killed two French spies and were bringing a hundred men, women, and children to join the British. Some Ottawas reported in May about five hundred men were even then at Saginaw Bay, waiting to display their loyalty to the King the moment his troops arrived. In addition, about ninety of Roundhead's old Wyandot followers arrived at the head of Lake Ontario with the news that even though the chiefs Blackbird and Splitlog had gone over to the enemy, many other tribesmen would have slipped away to the British forces had they been under looser surveillance.[55]

It was British inaction that ultimately decided the issue of Indian allegiance on the Detroit. There is not the slightest doubt that had Britain fielded an army, it would have been well supported by the Indians of the Old Northwest, but while the Americans held the frontier and the Redcoats remained supine, the natives sat smoldering resentfully in their lodges, held in sullen obedience to the United States by its arms and the provisions it could supply to the starving tribesmen. As one Ottawa chief remarked, the British had promised to return to the Detroit in the winter, "but I have got weary of waiting . . . ."[56] Despairing of a British resurgence, chiefs of the Wyandot, the Seneca, the Shawnee, the Miami, and the Deleware tribes assembled at Greenville, Ohio, in the summer of 1814 to sign a permanent cease-fire agreement with the United States on July 22. Sensibly, the government accepted Harrison's advice (rejecting that of Cass and the representatives of Ohio and Indiana) and resisted the temptation to punish the Indians with land seizures. The tribes were simply asked to acknowledge a cessation of hostilities, and to agree, by Article 2, to assist the United States in the war if required. The last condition was never met.[57]

If the Americans believed that the Greenville Treaty would extinguish unrest among the Indians of Ohio, Indiana, Michigan, and Illinois, they were mistaken. Many of the chiefs who signed it, like those of the Shawnee, belonged to the pacifist factions of their tribes that had long supported the United States, and there were notable absentees whose pacification was esssential for tranquility in the Old Northwest. The Potawatomis, in particular, were still at large. From Main Poc's camp on the Yellow River in Indiana Territory warriors continued to ride in search of plunder. The old chief was fading now, his influence much diminished, his frame aged and sick, and he was hard of hearing and too often sought refuge in drink to represent the threat he had once been. But a new focus of resistance was also developing on the Theakiki River, where Bad Sturgeon ("a Pottewattamie chief zealously attached to us," McDouall said) repudiated the Greenville Treaty and rallied dissident Potawatomis and Kickapoos. These sources of irritation outlived the War of 1812; Bad Sturgeon made his peace with the Americans at Fort Wayne in May, 1815, and Main Poc died incorrigible the following year.[58]

Britain's neglect slowly strangled what was left of the British-Indian alliance in the area between and south of Lakes Michigan, Huron, and Erie, but in the Far West the King controlled Michillimackinac, Saint Joseph, and Prairie du Chien, and it was here that the only effective Indian cooperation after Moraviantown occurred. The ailing economies of the tribes of the Upper Lakes and Mississippi contributed to their commitment to their great father.

Insufficient corn had been planted, few traders had appeared in the Indian villages during the war years, and ammunition for hunting was scarce. Long since unable to sustain themselves independently of the white men, the tribes exhibited a condition of general want. The Sioux chief Little Crow told the British:

> My Father, we are sorry to learn that we are to have no traders this year—although you give assistance to all your children, yet you have too many to take care of, before it can reach us. We have of late not had much assistance through you my Father, for one half of our nation have died of hunger with shreds of skins in their mouths for want of other nourishment. I have always thought and do so still, that it arises from no other cause but the trouble you have with the Americans.[59]

In the winter of 1814–1815 the Indians at Green Bay were "a most distressing sight; men, women & children, naked and in a state of starvation," and those at Prairie du Chien "in a starving condition owing to the want of ammunition."[60] Such circumstances induced the Indians to cling desperately to the meager rations afforded by the British, lacking as they did comparable alternatives. Dickson doubted the intrinsic loyalty of these tribesmen. According to him, "The Sioux have behaved like villains as they are . . . "; "The Poutewatamies have always been villians [villains] to both parties & will continue so untill the end of the chapter"; and the "Renards [Foxes] . . . [and] the Sauks are playing a double game . . . ."But he knew that whoever commanded the supplies would dictate the play.[61] Not surprisingly, British commanders turned the misery of the natives to their own advantage. Prevost's promises that the King would assist the Indians to regain "their old boundaries" and that peace would only be granted the United States "on the express condition that your interests shall be first considered, your just claims admitted, and no infringement of your rights permitted in future," were combined with the pledge that traders would soon be revisiting the villages and "the days of your prosperity will return . . . ." To help the British, the tribes must remain united and ready to march with the Redcoats.[62] McDouall instructed his subordinate at Prairie du Chien to inform the tribesmen that "their Great Father . . . is . . . endeavoring to

. . . relieve their distresses, but that the road being blocked up, the supplies which used to come in ships, now creep along by stealth in canoes, & are of course both small & precarious . . . ."[63]

In the field the Indian performance was indifferent. When the Americans attacked Michillimackinac in August, 1814, the Menominees under Chief Thomas were of material assistance to the British on the flanks, but the lack of enterprise among the other Indians convinced McDouall "of the great danger of depending upon these people . . . they are fickle as the winds . . . ."[64] Their efforts on the expedition to Prairie du Chien were even worse. Several hundred warriors from Michillimackinac and Green Bay, assembled with the aid of the Winnebago Teté de Chien, a chief McDouall regarded as "scarcely inferior to Tecumseth," accompanied McKay on his campaign of July, 1814. During the siege of Fort Shelby they were "perfectly useless" and "impossible to controul," raiding farms and houses about the town and for the most part quitting the army as soon as they had received a share of the spoils.[65] But this time they redeemed themselves. An American relief force under Major John Campbell was repulsed on the Mississippi, near the mouth of the Rock River, on July 21 by Sacs, Foxes, and Kickapoos in the first significant Indian engagement since Moraviantown. Sixteen Americans were killed or fatally wounded and fifteen wounded.[66] And when Major Zachary Taylor led another expedition up the Mississippi to chastize the Indians, hundreds of braves gathered to watch a British detachment commanded by Lieutenant Duncan Graham of the Indian Department turn it back near the Rock River on September 6. Inspired, some Sacs followed the Americans downriver and so harassed members of Taylor's party attempting to establish Fort Johnson at the Des Moines River that the fort was evacuated and burned the following month.[67]

On the whole, it must be admitted that Britain's Indian alliance ceased to function as an important feature of the War of 1812 after the Battle of Moraviantown. The victories at Detroit, at the River Raisin, and at Fort Meigs contrast vividly with the petty skirmishing of 1814 and 1815. At face value it seemed, therefore, that the defeat on the Thames and the death of Tecumseh had broken the multitribal confederacy and closed the Indian war, but this was scarcely so. Thousands of Indians were still in British service in 1814, and many more wanted only the opportunity to join them. Throughout the year the Sioux, the Iowas, the Winnebagoes, the Sacs, the Foxes, and the Menominees held fast to their great father, strengthened by supplies of food and ammunition and assurances that no peace would be concluded "till the lands plundered from the Indians, are restored."[68]

Farther east, most of the tribes tired of British inactivity and treated with the Americans at Greenville, but militants still afflicted the frontier with a predatory warfare in which civilians were often in the front line. During a raid on a settlement at Whiteside on the upper Illinois in July a Kickapoo war party pillaged the houses and took at least seven scalps.[69] Finally, at the head of Lake Ontario there resided more than six hundred fit warriors under Naiwash and Tenskwatawa, the survivors of Tecumseh's immediate following. The war in the West did not falter primarily because the Indians had forsaken the British. It was rather that they were destitute of provisions and lacked the purpose and direction that Tecumseh's leadership had previously given them, and most of all that the British simply failed to reopen the western theater. Not until a full nineteen months after the Battle of Moraviantown did the British-Indian alliance come to its end, after word of the Treaty of Ghent, signed on December 24, 1814, and the formal cessation of hostilities between Britain and the United States reached the remote wilderness posts of the upper Mississippi.

The Indians were shaken by the news because they had been led to believe that the peace would restore those lands in the Northwest that had been ceded, as some said fraudulently, in agreements with the United States since the Treaty of Greenville in 1795. Native claims to these territories had been pressed since the beginning of the conflict, passing from Tecumseh to the British prime minister, Lord Liverpool, via Major General Isaac Brock, Prevost, Bathurst, and Viscount Castlereagh, the foreign secretary. Brock became acquainted with the Indians' grievances when he collaborated with Tecumseh's warriors in August, 1812, for the successful campaign against Detroit. Grateful for the aid he then received, impressed by Tecumseh's arguments, and sensible of the value of the Indian alliance to the safety of Upper Canada, he committed Britain by promising that no peace negotiations would be conducted with the United States that did not embrace the claims of the tribesmen. Seconded by Prevost, who emphasized the reliance of the security of western Canada upon Indian goodwill, he lobbied the home government and on December 9, 1812, Bathurst declared that the tribal lands would be an issue in any discussions of peace. At the same time, the Canadian mercantile interests, fearful for their fur empire south and west of the Great Lakes, urged Whitehall to create a permanent Indian barrier state in the Northwest as "a sine qua non of any treaty whatsoever negotiated . . ." By June, 1814, Bathurst was talking about the restoration of "the whole of the Michigan country to the Indians."[70]

True to their word, when representatives of the two principal belligerents met in Ghent, Belgium, in August, 1814, the British demanded as a sine qua non for a settlement the establishment of an Indian buffer state between the United States and the King's possessions in North America. Neither power would be able to purchase land within the area, which would be set aside as a permanent Indian boundary and which would approximate, with modifications, the Greenville Treaty line of 1795. The reaction of the American commissioners at Ghent was predictable. They had not been furnished by their government with instructions covering the Indians and found the British proposals preposterous. The Indians were not, in their view, independent nations, but wards of the United States, residing in territory acknowledged by Britain in the Treaty of Paris in 1783 to belong to the Americans. The matter was a domestic concern in which no interference by a foreign power could be tolerated. Moreover, the creation of such an Indian state was tantamount to the United States ceding territory since they were determined to settle the Old Northwest. On August 25 the American plenipotentiaries rejected the sine qua non, and the talks tottered upon the brink of extinction.[71]

Eager to profit from even the impasse, Prevost ordered his

commanders to regale the tribesmen with the story of Britain's efforts at Ghent, accentuating the intransigent resistance of the Americans to the just claims of the Indians and stressing that the war was now being prosecuted by the King purely on their account. Whether the governor in chief and his subordinates really believed that their war-weary country was prepared to fight solely upon the Indian question may be doubted, but they gave pledges to the tribes that were incapable of fulfillment and ultimately caused the Redcoats considerable embarrassment. McDouall learned of the rupture in the peace negotiations in February, 1815, and in a speech to the Menominees, Winnebagoes, Ottawas, Ojibwas, Sacs, Foxes, and Sioux boasted that the King "would not listen to any proposal of the American government unless they would first agree to . . . restore to you again all the lands which they have robbed you of since their General Wayne's treaty of Greenville . . . ." Because the Americans were adamant in refusing the tribes justice, Britain was sending her troops, victorious in Europe, across the sea to attack the United States "on your account." As a comment upon the slowness of communications at this time, it is worth noting that the difficulties at Ghent had been resolved and a peace signed two months before McDouall dispatched a copy of his speech to his officer at Prairie du Chien.[72]

Of course, the British negotiators gave way. On September 19, 1814, upon instructions from Whitehall, they stripped the sine qua non of the idea of the buffer state so that it simply guaranteed the Indians the rights, privileges, and territories they had possessed in 1811, before the war, in effect protecting them from reprisals. When the Americans continued to procrastinate, Britain framed the new sine qua non into an article and presented it as an ultimatum, threatening to close negotiations if it was not provisionally signed or referred to the government of the United States. On October 14 the American diplomats consented to the article, and it passed into the more comprehensive peace concluded on December 24, 1814. Shorn of the radical suggestions about the barrier state, it was far less than the Indians had anticipated or been promised; it did not restore one acre of land lost in the cessions between 1795 and 1809. The dream of Tecumseh had survived the marshes of the River Thames to die more than a year later on Christmas Eve, in the wintry city of Ghent. Bathurst weakly urged Prevost to persuade the Indians to accept the peace ("we cou'd not be justified, in offering them further assistance, if they should persist in hostilities") with nothing more than the advice that the warriors, in bargaining with the United States, should emphasize their independence by styling themselves "nations" rather than "tribes."[73]

Great was the chagrin of Britain's officers in Canada when they received details of the Treaty of Ghent and realized the impropriety of their earlier remarks to the Indian allies. Prevost's attempt to gild the pill in a speech he prepared to be read at Burlington, Sandwich, Saginaw Bay, Michillimackinac, Green Bay, and Prairie du Chien, was considered by William Claus so inappropriate that he substituted one of his own. The Iroquois and western Indians in Canada were assembled at Burlington to hear it on April 24, 1815. Claus consoled the Indians for those they had lost in the war, and stated that he could now distribute compensation to squaws whose husbands had been killed or wounded. But peace had been made and the hatchet must be buried. The Indians had not been neglected, for the territories they held before the war were secure, and Britain would continue to regard them as friends and issue them presents through Fort Malden, when it was reoccupied. On the next day more than £2,300 was paid out in compensation before the chiefs replied on the twenty-sixth and twenty-seventh. Most of the speakers were Iroquois, who were unaffected by the land issue in the Old Northwest, and they dwelt upon the topical money matters rather than Indian boundaries. Claus must have been thankful for the diversion because he was fully aware that the Treaty of Ghent differed widely from repeated assurances given the Indians that peace would not be concluded until a permanent and satisfactory Indian boundary line had been established.[74]

Farther west McDouall confronted a similar predicament. Writing to Andrew H. Bulger, who commanded at Prairie du Chien, he complained that the peace was "contrary to reiterated & incessant suggestions from this country" and recommended that the Indians be told that the end of the war would enable traders to return to the tribes. Bulger should explain that the King would have continued fighting for the Indians if they had not become disunited. Some of those who had met the United States commissioners at Greenville in July, 1814—nations that had lost the most by the previous decade's land cessions—had even agreed to act against Britain's Indian allies, and the Redcoats could not expose their friends to a civil war. But words such as these were manifestly transparent, and when Captain Bulger heard the official news of the treaty on May 22, 1815, he was so afraid of the Indians' reaction that he transmitted the information to them as quickly as possible and withdrew his garrison on May 24 before the tribesmen could gather in large numbers to demonstate their fury. Retiring to Michillimackinac, Bulger consoled himself with the belief that through the issue of provisions and ammunition he had at least alleviated the material wants of the Indians during his brief occupation of Fort McKay.[75]

The peace and Bulger's withdrawal from the upper Mississippi symbolized the end of the British-Indian alliance far more than did the Battle of Moraviantown. Until that moment the fighting in the West, admittedly no longer more than a desultory guerrilla activity, had continued, and the very day that the British left Prairie du Chien after putting Fort McKay to the torch, a party of Sacs wrote a finale to the border war. Near Fort Howard, on the Cuivre River, they attacked an American detail, and during their retreat repulsed a pursuing force in a sink hole, leaving their adversaries with total losses of fourteen killed, one missing, and three wounded.[76] Without the British, however, further resistance was useless, and for the Indians nothing remained but to reestablish diplomatic relations with the Americans and accept the cease-fire. In accordance with the Treaty of Ghent, both sides surrendered captured territory, and Fort Malden was restored to the British as Michillimackinac, which had been taken in 1812, was returned to the United States.

And so in May, 1815, British troops and the western Indians from Burlington were ordered to Amherstburg, to retrace the route of their historic retreat and to pass, no doubt pensively, the site of the battle on the Thames in which many had participated.[77] A series of conferences followed. Most of the following of Naiwash and Tenskwatawa were repatriated after the council at Spring Wells, Detroit, in August and September, while to the northwest, at Michillimackinac, Portage des Sioux, Saint Louis, and elsewhere, the dissident warriors came to terms with the Big Knives throughout 1815 and 1816.

In treating the War of 1812 in the Northwest historians have understandably emphasized the first seventeen months of the fighting, and little was said about the period between October, 1813 and May, 1815. To them it seemed that the victories of Perry and Harrison wrought a decisive change in the course of the conflict. From the perspective given by the events after Moravian-town, the battle on Lake Erie appears to have been far more significant than the action on the Thames. It was Perry's naval supremacy that had driven Procter and Tecumseh into the interior and given the United States command of the Detroit, which enabled them to suppress the more severe enemy attacks on the American frontier. In 1814, despite Procter's defeat and Tecumseh's death, the Americans had little more. Beyond the captured towns of Detroit, Amherstburg, and Sandwich, British and Indians continued to dispute the ground with their adversaries, while thousands of braves waited in the Northwest to take up the hatchet whenever a British resurgence took place. Britain's military alliance with the Indians survived into 1815. Even the loss of between six and seven hundred soldiers on the Thames was perhaps of relatively little importance at a time when reinforcements were crossing the Atlantic after contributing to the defeat of Bonaparte in Europe.

This is not to say that Harrison's victory achieved nothing. It certainly deprived Britain of the immediate resources to worry the garrisons of the Detroit River and substantially impaired her prospects for future operations involving the Indians. Warriors had to be recruited, managed, and led, but the British retreat of 1813 had done nothing to improve native opinion of the Redcoats. Moreover, it cost the alliance Tecumseh, the man most capable of welding it together. Then, too, the battle restored honor to the arms of the United States in the Northwest and enabled their generals to turn their backs upon the frontier. Some of the first battles of the war had been fought in the West, where the Americans had been goaded by the prospect of an easy conquest; instead they led to the national humiliation of Hull's surrender of Detroit and to the British-Indian invasions of the American borders. Thereafter, the West had been a preoccupation that diverted the resources of the United States from areas in which they could have been more decisive.

Moraviantown finally laid the ghost of the Indian menace and expunged the ignominy of Hull's defeat; it permitted the Americans to look elsewhere. Unfortunately for them, it had come too late. The principal significance of the active British-Indian effort in the West between 1812 and 1813 was that it prevented the United States from concentrating its strength entirely upon Britain's weak defenses at Niagara and the Saint Lawrence during the first two years of the war, when Canada was the most vulnerable. In 1814 and 1815 the rundown of the European conflict began to change the balance of forces in North America, and Canada was in a stronger position.

After the Battle of Moraviantown, Britain found the threat posed by the enemy in the West to be a modest one. If the United States commanded the Detroit, the British reigned uncertainly on the Upper Lakes and the Mississippi, and neither side invested enough to break the stalemate in 1814. As activity in the West diminished, both flung themselves into some of the sharpest fighting of the War of 1812 on the Niagara frontier. Before the end of 1813 the Americans had a naval advantage on Lake Ontario, but the British had reoccupied the west bank of the Niagara and raided American towns across the river. Farther east, two American armies had collaborated inharmoniously in a campaign against Montreal. One force retired while the other was yet in the field, and both were independently mauled by the enemy and entered winter quarters with little to their credit before the end of November. The British survived 1813 despite the defeats of Lake Erie and Moraviantown, battles which shone all the brighter in the United States when set against a record of mismanagement and failure.

The following year saw an intensification of the struggle, both contestants exhausting themselves in gallant but bloody encoun-

ters on the Niagara during the summer. When it was over, the
opportunity of the United States to invade Canada had been lost
because Britain was shipping its Peninsular War veterans to America. Coupled with the might of the Royal Navy, these battalions
forced the Americans onto the defensive, both on the Canadian
border and along an enormous new front of the Atlantic seaboard
and gulf coast. A year after the retreat of Procter and Tecumseh,
Prevost commanded thirteen thousand regulars in Canada and the
launching of the *Lawrence* ship of the line restored his naval
supremacy on Lake Ontario. Ironically, however, the British
proved themselves as inept as their opponents had been on the
offensive, and Prevost's unsuccessful march to Plattsburg earned
the governor in chief a court-martial, which he did not live to
experience. When peace was finally concluded at Ghent, neither
the United States nor Britain were able to bargain from a decisive
advantage and the treaty largely restored the pre-war status quo.

The Moraviantown campaign deserves to be remembered less for
what it achieved than for what it represents. It was the last great
battle to be fought in a theater that had been a vortex of conflict for
more than half a century, a tradition embracing the French and
Indian War, Pontiac's uprising, the Revolution, and the Northwestern Indian War, as well as the War of 1812. No more were
Indian and white armies to march in common cause over the great
Northwest; no longer were the natives of those wide regions to
defend their birthright in a major battle; never again were the
Indians of North America an international force, affecting the
imperialist adventures of the great nations. They were merely a
domestic problem of no great import to national security. In this,
as in other respects, the campaign marks a major watershed in
frontier history, signifying that the most spectacular phase of
Indian-white conflict had come to an end.

Appendix

THE DISPUTE OVER
TECUMSEH'S BURIAL

A curious twentieth-century legacy of the retreat of 1813 was a dispute that for a time raged in Canada about the location of Tecumseh's remains. The literature still displays confusion on the subject, and it seems worthwhile to devote some paragraphs toward improving the discussion. In this quest, the contemporary evidence affords little assistance. An American account avers that Harrison left a burial party on the battlefield of Moraviantown to attend to the dead, and this was probably so because when Abraham Holmes later saw the ground he could only find two Indian bodies, neither of them Tecumseh's. Pierre Navarre, one of the American soldiers, always boasted that he had been delegated to inter the chief, but his story contained the fallacious claim that Tecumseh was buried in his regimentals.[1] This tradition would indicate that the Shawnee's grave was on or close to the scene of the battle, but Peter Trisler wrote on October 8, 1813 that Tecumseh's body was presented to the British, by which he must have signified noncombatants, who took it to Sandwich for burial.

Trisler's statement salvages some credibility for late secondhand material that would otherwise be deemed unimportant. Some of it, to be sure, is inordinate drivel that need detain no one. W. K. Merrifield's fable—that Joe Johnston (who reputedly supplied the information) and two other whites formed half of Tecumseh's personal bodyguard that protected the wounded chief as they retired from the battle and secretly buried him—is of this order.[2] But the strong local tradition that Tecumseh was interred by British sympathizers demands to be reevaluated in the light of Trisler's comment. It is alleged that the Sherman family helped bury the dead in a mass grave on October 6. David Sherman, then a boy, is supposed to have

215

told his son that Tecumseh was buried between two parts of a fallen walnut tree, situated on some high ground behind the swamp and east of the battlefield. On a nearby beechtree Indian mourners carved appropriate hieroglyphics, one of them the totem of a turtle.[3]

Joe Johnston is also represented to have known where Tecumseh lay buried and to have shown Christopher Arnold's son the spot, between two beech trees ornamented with Indian symbols.[4] Johnston's wife was said to have told Joseph Laird that her husband was beside Tecumseh during the battle. When the chief was wounded in the first minute of the action, Johnston propped him against a tree, from which he continued to direct the fight until receiving a fatal bullet above the heart. The body was secreted beneath the leaves of a fallen giant whitewood, but recovered in the night, amid fog and rain, by Johnston and two Shawnees, who bore it through the black forest in a blanket and buried it in a shallow grave beside a stream where a fallen oak lay lodged between a hickory and a basswood tree. When some obstructions damming the stream above were removed, the rushing water assisted the rain to obliterate telltale marks so that the sepulcher would remain a secret. This particular story was offered in 1913 by Albert Greenwood, who claimed to have heard it from Laird sixty-two years before. Furthermore, Greenwood said that he had spoken to the owner of the land on which he judged Tecumseh must have been buried, and that the settler had informed him that in 1851 he had discovered a human skeleton, upon a thigh bone of which "a ridge had grown . . . ." Greenwood knew in 1913 that such a disfigurement identified Tecumseh, but one wonders if a settler in the middle of the last century would have remembered or even noticed such a detail.[5]

The Johnston tradition, as given by Greenwood, has little to commend it, but it is possible that either Johnston or the Shermans had a hand in Tecumseh's burial. Another, though different case, has been made for George Ironside, who was related to Tecumseh by marriage and who lived at Amherstburg until his death in 1830. According to Dr. C. C. Graham, Ironside once related that Tecumseh had been shot in the heart at Moraviantown and collapsed across a fallen tree. He was carried away unmutilated by his followers for a secret burial, but afterwards, fearing that the bones would be stolen by some unscrupulous showman, Ironside exhumed them for reinterment beneath the floor of his own house. It was the opinion of Ironside's grandson, however, that his father believed Tecumseh to have been buried by his friends.[6]

The possibility exists that some of these traditions had their origin in a grave that was once pointed out in the locality as that of Tecumseh. James

B. Gardner found it within twenty years of the chief's death at the northeastern termination of a willow marsh on the north line of the battlefield, close to a large fallen black oak. About it flourished wild rose and marsh willow, but the modest hillock itself was so free of undergrowth, excepting a young gooseberry bush, two or three white ash shrubs, and the occasional weed, that it was rumored to be regularly attended by the neighboring Indians. A hewn post, three inches square by five feet in length and bearing faint traces of Indian characters drawn with red paint, had fallen from its place and lay beside the grave.[7] Gardner's story was picked up by other writers, but no other authentic descriptions of the grave have been found and what became of it is a mystery.

The subject seems to have become a controversy about 1876 when some remains alleged to be those of Tecumseh were examined by a Professor Wilson and others and declared to be a mixture of several human skeletons and animal bones. Wilson saw no reason to believe that any of them had belonged to the Shawnee chief. At that time probably no one knew where Tecumseh lay buried, if anywhere. In the summer of 1876 the Ojibwa Grand council, representing seventeen Ontario bands, pressed the Canadian government to place Tecumseh's body next to that of General Brock, but since the Indians were unable to say where the Shawnee might be found nothing came of the proposal.[8]

Of course, many, like Greenwood, affected to know more. Stories of secrets passed down from one generation to another intermittently tantalized the public when newspapers were short of copy. In the later nineteenth century it was an old Indian, Jacob Pheasant, who related how the Shawnees retrieved Tecumseh's corpse for a clandestine funeral. A boy of the Muncey Reservation, Jacob Logan, who listened to Pheasant about 1860, recalled many years later that Pheasant said he was at the Battle of Moraviantown and told how Tecumseh had been disturbed by a premonition of death. He was mortally wounded in the fray and carried by Pheasant, Bull Horn, and Yellow Fish to the north side of the Long Wood Road, where he died and was buried, with a musket, bayonet, and tomahawk, beneath the upturned roots of a tree merely a few yards from the spot on which the battle memorial was later erected.[9] In 1913 an aged charlatan on the Grand River Reservation posed as a nephew of Tecumseh, informing a gullible biographer of Joseph Brant that he held the secret of the Shawnee's last resting place. Thirteen years later one Cornelius Shawano of the Kettle Point Reservation also claimed descent from Tecumseh's band and spread the tale that two nephews had taken the great chief's body from the battlefield, substituting another who resembled him at the place where he had fallen, and buried him secretly. Yet another report said that Tecumseh's skull had been preserved at McGill University, Montreal, before its convenient destruction by fire on April 16, 1907. Thus the legend of Tecumseh marched on, the fictions themselves reworked and distorted. [10]

None of these items aroused the popular enthusiasm that followed the sensational discovery of a skeleton on Saint Anne's Island, in the Saint Clair River at the head of Lake Saint Clair, on June 2, 1910. Again, the story was rooted in oral tradition, this time featuring Chief Sha-wah-wan-noo, who, it will be remembered, had fought at Moraviantown and had been erroneously named by Benson J. Lossing as the Indian second-in-command in that action. He was probably a fairly young warrior of no great status in 1813, and from 1846 until his death in 1870 lived in retirement on Walpole Island, next to Saint Anne's Island. [11] Somehow it eventually got around that Sha-wah-wan-noo (or John Naudee, as he was also called) had acquired the bones of Tecumseh. In 1910 a mixed-blood Indian, Matthew Fisher, said that his uncle, John Fisher, had known Sha-wah-wan-noo and maintained that during the 1860s when the old Moraviantown battlefield was being cleared, the chief had exhumed Tecumseh's remains to reinter them on Saint Anne's Island. He used to fly a flag over the grave. This story was confirmed by Sha-wah-wan-noo's grandson, Edward Jackson, who had been only nineteen at the time of his grandfather's death. Jackson reported that Sha-wah-wan-noo had hidden Tecumseh's body during the Battle of the Thames and later buried it near Tilbury. Finally he moved it to Saint Anne's Island. In 1931, Johnston Peters, a young man of twenty-five in 1870, supported the statements of Fisher and Jackson, and there were other witnesses. A woman called Hubble remembered that as a girl picking plums on Saint Anne's Island, she had seen Sha-wah-wan-noo performing rituals over what he said was Tecumseh's grave, and a boatman, William Leonhardt, claimed to have also seen the old chief at such work. [12]

The physician to the Indians on Walpole Island, Dr. George Mitchell, evidently encountered some of these rumors and assembled a party of citizens from nearby Wallaceburg to investigate the story. Guided by Fisher and Jackson, they located Sha-wah-wan-noo's grave, near Mitchell's Bay, Saint Anne's Island, and seven feet east of it the supposed sepulcher of Tecumseh. The fragments of a wooden box, some three-foot-square, were unearthed, inside of which was a skeleton, the skull in two pieces, and a black stovepipe. After photographs had been taken, the bones were carried to Wallaceburg in the folds of a flag and placed in the doctor's custody. Three days later, however, three Indians from Walpole Island, Chief Joseph White, Bill Sands, and Johnston Peters, arrived in the town and repossessed the skeleton; according to White, it was reburied. Mitchell had been allowed little opportunity to examine the bones, but believed that they belonged to a male about five feet ten inches in height. He had neither noticed nor sought the leg fracture that Tecumseh was thought to have sustained as a youth.

Perhaps the whole doubtful matter would have been forgotten had not Constable Thomas Corless of the Sarnia Royal Canadian Mounted Police decided in January, 1931, to inquire into a report that the bones of Tecumseh had reappeared in the attic of Sarah White, widow of Joseph White, who had died in 1929. These proved to be animal bones, but Silas Shobway, White's stepson, professed to know where the genuine skeleton was hidden. He explained that his stepfather had protected and regularly cleaned Tecumseh's bones, and that they had subsequently passed into Shobway's custody and been placed in various hideouts. On January 17, Corless and Shobway recovered a rotting burlap sack from beneath snow and leaves on Walpole Island and deposited the contents—a complete human skeleton minus a kneecap, some rib bones, and part of the skull—with the Walpole Island Soldiers' Club pending further inquiries.

There was small doubt that the skeleton was the same originally produced from Saint Anne's Island, but this time the bones were thoroughly examined on January 21 by Dr. W. B. Rutherford in the presence of a member of Parliament, Ross Gray, the biographer of Tecumseh, Norman St. Clair Gurd, and Constable Corless. Although the height was right for Tecumseh, the leg bones had not been fractured. Nevertheless an extraordinary Grand Council of the Indians of Ontario was convened on Walpole Island on February 25, attended by representatives from eight reservations, and evidence was given by Gurd, Corless, and others as a preliminary to a heated exchange in which the Moravians of the Thames insisted that Tecumseh was buried near the old battlefield and others as vociferously championed the recent discovery. Eventually the meeting declared the Walpole Island skeleton to be the remains of the celebrated Shawnee chief by 11 votes to 10 and resolved that they be interred on the island and that the Historic Sites and Monuments Commission be requested to consider whether a national memorial might be erected over the grave.[13]

Unconvinced, the Canadian government declined to act. For one thing, the Moravian Indians repudiated the findings of the Grand Council and demanded that any monument be established on the site of the

Battle of Moraviantown. For another, the historian E. A. Cruikshank, though enthusiastic about a Tecumseh monument, stressed the obvious weaknesses in the second- and third-hand testimony upon which the Walpole Island case had been based. Instead, the Historic Sites and Monuments Board of Canada, encouraged by Cruikshank, determined to proceed with their own national memorial to Tecumseh, a project that was never completed.[14] In the absence of government support, the Walpole Island Indians and the Soldiers' Service Club raised funds privately and a start was made to the building of a memorial cairn on the island on August 11, 1934. It took seven years to complete and even then lacked the statue originally intended to complement it. An official ceremony on August 23, 1941, organized by members of the Ojibwa and Potawatomi tribes, closed the saga of the Walpole Island skeleton with an impressive send-off. Hundreds of spectators filed past the bones as they lay in the local Anglican church, and the speakers for the occasion included a member of Parliament, a mayor, and the secretary of the Department of Indian Affairs. The remains were placed in the cairn and received the rites of the church, and a colorful Indian pageant depicted events in the life of the great Shawnee chief.[15]

Unfortunately, these bones, so reverently laid to rest, were not those of Tecumseh. The most satisfactory evidence, from competent and independent witnesses, establishes that Tecumseh suffered a severe thigh injury as a young man. According to Anthony Shane, he fell from his horse during a buffalo hunt and broke both thighs. Tecumseh was left with a permanent and prominent disfigurement that earned him a nickname among the Indians. Stephen Ruddell, a white man raised by the Shawnees, wrote that Tecumseh broke a thigh in a fall from his horse one autumn, and the following spring could only keep up with his party by using crutches. Another white captive of the Shawnees was Christopher Miller, who met Wickliffe in 1812. "Miller knew Tecumsie well," Wickliffe recollected, "and described him to me. He said that Tecumsie had his leg broken by a fall from his horse, that he had tried once to kill himself because he said 'he could not be a warrior or a hunter,' that one of his legs was shortened by the wound . . . ." There can be no doubt, from these records, that the Walpole Island skeleton, neither of the thigh bones of which had been broken, was not Tecumseh.[16]

That being so, the location of the chief's grave remains an enigma, one which, barring the unlikely discovery of further documentation, will probably never be solved. Almost two centuries must surely have now drawn the veil of oblivion over the resting place of the Indian leader.

ABBREVIATIONS

Adm.	Admiralty Papers, Public Record Office, Kew, England.
CO	Colonial Office Papers, Public Record Office, Kew, England.
Cochran Narrative	Narrative of James Cochran, Welch Regiment Museum, Cardiff Castle, Cardiff, Wales.
Cochran Notes	James Cochran's marginal notes to his copy of Richardson's *War of 1812* (1842), cited by the page of the text to which the note refers. Welch Regiment Museum, Cardiff.
Draper Mss.	Papers of Lyman C. Draper, State Historical Society of Wisconsin, Madison, Wisconsin (microfilm).
LOC	Department of Manuscripts, Library of Congress, Washington, D.C.
MPHC	*Michigan Pioneer and Historical Society Historical Collections*, 40 vols. (Lansing: George, Thorp, Godfrey, Smith and others, 1877–1929).
PAC	Public Archives of Canada, Ottawa. Indian Affairs records are cited by Record Group, volume and page number, for example, PAC RG 10, 3:1558–59. Military records are cited by Record Group, volume (C series) and

	page number, for example, PAC RG 8, C257:300–01
PCM	Court-martial of Henry Procter, War Office Papers, Public Record Office, Kew, England, WO 71/243.
Procter Papers	Papers of Henry Procter, War of 1812 Papers of the Department of State, 1789–1815, Intercepted Correspondence, National Archives, Washington, D.C.
Sec. of War, LR, Reg.	Letters Received by the Secretary of War, Registered Series, National Archives, Washington, D.C.
Sec. of War, LR, Unreg.	Letters Received by the Secretary of War, Unregistered Series, National Archives, Washington, D.C.
WO	War Office Papers, Public Record Office, Kew, England.

NOTES

1
Introduction

1. Hall to Harvey, Oct. 5, 1813, PAC RG 8, C680: 205–06a.
2. Reginald Horsman, "The Role of the Indian in the War," in Philip P. Mason,ed., *After Tippecanoe*, p. 73.
3. John Richardson, *Tecumseh; or, the Warrior of the West: a Poem in Four Cantos, with Notes*, p. *v*.
4. Correspondence in PAC RG10, vol. 1993, file 6828.
5. *Toronto Globe*, Oct. 2, 17, 1913; Katherine B. Coutts, "The Tecumseh Memorial Boulder," *Kent Historical Society* 6 (1924):85–87.
6. Anderson Chenault Quisenberry, *Kentucky in the War of 1812*, p. 96
7. Charles O.Z. Ermatinger, "The Retreat of Proctor and Tecumseh," *Ontario Historical Society Papers and Records* 18 (1919): 11–21; Victor Lauriston, "The Case for General Proctor," in Morris Zaslow and Wesley B. Turner, eds., *The Defended Border: Upper Canada and the War of 1812*, pp. 121–29.
8. William S. Hatch, *A Chapter of the History of the War of 1812 in the Northwest*, pp. 116–17.
9. Procter to Major General Francis de Rottenburg, Oct. 16, 1813, PAC RG 8, C680:259–60.
10. Chambers to Lieutenant Colonel Christopher Myers, Jan. 5, 1814, WO 71/243.
11. John Richardson, "A Canadian Campaign, by a British Officer," *The New Monthly Magazine and Literary Journal* 19 (1827):253.
12. Cochran notes, p. 127; Cochran Narrative, p. 64.

2

A Prologue: August and September, 1813

1. Prevost to Lord Liverpool, May 18, 1812, WO 1/96. Contemporary material on Amherstburg and Fort Malden can be found in Ernest J. Lajeunesse, ed., *The Windsor Border Region*, pp. *cxvii–cxxix*, 189–226; Gother Mann to Lord Dorchester, Dec. 6, 1788, *MPHC* 12 (1888):30–37; Diary of Captain James Sympson, quoted in Anderson Chenault Quisenberry, *Kentucky in the War of 1812*, pp. 102–03; reminiscences of Elias Darnell, quoted in Francis Cleary, "History of Fort Malden or Amherstburg," *Essex Historical Society Papers and Addresses* 2 (1915):44; Samuel R. Brown, *An Authentic History of the Second War for Independence*, 1:120; Shelby to his wife, Oct. 1, 1813, Shelby Papers, vol. 4, LOC; John Richardson, *The Canadian Brothers; or, The Prophecy Fulfilled*, 1:2–8. Two maps of the area are preserved in the William Henry Harrison papers, LOC, and a plan of 1808 in the National Map Collection of the PAC, H3/440/Amh. 1808.

2. Sandwich was situated on a small plain near the river and contained a windmill, houses, a Huron church, and parks in its rear. *Montreal Gazette*, Jan. 4, 1814.

3. Earl Bathurst to Prevost, Dec. 9, 1812, CO 42/147:237–41.

4. Return of the Right Division, Sept. 22, 1813, PCM, pp. 427–29.

5. Edward Baynes to Procter, Aug. 12, 1813, PCM, p. 401; testimony of William Evans, PCM, pp. 59, 65; Matthew Charles Dixon, PCM, p. 96.

6. Evans, PCM, pp. 59–60; Procter to Noah Freer, Sept. 3, 1813, PAC RG 8, C680:7–10.

7. *Quebec Gazette*, July 25, 1805; War Office, *A List of all the Officers of the Army and Royal Marines*, pp. 220–21; L. Homfray Irving, *Officers of the British Forces in Canada During the War of 1812–15*, p. 11; D.A.N. Lomax, *A History of the Services of the 41st (Welch) Regiment*, p. 369; Interview with Captain William Caldwell by Lyman C. Draper (1863), Draper Mss., 17S229; Procter file, WO 42/38/295. Procter's three daughters were Susannah Ann (born Leominster, November, 1794), Frances Sarah (born July 15, 1803), and Augusta Margaret Firth (born November 19, 1808).

8. *Quebec Gazette*, Aug. 8, 1811.

9. Cochran Narrative, pp. 55–56.

10. Felix Troughton, PCM, p. 106.

11. Procter, PCM, p. 370.

12. Jones, PCM, p. 178.

13. Colonel William Caldwell, PCM, p. 176; Captain John Hall, PCM, p. 239; Richard Mentor Johnson to William Henry Harrison, Sept. 20, 1813, Harrison Papers, LOC.

14. Edward Baynes, General Orders, July 26, 1813, PAC RG 10, 28:16484–85.

15. Shawnee prophet to Colonel William Caldwell, Nov. 20, 1814, PAC RG 10, 29:17381–82; Askin to John Askin, June 2, 1813, "Askin Papers," MPHC 32 (1903):502–05.

16. Procter to Roger Sheaffe, Nov. 20, 1812, Procter Papers. The Wyandots were considered by the Indians to be the leading tribe, keepers of the great calumet which kindled the intertribal council fire. William Henry Harrison to John Armstrong, Mar. 22, 1814, Logan Esarey, ed., *Messages and Letters of William Henry Harrison*, 2:636–41.

17. Procter, PCM, p. 411.

18. This chief appears as Ustaiechta, or Roundhead, in a signature on a deed of sale to land south of the Detroit River in September, 1800. Ernest J. Lajeunesse, ed., *The Windsor Border Region*, pp. 205–09. Particulars of the Roundhead's career may be found in Frederick W. Hodge, ed., *Handbook of American Indians*, 2:397, and the unreliable but interesting Peter D. Clarke, *Origin and Traditional History of the Wyandotts*.

19. George C. Chalou, "The Red Pawns Go to War: British-American Indian Relations, 1810–15." Ph.D. diss., Indiana University, 1971, and R. David Edmunds, *The Potawatomis: Keepers of the Fire*, discuss Main Poc.

20. Colonel William Caldwell to William Claus, June 15, 1815, PAC RG 10, 30:18051–52; memoranda of Lieutenant Colonel William James, PAC RG 10, 12:10644–61; Lewis Cass, "Indians of North America," *North American Review* 22 (1826):99.

21. John Marshall, *Royal Navy Biography*, vol. 3, pt. 1, pp. 186–95; statements of the British squadron, 1813, CO 42/151:100, CO 42/152:55.

22. Procter to Prevost, Sept. 13, 21, 1813, CO 42/151:157–58, 217–18; Warburton, PCM, p. 8; John Richardson, "A Canadian Campaign, by a British Officer," 19:251.

23. British-American relations before the war are studied in A.L.

Burt, *The United States, Great Britain and British North America 1783–1815*, and Bradford Perkins, *Prologue to War: England and the United States, 1805–1812*. A particularly clear resume of the debate about the origins of the war can be found in Harry L. Coles, *The War of 1812*, pp. 1–37.

24. The most recent scholarly surveys of the war are Reginald Horsman, *The War of 1812*; John K. Mahon, *The War of 1812*; and J.C.A. Stagg, *Mr. Madison's War: Politics, Diplomacy, and Warfare in the Early American Republic, 1783–1830*.

25. Dwight L. Smith, "Indian Land Cessions in the Old Northwest, 1795–1809." Ph.D. diss., Indiana University, 1949, reviews these developments between the treaties of Greenville (1795) and Fort Wayne (1809).

26. Few histories show insight into the changes occurring in Indian societies during this period. Among the exceptions are A.F.C. Wallace, *The Death and Rebirth of the Seneca*; Raymond E. Hauser, "An Ethnohistory of the Illinois Indian Tribe, 1673–1832." Ph.D. diss., Northern Illinois University, 1973; and H. Hickerson, *The Chippewa and their Neighbours*.

27. The latest studies of this movement are Herbert C.W. Goltz, "Tecumseh, the Prophet and the Rise of the Northwestern Indian Confederacy." Ph.D. diss., University of Western Ontario, 1973; R. David Edmunds, *The Shawnee Prophet*; and R. David Edmunds, *Tecumseh and the Quest for Indian Leadership*.

28. The Miamis were the best example of Indians driven from neutrality by the American campaigns. Because Indians were bound by their law to avenge injury against their relatives or fellow clan or totem members, American attacks almost inevitably provoked retaliation. See Bert Anson, *The Miami Indians*, ch. 5.

29. Useful accounts of the naval rivalry on Lake Erie are Ernest A. Cruikshank, "The Contest for the Command of Lake Erie in 1812–13," and C.P. Stacey, "Another Look at the Battle of Lake Erie," both reprinted in Morris Zaslow and Wesley B. Turner, eds., *The Defended Border: Upper Canada and the War of 1812*, pp.84–113.

30. Perry to Duncan McArthur, Aug. 31, 1813, McArthur Papers, vol. 3, no. 565, LOC.

31. Prevost to Bathurst, Oct. 17, 26, Nov. 5, 1812, CO 42/147:215–19, Co 42/148:3, 7–15.

32. Warren to John W. Croker, May 9, 1813, Adm. 1/503:269–70.

33. Barclay's narrative for his court-martial, William Wood, ed., *Select British Documents of the Canadian War of 1812*, 2:298–300.

34. Procter to Prevost, Aug. 18, 1813, Wood, *British Documents*, 2:260–61; Procter to R. McDouall, June 16, 1813, ibid., 2:243–45; Barclay to John Vincent, June 17, 1813, ibid., 2:245–47.

35. Prevost to Warren, June 24, 1813, Adm. 1/504:142–43.

36. Lewis Cass to John Armstrong, Dec. 4, 1813, Sec. of War, LR, Reg.

37. Procter to McDouall, June 16, 1813, Wood, *British Documents*, 2:243–45.

38. Robert Gilmore, the deputy assistant commissary, complained of the gross wastage among the Indians. Sheep and hogs were unnecessarily butchered by them, and cattle were sometimes killed merely for a horn and the tail. Gilmore to Edward Couche, Aug. 6, 1813, *The Weekly Register*, Jan. 15, 1814,5:328–29; Procter to Freer, Sept. 6, 1813, Wood, *British Documents*, 2:269–70; Richardson, "Canadian Campaign," 19:250.

39. Prevost to Procter, July 11, 1813, Wood, *British Documents*, 2:251–53; Procter to Baynes, Aug. 19, 1813, ibid., 2:261–63; Freer to Procter, Sept. 2, 1813, Procter Papers; Prevost to Procter, Oct. 6, 1813, PCM, pp. 397–98; R.H. Sheaffe, Aug. 26, 1813, PAC RG 8, C257:132–35; William Claus to Edward M'Mahon, Oct. 9, 1813, PAC RG 10, 3:1289. The annual shipment of English presents included ornaments such as earbobs, armbands, bells, beads, brooches, and medals; items of clothing, including sheets and blankets, hats, buttons, buckles, bunting, handkerchiefs, feathers, lace, ribbons, and shoes; weapons and implements such as rifles, muskets, pistols, powder and ball, flints, swords, spears, tomahawks, knives, saddles and bridles, awls and needles, thread and twine, scissors, basins, pans, kettles, pipes and tobacco, mirrors and combs, razors, hoes, hooks, iron and steel, nails, locks and red leather trunks; and miscellaneous trifles such as oil, vermilion, and mustard seed. List of presents, 1813, CO 43/23:123–29.

40. Procter to Prevost, July 13, 1813, Wood, *British Documents*, 2:256–57; Procter to Baynes, Aug. 19, 1813, ibid., 2:261–63; Procter to McDouall, June 16, 1813, ibid., 2:243–45; Captain Richard Bullock to Freer, Sept. 28, 1813, PAC RG 8, C257:156–58; Orders for R. Dickson, Aug. 31, 1813, PAC RG 8, C257:144–45; Elliott to William

Claus, Aug. 29, 1813, PAC RG 10, 28:16527–29; Billy Caldwell, PCM, p. 161.

41. Procter to Prevost, July 11, 1813, Wood, *British Documents*, 2:253–54; Barclay to Prevost, July 16, 1813; ibid., 2:257–59.

42. Barclay to Prevost, July 16, 1813, ibid., 2:257–59.

43. Procter to Prevost, Aug. 26, 29, 1813, ibid., 2:264–67.

44. Procter to Baynes, Aug. 19, 1813, ibid., 2:261–63.

45. Prevost to Bathurst, July 20, 1813, CO 42/151:78–79.

46. Prevost to Procter, June 20, July 11, 12, 1813, Wood, *British Documents*, 2:247–48, 251–53, 255–56; letter to Procter, Aug. 26, 1813, PAC RG 8, C679:500–01; Prevost to Procter, Aug. 22, 1813, PAC RG 8, C679:476–79; Prevost to the Duke of York, June 23, 1813, WO 1/96.

47. Warren to Croker, Aug. 21, Sept. 24, Oct. 14, 1813, Adm. 1/504:140–41, 175–76, 199–200; Prevost to Warren, Sept. 26, Oct. 11, Nov. 13, 1813, Adm. 1/504:201–02, 357–58, 367–68.

48. Bathurst to Prevost, Aug. 14, 1813, CO 43/23:119; Prevost to Bathurst, July 20, Aug. 25, Nov. 4, 1813, CO 42/151:78–79, 138–44, CO 42/152:5–6; Prevost to Procter, Sept. 6, 1813, Procter Papers; de Rottenburg to Procter, Aug. 29, Sept. 10, 1813, Procter Papers.

49. Prevost to Procter, July 23, 1813, Procter Papers; de Rottenburg to Procter, Aug. 6, 16, 29, 1813, Procter papers; Barclay to Yeo, Sept. 6, 1813, Wood, *British Documents*, 2:292–93, Barclay Narrative, ibid., 2:303.

50. Procter to Prevost, Aug. 26, 29, 1813, Wood, *British Documents*, 2:264–67; Barclay narrative, ibid., 2:302; Elliott to Claus, Aug. 29, 1813, PAC RG 10, 28:16527–29.

51. Barclay to Yeo, Sept. 12, 1813, Wood, *British Documents*, 2:274–77; Gilmore to Procter, Aug. 14, 1813, *The Weekly Register*, Jan. 15, 1814, 5:327.

52. Barclay Narrative, Wood, *British Documents*, 2:304; de Rottenburg to Procter, Aug. 6, 16, 1813, Procter papers; Harvey to Procter, Aug. 28, 1813, Procter Papers; de Rottenburg to Baynes, Sept. 10, 1813, PAC RG 8, C680:58–61.

53. John Johnston to John Armstrong, Aug. 3, 1813, Esarey, *William Henry Harrison*, 2:509; Harrison to Armstrong, Aug. 22, 1813, ibid., 2:525–26.

54. Peter Latouche Chambers had been made an ensign in the Forty-

first in 1803 and became a captain within a few years. He was eventually commissioned a lieutenant colonel, served in France, Burma, and India, and died at Madras on August 29, 1827. Lomax, *Services of the 41st*, p. 372.

55. Elliott, minutes of council, Aug. 23, 1813, PAC RG 8, C257:139–42.

56. Caldwell, PCM, p. 158.

57. Lewis Cass, "Policy and Practise of the United States and Great Britain in Their Treatment of Indians," *North American Review* 24 (1827):426. Cass's informants were Isaac and William Walker and their mother, and an agent with the Wyandots who had been present when Tarhe, the chief who sent the emissaries, reported on the mission to Harrison.

58. Chambers to Freer, Aug. 26, 1813, PAC RG 8, C679:445–46. Roundhead died of natural causes shortly after the council, certainly before mid-September. Procter acknowledged that: "The Indian cause and ours experienced a serious loss in the death of Roundhead." Procter to de Rottenburg, Oct. 23, 1813, Wood, *British Documents*, 2:323–27; R.M. Johnson to Harrison, Sept. 20, 1813, Harrison Papers, LOC; *The Lucubrations of Humphrey Ravelin*, p. 335.

59. Harrison to Armstrong, Sept. 8, 1813, Mar. 22, 1814, Esarey, *William Henry Harrison*, 2:537–39, 636–41; Cass, "Policy and Practise," pp. 425–28. The messengers of Tecumseh and Elliott were also circulating in the Indian country. In August a Mohawk report about the conduct of the Senecas, who had supplied men for Harrison, was received by British Chiefs and forwarded to the southern Indians, presumably the Creeks, with some of whom Tecumseh was in alliance. The next month a few Wyandots dispatched by Elliott to speak to the Crane's people at Sandusky returned to report that the Crane had moved to the Mad River on the Ohio. The chief urged all Indians to join him there, safe from the forthcoming campaign, and his message to that effect was delivered to the British Indians on September 7 in Elliott's presence. Elliott to Claus, Aug. 29, 1813, PAC RG 10, 28:16527–29; Elliott to Procter, Sept. 8, 1813, *The Weekly Register*, Jan. 15, 1814, 5:327.

60. Chambers to Freer, Aug. 26, 1813, PAC RG 8, C679:445–46; Interview with Anthony Shane by Benjamin Drake (1821), Draper Mss., 12YY71–72.

61. Moses Dawson, *Historical Narrative of the Civil and Military Services*

of Major-General William Henry Harrison, p. 437; see also *The Weekly Register*, Sept. 18, 1813, 5:43.

62. Procter to Prevost, Aug. 26, 1813, Wood, *British Documents*, 2:264–65.

63. Elliott to Claus, Aug. 29, 1813, PAC RG 10, 28:16527–29; John Johnston, letter apparently dated Sept. 12, 1813, *The Weekly Register*, Oct. 9, 1813, 5:97; Cochran Notes, pp. 60, 90.

64. Barclay to Yeo, Sept. 12, 1813, Wood, *British Documents*, 2:274–77; Procter to de Rottenburg, Sept. 12, 1813, ibid., 2:272–73; Barclay court-martial, ibid., 2:289–319; casualty list, ibid., 2:279–81.

65. *The Weekly Register*, Sept. 25, 1813, 5:55.

3
The Painful Decision: September, 1813

1. John Armstrong, *Notices of the War of 1812*, 1:183–84.

2. Andrew Willima Cochran, PCM, pp. 296–98.

3. Armstrong to Harrison, Oct. 20, 1813, Logan Esarey, ed., *Messages and Letters of William Henry Harrison*, 2:588; Journal of Lewis Bond, LOC, p. 76; Moses Dawson, *Historical Narrative of the Civil and Military Services of Major-General William Henry Harrison*, pp. 421–24.

4. Gilmore to Edward Couche, Aug. 6, 1813, *The Weekly Register*, Jan. 15, 1814, 5:328–29; Gilmore to Couche, Sept. 5, 1813, CO 42/151:152; Richard Pattinson, PCM, p. 166.

5. Isaac Shelby to his wife, Oct. 28, 1813, Shelby Papers, vol. 4, LOC; Cass to Armstrong, Oct. 28, Nov. 28, 1813, Sec. of War, LR, Reg.

6. Gilmore to Procter, Aug. 14, 1813, *The Weekly Register*, Jan. 15, 1814, 5:327; Pattinson, PCM, p. 166; Gilmore, PCM, pp. 181–85; Talbot, PCM, pp. 186–87, 189; A.W. Cochran, PCM, p. 328; R. Gourlay, *Statistical Account of Upper Canada*, pp. 128–43; Fred Coyne Hamil, *The Valley of the Lower Thames, 1640 to 1850*, pp. 57, 83. Thomas Talbot had founded the haven of Port Talbot in 1803.

7. Procter, declaration of martial law, Sept. 13, 1813, Sec. of War, LR, Reg.

8. *Montreal Gazette*, Oct. 5, 1813, Others whose consideration of Procter's situation lacked depth were less generous. "Proctor is certainly a

grand coward . . ." wrote an American with Harrison's army. Letter to the *Chillicothe* (Ohio) *Fredonian*, Oct. 11, 1813, *The Weekly Register*, Nov. 6, 1813, 5:174.

9. Cochran, PCM, pp. 305–06, 312.

10. These episodes have recently been reexamined by J. Leitch Wright, *Britain and the American Frontier, 1783–1815*, pp. 37–39, 96.

11. Caldwell, PCM, pp. 175–76.

12. Procter to Prevost, Sept. 13, 1813, CO 42/151:157–58.

13. The history of the two Indians in the Battle of Lake Erie is obscure. Contemporary press gossip erroneously identified them as the Wyandot chiefs Walk-in-the-Water and Splitlog. *The War . . .*, no. 68, Oct. 5, 1813, 2:67. In fact the adventurers were both young warriors, Ensign Cochran believed Delawares. They apparently served aboard the *Detroit* without distinction. *The Weekly Register*, Oct. 30, 1813, 5:149, describes how they were placed in the fighting tops, but skulked below during the battle. Held as prisoners of war in Ohio, they either escaped or were turned over to the Indians friendly with the United States. Johnson to Harrison, Sept. 20, 1813, Harrison papers, LOC; John Richardson, "A Canadian Campaign, by a British Officer," 19:547–48; Cochran Narrative, 54–55; Chamblee and Billy Caldwell to Harrison's friends, Mar. 23, 1840, reprinted form the *Chicago Daily American* of June 9, 1840, in John Wentworth, *Early Chicago: Fort Dearborn. An Address*, p. 61; Alfred Brunson, *A Western Pioneer, or, Incidents in the Life and Times of Rev. Alfred Brunson*, 1:131.

14. Johnson to Harrison, Sept. 20, 1813, Harrison papers, LOC; Francis Baby, PCM, p. 149; Captain W. Caldwell, PCM, p. 156; Billy Caldwell, PCM, p. 159; Colonel Caldwell, PCM, pp. 176–77; William Jones, PCM, p. 178.

15. Barclay to Prevost, July 16, 1813, William Wood, ed., *Select British Documents of the Canadian War of 1812*, 2:257–59; Harvey to Procter, Sept. 6, 1813, Procter Papers; Procter, PCM, pp. 353, 358; Harrison to Armstrong, Sept. 15, 1813, Esarey, *William Henry Harrison*, 2:540–41; Armstrong to Harrison, Sept. 22, 1813, ibid., 2:544–45.

16. Procter, PCM, p. 352.

17. Procter to Prevost, Sept. 21, 1813, CO 42/151:217–18.

18. Procter to de Rottenburg, Sept. 12, 1813, Wood, *British Documents*, 2:272–73.

19. Dixon, PCM, p. 96; Troughton, PCM, pp. 106, 112; Captain

John Hall, PCM, p. 236. Dixon lived to become a major general in 1854 and died in Southampton in 1860. Troughton, less fortunate, died on his way to England on June 26, 1815.

20. Procter to Prevost, Sept. 13, 1813, CO 42/151:157–58.

21. Procter to Prevost, Sept. 21, 1813, CO 42/151:217–18.

22. Procter to de Rottenburg, Oct. 23, 1813, Wood, *British Documents*, 2:323–27.

23. Harvey to Procter, Sept. 17, 1813, PAC RG 8, C680:75–77.

24. Harvey to Procter, Sept. 26, 1813, Sec. of War, LR, Reg.

25. De Rottenburg to Prevost, Sept. 30, 1813, PAC RG 8, C680:123–25.

26. Baynes to Procter, Sept. 18, 1813, Esarey, *William Henry Harrison*, 2:582–84.

27. Prevost to Procter, Sept. 23, 1813, Wood, *British Documents*, 2:284–85; Prevost to Warren, Sept. 26, 1813, Adm. 1/504:201–02.

28. Prevost to Bathurst, Sept. 22, 1813, CO 42/151:154–56.

29. Prevost to Procter, Oct. 6, 1813, PAC RG 8, C680:149–50.

30. Prevost to Bathurst, Oct. 8, 1813, CO 42/151:163–72.

31. Warburton, PCM, p. 8; Dixon, PCM, p. 96; Troughton, PCM, pp. 106, 112; Le Breton, PCM, p. 167; Hall, PCM, p. 236.

32. Hall, PCM, p. 236.

33. Dixon, PCM, p. 96; Le Breton, PCM, p. 168.

34. Warburton, PCM, p. 8.

35. R.M. Johnson to Harrison, Sept. 20, 1813, Harrison papers, LOC.

36. Elliott to William Claus, Oct. 24, 1813, PAC MG 19/fl/10:111–13.

37. Warburton, PCM, pp. 8–9. He is supported by Ensign Cochran, who gives the dates September 18 and September 20. Cochran Narrative, p. 56. James Cochran had been sent from Europe as part of the Second Battalion of the Forty-first under Evans and joined Procter's division in Sandusky Bay on August 3, 1813. Cochran Notes, p. 107. He subsequently became a lieutenant (1815) and a brevet major (1841) and retired in 1845.

38. Procter, PCM, p. 19; Jones, PCM, pp. 180–81; Hall, PCM, p. 237; *The Weekly Register*, Nov. 6, 1813, 5:174–75; Bond Journal, LOC, p. 64.

39. In the map of 1808 the Indian council house is shown close to Fort

Malden, by the farthermost bastion from the town and overlooking the river (PAC H3/440/Amh. 1808). A map in the Harrison Papers of the Library of Congress places a brick meetinghouse about 80 yards above the fort, near the same bastion, and although the distance from the fort is greater, it may be the same building. Thse two maps are not entirely in agreement in other particulars.

40. *The Lucubrations of Humphrey Ravelin*, p 354. Although the Canadian historian, E.A. Cruikshank, identifies the anonymous author of this work as Henry Procter, who appears on army lists as an ensign of the Forty-first in 1813, other evidence shows that the writer was George Procter, an army officer who married Susannah Ann Procter, the daughter of the general, in 1819. George Procter became a brevet major in 1837 and was later promoted to lieutenant colonel, but died suddenly at sea off Aden in 1842. WO 42/38/294. His material in *Humphrey Ravelin* demonstrates that he possessed accurate information about the Right Division's operations, and he stated that "whatever fell not under my own observations is given upon authority which it would be impossible to doubt for an instant" (p. 323). That "authority" might well have been General Procter himself.

41. Richardson, "Canadian Campaign," 19:252. Richardson also wrote of the council in ibid., 19:252–53; *Tecumseh*; or, *the Warrior of the West: A Poem in Four Cantos, with Notes*, pp. 116, 128; and *Richardson's War of 1812*, pp. 204–07, 226–27.

42. Speech of Tecumseth, PCM, pp. 381–82.

43. Interview with McCormick by L.C. Draper (1863), Draper Mss., 17S208; Bond Journal, LOC, p. 63.

44. Speech of Tecumseth, PCM, pp. 381–82.

45. Lewis Cass, "Indians of North America," p. 99, advances a silly story from Mrs. Walker, a half-blood Wyandot, that Tecumseh's speech had been composed by Walk-in-the-Water, the Grey-Eyed Man, and Isidore, three Wyandots, at her home. "Tecumthe," adds Cass, "was not an able composer of speeches. We understand he was particularly deficient in those powers of the imagination, to which we have been indebted for the boldest flights of Indian eloquence. He was sometimes confused, and generally tedious and circumlocutory." It is true that the Indians were democratic people, and their leaders conferred to determine, as far as possible, a common policy. In these councils Tecumseh's influence was profound. At the British council at Amherstburg he would

have presented the agreed policy of the Indians, either freely or by interpreting symbols on a wampum belt as aids to the memory on the points that were to be made. In the latter case, the orator's powers of imagination and eloquence were required to convey the ideas represented by the symbols. The Indians were not literate and did not compose or rote-learn speeches word for word. Cass's remarks must also be viewed in their context, for they were part of a vigorous and unfair review of a book by John Dunn Hunter, which had included a tribute to Tecumseh's eloquence. In his eagerness to attack Hunter, Cass showed only a marginal interest in the truth. Cass's articles for the *North American Review* were published anonymously, but the authorhsip is revealed in, among other sources, Henry Rowe Schoolcraft, *Personal Memoirs of a Residence of Thirty Years with the Indian Tribes*, pp. 217–18, 259.

Among many other stories generated by Tecumseh's rebuke of Procter, one of the oldest appears in Francis Hall's *Travels in Canada, and the United States, in 1816 and 1817*, p. 228: "On another occasion, when by way of pacifying his [Tecumseh's] remonstrances with a metaphor, in the Indian manner, our commander [Procter] professed his readiness to lay his bones by his side, 'Tell the dog,' said the angry warrior, 'he has too much regard for his carcass, to lay his bones any where.'" In 1885, John Bertrand, a citizen of Amherstburg, remembered that when he was a boy of nearly twelve years of age he saw Tecumseh—"about 5 feet 9 inches—a great, stout broad shouldered man"—on the large stone "at the foot of Gore St. near the docks." He claimed to have heard the chief denounce Procter for cowardice. The date he assigns to the incident (September 10, 1813) raises several questions. Tecumseh did not have grounds for charging Procter with cowardice at that time, and there is no evidence to show that the latter was then in Amherstburg rather than at his headquarters at Sandwich. A.A. Falls to Draper, Jan. 21, 1885, Feb. 9, 1886, Draper Mss., 6YY109, 6YY111.

46. Procter, PCM, pp. 351–52.

47. Hall, PCM, pp. 237–38. It was rumored that Tenskwatawa, Tecumseh's brother, supplied Elliott with the information about the Indians' intention to sever the wampum belt that had symbolized British-Indian union. Jones, PCM, pp. 180–81.

48. Warburton, PCM, p. 20; Billy Caldwell, PCM, p. 137; Hall, PCM, p. 239; Procter, PCM, pp. 419–20.

49. Warburton, PCM, p. 9; Hall, PCM, p. 280; Elliott to Claus,

Oct. 24, 1813, PAC MG 19/fl/10:111–13. Richardson's account has the Indians being told that the fort could not be defended easily because the heavy guns had been removed to arm Barclay's squadron, and has Tecumseh making a final short speech consenting to the retreat.

50. Cochran, PCM, pp. 293–95.

51. Lieutenant James Fraser, PCM, p. 287.

52. Billy Caldwell, PCM, pp. 161–62; Elliott to Claus, Oct. 24, 1813, PAC MG 19/fl/10:111–13.

53. Warburton, PCM, p. 19; Harrison to Armstrong, Sept. 30, Oct. 10, 1813; Esarey, *William Henry Harrison*, 2:554–56, 573–75; Bond Journal, LOC, p. 65; McArthur to Armstrong, Oct. 6, 1813, Sec. of War, LR, Unreg.; R. David Edmunds, *The Potawatomis: Keepers of the Fire*, pp. 197–98; A.R. Gilpin, *The War of 1812 in the Old Northwest*, p. 220.

54. *Quebec Gazette*, Oct. 14, 1813.

55. Milo M. Quaife, ed., *War on the Detroit: The Chronicles of Thomas Verchères de Boucherville*, pp. 138–43.

56. Baby, PCM, pp. 145–46; Procter, PCM, p. 356.

57. British officer to his parents, Sept. 26, 1813, *New York Commercial Advertiser*, Nov. 18, 1813.

58. Shane interviewed by Drake (1821), Draper Mss., 2YY56, 12YY69–71. Jim, George, and Mary Blue-Jacket were the children of the famous Shawnee chief Blue Jacket by his French-Canadian-Shawnee wife, a daughter of Jacques Duperon Baby. Mary died in 1806. George was employed as an Indian interpreter by the British at Amherstburg in 1813. Jim, according to his nephew, married a Wyandot and died in Kansas about 1845, aged some eighty years. An unmarried daughter was said to have survived him. Charles Blue-Jacket interviewed by Draper (1868), Draper Mss., 23S167; Interviews with Nannette Caldwell and Mrs. P. Drouillard by Draper (1863), Draper Mss., 17S175–76, 17S187; Milo M. Quaife, ed., *The John Askin Papers*, 1:561, 2:34; establishment of the Indian Department, Apr. 15, 1813, PAC RG 10, 28:16452–53.

59. Folder, "Stories re Detroit,"Lacey Papers, Burton Historical Collection, Detroit Public Library. The tone of the document is as much sensational and polemical as historical. Information may have come from Hamtramck through Lacey's grandfather, B.F.H. Witherell, an early Detroit historian, or even have been invented by Lacey herself in the twentieth century.

60. Procter, PCM, pp. 361–62.

61. *Montreal Gazette*, Jan. 4, 1814.

62. Talbot, PCM, pp. 185–86; Crowther, PCM, pp. 190, 198.

63. Crowther, PCM, pp. 191–92, 197.

64. Talbot, PCM, pp. 186–87, 189.

65. Troughton, PCM, pp. 106, 111; Bond journal, LOC, p. 64.

66. Warburton, PCM, pp. 9, 15, 24; Chambers PCM, p. 85; Hall, PCM, p. 279.

67. Warburton, PCM, p. 26; PCM, pp. 48, 53, 65–66; Hall, PCM, p. 240; Procter, PCM, pp. 355–56; William F. Coffin, *1812: The War, and its Moral: A Canadian Chronicle*, p. 225.

68. His career is respectably described by Consul W. Butterfield, *History of the Girtys*.

69. Evans, PCM, pp. 58–59; Billy Caldwell, PCM, p. 159; Hall, PCM, pp. 239, 279; Procter, PCM, p. 358.

70. Billy Caldwell, PCM, pp. 137, 158.

71. Cass to Armstrong, Dec. 17, 1813, Sec. of War, LR, Reg.; George F.G. Stanley, "The Contribution of the Canadian Militia During the War," in Philip Mason, ed., *After Tippecanoe: Some Aspects of the War of 1812*, pp. 28–48.

72. Benson J. Lossing, *The Pictorial Field-book of the War of 1812*, pp. 299–300; Interview with Reynolds by Draper (1863), Draper Mss., 17S245. The accuracy of Reynolds's memory may be judged in the light of his statement that Tecumseh claimed to have watched the battle on Lake Erie from a tree and was satisfied that Barclay had done his best. In reality the chief seems to have been utterly ignorant of the battle.

73. Holmes to Hall, Sept. 27, 1813 (two letters), PCM, pp. 383–84.

74. Holmes, PCM, p. 136; Hall, PCM, pp. 271, 275; Procter, PCM, pp. 359, 415.

75. Evans, PCM, p. 54; Holmes, PCM, p. 136.

76. Warburton, PCM, p. 9; Evans, PCM, p. 49; Muir, PCM, pp. 74–75.

77. Reginald Horsman, *Matthew Elliott, British Indian Agent*.

78. Harrison to Armstrong, Sept. 27, 1813, Esarey, *William Henry Harrison*, 2:550–51; Robert B. McAfee, *The Late War in the Western Country*, pp. 366–69; Bond Journal, LOC, p. 64.

79. Alfred M. Lorrain, *The Helm, the Sword, and the Cross: A Life Narrative*, pp. 150–51.

80. Harrison to Armstrong, Sept. 30, Oct. 9, 1813, Esarey, *William Henry Harrison*, 2:554–56, 558–65; Gilpin, *The War of 1812, in the Old Northwest*, pp. 220–21.

4
From Sandwich to Moraviantown: September 27 to October 5, 1813

1. Fred Coyne Hamil, *The Valley of the Lower Thames, 1640 to 1850*, p. 84; R. Gourlay, *Statistical Account of Upper Canada*, pp. 129, 132, 135, 138; Bond Journal, LOC, p. 65; Isaac Shelby to his wife, Oct. 28, 1813, Shelby Papers, vol. 4, LOC; James Sympson Diary, quoted in Anderson Chenault Quisenberry, *Kentucky in the War of 1812*, pp. 103–04; Chambers, PCM, p. 88; Allan McLean, PCM, p. 230; Askin Diary, Sept. 29, Oct. 2, Oct. 6, 1813, "Extracts from the Diary of John Askin," *MPHC* 32 (1903):468–74.
2. Warburton, PCM, pp. 9–10; Evans, PCM, pp. 49–50; Hall, PCM, pp. 240–41; Cochran Narrative, p. 58.
3. Baby, PCM, p. 150; Hall, PCM, pp. 241–42, 276; Procter, PCM, p. 372.
4. Procter, PCM, p. 159.
5. Evans, PCM, pp. 58–59; McLean, PCM, p. 221; Hall, PCM, p. 276; Procter, PCM, p. 372.
6. Elliott to Claus, Oct. 24, 1813, PAC MG 19/fl/10:111–13.
7. Edwin C. Guillet, *Early Life in Upper Canada*, p. 148; certification of Baby's claims, PAC RG 10, 4:1723–24.
8. Baby, PCM, p. 146.
9. Warburton, PCM, p. 10; Troughton, PCM, pp. 107, 111; Samuel Wood, PCM, p. 206; McLean, PCM, p. 224; Hall, PCM, pp. 244, 263, 282.
10. Billy Caldwell, PCM, p. 138; Hall, PCM, p. 245; Procter, PCM, p. 364.
11. Diary of a British officer, John Richardson, *Richardson's War of 1812*, p. 226.
12. Cochran Notes, p. 134. The references are to Major Muir and Lieutenant Benjamin Geale.
13. Warburton, PCM, pp. 14, 24; Crowther, PCM, p. 198; Hall,

PCM, pp. 244, 264; A.W. Cochran, PCM, pp. 302–03; William F. Coffin, *1812: The War, and its Moral: A Canadian Chronicle*, p. 225.

14. Procter to de Rottenburg, Oct. 23, 1813, William Wood, ed., *Select British Documents of the Canadian War of 1812*, 2:323–27.

15. Dixon, PCM, p. 97.

16. McLean, PCM, p. 222; Procter, PCM, p. 362.

17. Crowther, PCM, pp. 192–93; Hall, PCM, p. 246. The foregoing discredits the much published story that Procter and Tecumseh reconnoitered Chatham together. It was first printed in 1824 by Moses Dawson upon the authority of an unnamed British sergeant who reportedly commanded the accompanying escort. Procter and Tecumseh are alleged to have driven from Dolsen's in the general's gig and examined Chatham, where Procter promised a stand would be made. Tecumseh agreed that "it was a good place, and when he should look at the two streams, they would remind him of the Wabash and the Tippecanoe." Moses Dawson, *Historical Narrative of the Civil and Military Services of Major-General William Henry Harrison*, p. 438. This tale is apochryphal. Tecumseh reached Dolsen's on September 30 and was there two days later when he conferred with Billy Caldwell and Elliott on the afternoon of October 2. Caldwell, PCM, p. 138. Procter rejoined his division at Dolsen's on October 1. On the second he dispatched Dixon to reconnoiter Chatham and accompanied Hall on an expedition to the mouth of the Thames. The general relied upon Dixon's report for his information on the forks, and the next morning left for Moraviantown, leaving Tecumseh with the army at Dolsen's.

18. Dixon, PCM, p. 102; Crowther, PCM, p. 194; Hall, PCM, pp. 250, 269, 274; Fraser, PCM, p. 286.

19. Dixon, PCM, p. 97; Crowther, PCM, pp. 193–94.

20. Holmes, PCM, p. 136; Hall, pp. PCM, 243, 247, 257–58.

21. Warburton, PCM, pp. 11–12.

22. Crowther, PCM, pp. 194–95; Hall, PCM, p. 249; Lieutenant Richard Bullock to Major Richard Friend, Dec. 6, 1813, *Richardson's War of 1812*, pp. 230–34; Elliott to Claus, Oct. 24, 1813, PAC MG 19/fl/10:111–13.

23. Evans, PCM, p. 55.

24. Chambers, PCM, pp. 83–84; Baby, PCM, p. 147.

25. Cochran Narrative, p. 59.

26. Harrison to Armstrong, Oct. 9, 1813, Logan Esarey, ed., *Mes-*

sages and Letters of William Henry Harrison, 2:558–65; Hamil, *Lower Thames*, pp. 58–59; R.B. McAfee, map facing page 123 of Robert B. McAfee, "The McAfee Papers," *Register of the Kentucky State Historical Society* 26 (1928):4–23, 108–36, 236–48; Kent Historical Society, "Some Historical Notes on the County of Kent," PAC, p. 26.

27. Billy Caldwell, PCM, pp. 160, 162. McAfee's map of Chatham suggests that the Indians camped south of the creek on the night preceding the skirmish with the Americans.

28. Evans, PCM, p. 51; Muir, PCM, pp. 75, 80; Hall, PCM, p. 272.

29. The primary sources for the action at Chatham are: Harrison to Armstrong, Oct. 9, 1813, Esarey, *William Henry Harrison*, 2:558–65; journal of Eleazor D. Wood in George W. Cullum, ed., *Campaigns of the War of 1812–15, Against Great Britain*, p. 412; "McAfee Papers," pp. 123–24; Sympson diary, Quisenberry, *Kentucky in the War*, pp. 104–05; Cochran Narrative, p. 61; John Speed Smith to M.B. Corwin, Mar. 6, 1840, *Kentucky Gazette*, Apr. 9, 1840; Interview with James Bentley by Draper (1863), Draper Mss., 17S179–80; Robert B. McAfee, *The Late War in the Western Country*, pp. 385–86; Evans, PCM, p. 66; McLean, PCM, p. 224; Hall, PCM, p. 249; Elliott to Claus, Oct. 24, 1813, PAC RG MG 19/fl/10:111–13; John Chambers to M.B. Corwin, Feb. 28, 1840, in Isaac R. Jackson, *A Sketch of the Life and Public Services of William Henry Harrison*, pp. 31–32. The failure of the Indians to totally destroy the lower bridge over McGregor's Creek before the engagement merits comment. Conceivably they had not time to complete its demolition, but the laborious task of ripping up the planking suggests that the more obvious and potentially effective method of destruction by fire had failed. It must be remembered that rain had been falling for days and the wood was thoroughly drenched.

30. George Ironside to Duncan Cameron, Oct. 3, 1814, PAC RG 10, 29:17236–37. Two Americans were killed outright at Chatham, and Captain Elijah Craig died of his wounds a few days later. "McAfee Papers," p. 131; pay and muster rolls of Johnson's regiment, Voluntary Organizations and State Militia, War of 1812, RG 94, National Archives, Washington, D.C. Official British papers list no Indian fatalities for the skirmish, but local tradition claimed otherwise. Two bodies were supposedly buried by nearby settlers, and it was said that a year afterwards John Toll and another boy discovered the remains of a third near the mill while hunting squirrels. Kent Historical Society, "Historical Notes,"

pp. 25–26. This Toll is also alleged to have said that Tecumseh had found him playing by the riverside before the skirmish and told him to run home, a tale that recalls a more authenticated story given by David Sherman, to be dealt with later. Victor Lauriston, *Romantic Kent*, p. 89.

31. Caldwell, PCM, pp. 138, 162.

32. Harrison to Armstrong, Oct. 10, 1813, Esarey, *William Henry Harrison*, 2:573–75; McAfee, *Late War*, p. 385; Elliott to Claus, Oct. 24, 1813, PAC MG 19/fl/10:111–13. Walk-in-the-Water remained peaceful thereafter, and died aged about seventy years on a reservation on the Huron River in 1818.

33. Caldwell, PCM, pp. 160, 162.

34. Warburton, PCM, pp. 11–12; Dixon, PCM, pp. 97–98; Coleman, PCM, pp. 121–22; Procter, PCM, pp. 364–65.

35. Chambers, PCM, P. 86; Troughton, PCM, p. 107; Crowther, PCM, pp. 191, 196–97; Hall, PCM, p. 242; Procter to de Rottenburg, Nov. 16, 1813, Wood, *British Documents*, 2:338–41.

36. Warburton, PCM, pp. 12–13; Crowther, PCM, pp. 196–97; Richard Pattinson to John Vincent, Dec. 7, 1813, PAC RG 8, C257:196–97; "McAfee Papers," pp. 123–24.

37. Warburton, PCM, pp. 12–13; Evans, PCM, p. 51.

38. Evans, PCM, p. 49; Gilmore, PCM, pp. 141–42; Crowther, PCM, pp. 190–91.

39. Evans, PCM, p. 60–61; Gilmore, PCM, pp. 142, 144; Philip Brooks, PCM, p. 202.

40. Evans, PCM, pp. 56–57; J. Hill, PCM, p. 116; Lewis Fitzgerald, PCM, p. 127; Bent, PCM, pp. 132–34; Gilmore, PCM, pp. 140–44; Crowther, PCM, pp. 195–96; diary of officer, *Richardson's War of 1812*, p. 226; Cochran Narrative, p. 62.

41. Warburton, PCM, pp. 13, 28–29; Evans, PCM, pp. 52, 55; Chambers, PCM, pp. 84, 89, 93–94; Brooks, PCM, pp. 202–03; Grant, PCM, pp. 203–04; Hall, PCM, pp. 252–53, 257–58.

42. Procter to de Rottenburg, Oct. 5, 1813, PAC RG 8, C680:208; Dixon, PCM, p. 98; Samuel Wood PCM, p. 206.

43. Warburton, PCM, pp. 29–30; Dixon, PCM, p. 99; Hill, PCM, pp. 114, 116; Wood, PCM, pp. 206–07.

44. Hill, PCM, p. 116.

45. John Strachan to James Brown, Oct. 30, 1813, J.L.H. Henderson, ed., *John Strachan: Documents and Opinions*, pp. 46–48.

46. Cochran Narrative, p. 62; Warburton, PCM, pp. 13, 25.

47. Evans, PCM, p. 51; "McAfee Papers," p. 126; Robert Scrogin to the Committee of Correspondence and Vigilance of Warren County, Ohio, Nov. 16, 1835, *Kentucky Gazette*, Nov. 28, 1835. Scrogin served under Harrison as a lieutenant of militia but his account is manifestly dramatized.

48. T. K. Holmes to Draper, Apr. 20, 1882, Draper Mss., 7YY67.

49. T. K. Holmes to Draper, Apr. 20, 1882, Draper Mss. 7YY67, 7YY129; A. Jamieson to Draper, Mar. 13, 1882, Draper Mss., 7YY65–66; Hamil, *Lower Thames*, pp. 60, 342, 352. Holmes dictated his information to his son, Tecumseh K. Holmes. His description of Chief Tecumseh as a handsome man of medium height, strong build, and a broad chest and shoulders, is accurate. He had indistinct recollections of the chief's headgear, but guessed that it might have been a turban. Abraham Holmes died in February, 1890, according to *Commemorative Biographical Record of the County of Kent Onatario*, p. 36. Joseph Johnston (or Johnson) and his sister Margaret had been settled on the Thames for several years. Hamil (p. 342) asserts that Margaret was formerly an Indian captive, whereas Holmes speaks of Joseph as having lived with the Indians.

50. Harrison to Armstrong, Oct. 9, 1813, Esarey, *William Henry Harrison*, 2:558–64; Chambers, PCM, p. 94; Hall, PCM, p. 279; Procter, PCM, p. 369; A.R. Gilpin, *The War of 1812 in the Old Northwest*, p. 224.

51. *Columbus Sentinel*, Jan. 3, 1832.

52. Thaddeus S. Arnold, "Battle of the Thames and Death of Tecumseh," *Annual Transactions of the United Empire Loyalists Association of Ontario, 1901–1902* 4 (1903):30, 33–34.

53. Colin C. Ironside to Draper, May 4, 1885, Draper Mss., 7YY76; A.A. Falls to Draper, Jan. 21, 1885, PCM 6YY109.

54. David Sherman's son, Lemuel, was born in 1827 and thus nearly forty years of age at the time of his father's death. It is quite possible that he had a clear recollection of the Tecumseh story and preserved some accurate details. Lemuel Sherman survived into the twentieth century. *Commemorative Biographical Record of the County of Kent Ontario*, pp. 567–68; Benson J. Lossing, *The Pictorial Field-book of the War of 1812*, p. 560; Katherine B. Coutts, "Thamesville and the Battle of the Thames," in Morris Zaslow and Wesley B. Turner, eds., *The Defended Border: Upper*

Canada and the War of 1812, pp. 116–18.

55. C.A. Wickliffe to the editor of the *Bardstown Gazette*, Nov. 25, 1859, "Tecumseh and the Battle of the Thames," *Register of the Kentucky Historical Society* 60 (1962):45–46; "McAfee Papers," p. 125; Alfred Brunson, "Death of Tecumseh at the Battle of the Thames in 1813," *Report and Collections of the State Historical Society of Wisconsin* 4 (1859):370–71; J. Davidson to the editor of the *Louisville Journal*, Oct. 22, 1859, "Who Killed Tecumseh?" *Historical Magazine* (July 1866):205.

56. Shadrach Byfield, "A Narrative of a Light Company Soldier's Service, in the 41st Regiment of Foot, During the Late American War," *The Magazine of History with Notes and Queries* 11 (1910):80.

57. Warburton, PCM, pp. 15–16, 27; Evans, PCM pp. 53, 64; Hill, PCM, p. 116.

58. Evans, PCM, pp. 64; Chambers, PCM, pp. 86, 89, 92; Troughton, PCM, p. 110; Hill, PCM, pp. 113–14, 116; Bent, PCM, pp. 133–34; White, PCM, p. 139; Gilmore, PCM, p. 142; Pattinson, PCM, p. 166; Wood, PCM, pp. 206–07; Gowrie to Captain W. Shaw, Nov. 1813, Norman St. Clair Gurd, *The Story of Tecumseh*, pp. 182–83; documents regarding soldiers' compensation claims for loss of baggage, PAC RG 8, vols, 912–14.

59. Harrison to Armstrong, Oct. 9, 1813, Esarey, *William Henry Harrison*, 2:558–65.

60. Evans, PCM, pp. 54, 65–66; Chambers, PCM, pp. 93–95; Baby, PCM, pp. 152–53; Caldwell, PCM, p. 163; McLean, PCM, p. 221; Hall, PCM, p. 242; Procter, PCM, p. 372.

61. Dixon, PCM, p. 102; Holmes, PCM, p. 136; Hall, PCM, pp. 242–43; Procter, PCM, pp. 363–64. Harrison's dispatch suggests that Holmes was captured near Baptiste's Creek and that Hall had damaged the bridge over Jeannette's Creek.

62. Warburton, PCM, p. 28; Hall, PCM, p. 269.

63. "McAfee Papers," p. 125; Chambers, PCM, pp. 93–94; Billy Caldwell, PCM, p. 162; Pattinson, PCM, p. 166; John Dolsen, PCM, p. 285.

5
The Battle of Moraviantown: October 5, 1813

1. Chambers, PCM, p. 84; McLean, PCM, p. 232; *Montreal Gazette*, Jan. 4, 1814; Cochran Narrative, pp. 59–60; R.B. McAfee map, PAC F/440/Moraviantown/1813.

2. Warburton, PCM, pp. 12–13; Chambers, PCM, p. 87; Dixon, PCM, p. 98.

3. Troughton, PCM, p. 108.

4. Warburton, PCM, pp. 32–34; Evans, PCM, pp. 57–58; Chambers, PCM, p. 87; Dixon, PCM, p. 99; Talbot, PCM, pp. 186, 188–89.

5. Evans, PCM, p. 69; Captain W. Caldwell, PCM, pp. 155–56; Billy Caldwell, PCM, p. 161; Le Breton, PCM, p. 169; Talbot, pp. PCM, 188–89; Hall, PCM, p. 282.

6. Warburton, PCM, pp. 13–14, 26; Evans, PCM, p. 68; Chambers, PCM, pp. 84, 93–94; Hall, PCM, pp. 253–54; Bullock to Friend, Dec. 6, 1813, John Richardson, *Richardson's War of 1812*, pp. 230–34.

7. Warburton, PCM, p. 35; Evans, PCM, p. 52; Chambers, PCM, p. 84; Baby, PCM, pp. 147–48; Hall PCM, p. 278.

8. Norman St. Clair Gurd, *The Story of Tecumseh*, p. 183; Katherine B. Coutts, "Thamesville and the Battle of the Thames" (1908), reprinted in Morris Zaslow and Wesley B. Turner, eds., *The Defended Border: Upper Canada and the War of 1812*, p. 118.

9. Troughton, PCM, p. 106.

10. Procter, PCM, p. 369.

11. Billy Caldwell, PCM, pp. 161, 164; Hall, PCM, pp. 254–55, 279; Fraser, PCM, p. 288; Cochran Narrative, p. 63; Cochran Notes, p. 122.

12. D.A.N. Lomax, *A History of the Services of the 41st (Welch) Regiment*, p. 88.

13. Chambers, PCM, p. 84; Hall, PCM, pp. 252–53.

14. Return of the Right Division, Oct. 1, 1813, PCM, pp. 385–87; Warburton, PCM, p. 14; Troughton, PCM, p. 112.

15. Evans, PCM, pp. 67–68; Gilmore, PCM, p. 144; Hall, PCM, pp. 257–58.

16. Brooks, PCM, pp. 202–03; Bullock to Friend, Dec. 6, 1813, *Richardson's War of 1812*, pp. 230–34; Prevost to Bathurst, Oct. 30, 1813, William Wood, ed., *Select British Documents of the Canadian War of 1812*, 2:327–29.

17. Harrison to Armstrong, Oct. 9, 1813, Logan Esarey, ed., *Messages and Letters of William Henry Harrison* 2:558–65; Robert B. McAfee, *The Late War in the Western Country*, pp. 348–51; R.M. Johnson to Armstrong, Dec. 22, 1834, John Armstrong, *Notices of the War of 1812*, 1:232–34; Shelby to Ephraim McDowell, Sept. 10, 1813, Shelby Papers, vol. 4, LOC; Shelby to Armstrong, Nov. 19, 1813, Sec. of War, LR, Reg.; George C. Chalou, "The Red Pawns Go to War: British-American Indian Relations, 1810–15," Ph.D., diss., Indiana University, 1971, p. 289; Alfred Brunson, "Death of Tecumseh at the Battle of the Thames in 1813," *Report and Collections of the State Historical Society of Wisconsin* 4 (1859):371.

18. Harrison to Armstrong, Oct. 11, 1813, Esarey, *William Henry Harrison*, 2:576–77; statement of C.S. Todd to the *National Intelligencer*, *The Weekly Register*, Jan. 1, 1814, 5:301; A.R. Gilpin, *The War of 1812 in the Old Northwest*, p. 221; Benson J. Lossing, *The Pictorial Field-book of the War of 1812*, p. 549; John K. Mahon, *The War of 1812*, p. 182.

19. Warburton, PCM, pp. 34, 36; Evans, PCM, p. 57; Hall, PCM, pp. 255, 278; McAfee, *Late War*, p. 388; map in "McAfee Papers," facing page 126; map enclosed in R.M. Johnson to Armstrong, Nov. 21, 1813, Sec. of War, LR, Reg.; map contained in Henry Onderdonk's manuscript, "Life and Times of Tecumseh," approved by R.M. Johnson, LOC.

20. Procter, PCM, pp. 368–69, 380; Procter to de Rottenburg, Nov. 16, 1813, Wood, *British Documents*, 2:338–41.

21. Procter to de Rottenburg, Nov. 16, 1813, Wood, *British Documents*, 2:338–41.

22. McLean, PCM, p. 227.

23. Map enclosed in Johnson to Armstrong, Nov. 21, 1813, Sec. of War, LR, Reg.; Captain W. Caldwell, PCM, p. 155; Billy Caldwell, PCM, p. 164; Coutts, "Thamesville," p. 117. A half-blood son of Colonel William Caldwell, Billy Caldwell was an ideal link between the Indian and British forces. He had been appointed as Indian aide in August, 1813, with an allowance for a horse with which to visit and encourage the tribes. Caldwell, PCM, p. 158.

24. Thomas McKee to Sir John Johnson, Sept. 26, 1814, PAC RG 10, 29:17229–30. Twenty-five Creeks followed Tecumseh on his retreat and later served on the Niagara frontier until they were dispersed after the death of their leader at the siege of Fort Erie in 1814.

25. Annotations on map of the Thames by George Williams, Aug. 9, 1814, PAC H2/410/Thames/1814. This map appears to have been prepared with the assistance of members of the Indian Department, and as far as it can be checked, is accurate.

26. Baby, PCM, pp. 149, 151; Billy Caldwell, PCM, p. 164. Cochran, for example, records that upon the imminence of battle Tecumseh "instantaneously recovered his spirits and was all life, activity and good humour . . . ." Cochran Narrative, p. 65.

27. Shane interviews with Drake (1821), Draper Mss., 2YY56–57.

28. *The Weekly Register*, Apr. 16, 1814, 6:111–12, accurately points out that Tecumseh's "dress was plain—he was never known to indulge in the gaudy decoration of his person, which is the general practice of the Indians. He wore on the day of his death a dressed deerskin coat and pantaloons . . . ."

29. *The Lucubrations of Humphrey Ravelin*, p. 342.

30. *Army and Navy Chronicle* 7 (1838):295–96, reprinted from the *Baltimore American*. William Hickling said that his late friend George E. Walker obtained an account of Tecumseh's death from Black Hawk shortly after the Black Hawk War of 1832. Walker may have been "W." Hickling to Draper, Oct. 13, 1875, Draper Mss., 9YY110–11.

31. Donald Jackson, ed., *Black Hawk: An Autobiography*, p. 68.

32. Benson J. Lossing, "Was Tecumtha Skinned?", *American Historical Record* 1 (1872):285; Samuel Theobald to Benson J. Lossing, Jan. 16, 1861, Draper Mss., 7YY33–43; Interview with Mary Logan Smith by Draper (1863), Draper Mss., 18S164.

33. Caldwell, PCM, p. 164.

34. Interview with Bourassa by Draper (1868), Draper Mss., 23S185–89.

35. Interview with Caldwell by Draper (1863), Draper Mss., 17S222–24.

36. Gordon Hubbard to Draper, Sept. 4, 1875, Feb. 12, 1879, Draper Mss., 9YY104, 9YY106; Hickling to Draper, Oct. 13, 19, 1875, Draper Mss., 9YY110–12; William Hickling, "Caldwell and Shabonee," *Addresses Delivered at the Annual Meeting of the Chicago Historical Society . . . 1868 . . . Together with . . . Sketches of Billy Caldwell and Shabonee . . .*, p. 32.

37. Caldwell, PCM, p. 164.

38. Ibid.

39. Evans, PCM, pp. 52, 72; Coleman, PCM, p. 122; Fitzgerald, PCM, p. 129; James Lamb, PCM, p. 235; Hall, PCM, p. 255; Bullock to Friend, Dec. 6, 1813, *Richardson's War of 1812*, pp. 230–34.

40. *Richardson's War of 1812*, p. 212. In his historical novel, *The Canadian Brothers*, Richardson confirms these details. Tecumseh took the hands of the British officers ("we fancy we can feel the generous pressure of his fingers even at this remote period") and appeared confident of success, leaving "with a bounding step that proved not only how much his heart had been set upon the cast, but how completely he confided in the result." John Richardson, *The Canadian Brothers; or, the Prophecy Fulfilled*, 2:191.

41. William F. Coffin, *1812: The War, and its Moral: A Canadian Chronicle*, p. 228; "Campaigns in the Canadas," *Quarterly Review* 27 (1822):431–32. This account purports to be based upon some well-known histories of the war and "other sources of information" (p. 408), the latter of which seem to have supplied the data about Tecumseh's review of the troops. It says that the Shawnee chief returned to the Indians and harangued them before they were formed, which is not unlikely. William Hatch implies that he and others spoke to Indians at the treaty of Greenville in 1814 and heard that, just before firing began at Moravian-town, Tecumseh and some of his men passed along the Indian line urging the warriors to "be brave," "stand firm," and "shoot certain." William S. Hatch, *Chapter of the History of the War of 1812 in the Northwest*, pp. 155–56.

42. Hall, PCM, p. 256.

43. Chambers, PCM, p. 90.

44. Cochran Narrative, p. 63.

45. Bullock to Friend, Dec. 6, 1813, *Richardson's War of 1812*, pp. 230–34; Warburton, PCM, pp. 13–14, 17–18, 37, 41; Evans, PCM, p. 52; Muir, PCM, pp. 75–76; Bullock, PCM, p. 117; Coleman, PCM, p. 122; Fitzgerald, PCM, p. 132; McLean, PCM, p. 224; Hall, PCM, p. 255.

46. Chambers, PCM, p. 95.

47. Cochran Narrative, p. 63; Bullock to Friend, Dec. 6, 1813, *Richardson's War of 1812*, pp. 230–34; Warburton, PCM, pp. 34, 42; Evans, PCM, p. 71; Dixon, PCM, p. 103; Bullock, PCM, p. 118.

48. William Caldwell, PCM, p. 155; Hall, PCM, p. 255; Procter, PCM, p. 375.

49. Bullock to Friend, Dec. 6, 1813, *Richardson's War of 1812*, pp.

230–34; Warburton, PCM, pp. 13–14; Evans, PCM, p. 53; Chambers, PCM, p. 84; Hall, PCM, p. 258; Shelby to his wife, Sept. [Oct.] 8, 1813, Shelby Papers, vol. 4, LOC.

50. Harrison to Armstrong, Oct. 9, 1813, Esarey, *William Henry Harrison*, 2:558–65; McAfee, *Late War*, p. 389.

51. Harrison to Armstrong, Oct. 9, 1813, Esarey, *William Henry Harrison*, 2:558–65; Harrison to T. Corwin, July 2, 1840, Rufus King, *Ohio* pp. 412–14; John O'Fallon to M.B. Corwin, Feb. 26, 1840, J. Thomas Scharf, *History of Saint Louis City and County*, 1:347–48.

52. Johnson to Armstrong, Nov. 21, 1813, Sec. of War, LR, Reg.

53. Johnson to Armstrong, Nov. 21, 1813, Sec. of War, LR, Reg.; Johnson to Armstrong, Dec. 22, 1834, Armstrong, *Notices*, 1:232–34; McAfee, *Late War*, p. 390; Samuel R. Brown, *An Authentic History of the Second War for Independence*, 1:126–27; statement of Jeremiah Kirtley, Sept. 1, 1840, *Kentucky Gazette*, Sept. 24, 1840; Theobald to Lossing, Jan. 16, 1861, Draper Mss., 7YY33–43; Garrett Wall to Mann Butler, Aug. 30, 1834, Mann Butler, *A History of the Commonwealth of Kentucky*, pp. 547–48.

54. This and the following paragraph are based upon Bullock to Friend, Dec. 6, 1813, *Richardson's War of 1812*, pp. 230–34; Cochran Narrative, pp. 62–65; Warburton, PCM, pp. 13–14, 22, 35–36, 38; Evans, PCM, pp. 52–53, 57, 70–73; Muir, PCM, pp. 76–77; Chambers, PCM, pp. 84–85, 89–90; Dixon, PCM, pp. 103–04; Bullock, PCM, pp, 117–19; Lefevre, PCM, pp. 210–14; Benac, PCM, p. 216; McLean, PCM, pp. 224–26, 228–33; Lamb, PCM, pp. 234–35; Hall, PCM, pp. 258–60 265–66.

55. Warburton, PCM, p. 38.

56. Hall, PCM, p. 259. Procter's words are variously reported as "For shame 41st" (Dixon, PCM, p. 103; Coleman, p, PCM, 124); "41st, 41st, what are you about?" (Fitzgerald, PCM, p. 128); and "Halt 41st, halt 41st, for shame on you. Why do not you form?" (Lefevre, PCM, p. 211).

57. Lefevre, PCM, p. 212.

58. Hall, PCM, p. 260. The court-martial found that "as to any defect or reproach with regard to the personal conduct of Major General Procter during the action . . . the court most fully and honourably acquits the said Major General Procter." Court, PCM, p. 327. Despite the finding, Procter has repeatedly been accused of cowardice on the battle-field.

59. Troughton, PCM, pp. 108–09; Le Breton, PCM, p. 173; letter to the *Chillicothe* (Ohio) *Fredonian*, Oct. 11, 1813, *The Weekly Register*, Nov. 6, 1813, 5:174.

60. Bullock to Friend, Dec. 6, 1813, *Richardson's War of 1812*, pp. 230–34; Warburton, PCM, pp. 40–41; Evans, PCM, p. 52; Harrison to Armstrong, Oct. 9, 1813, Esarey, *William Henry Harrison*, 2:558–65.

61. Harrison to Armstrong, Oct. 9, 1813, Esarey, *William Henry Harrison*, 2:558–65.

62. Johnson to Armstrong, Dec. 22, 1834, Armstrong, *Notices*, 1:232–34; McAfee, *Late War*, p. 396; statement of R.B. McAfee, Aug. 1, 1840, *Kentucky Gazette*, Sept. 24, 1840.

63. Warburton, PCM, p. 22; Evans, PCM, p. 57; Muir, PCM, p. 77; Chambers, PCM, p. 85; Bullock, PCM, p. 119; Fitzgerald, PCM, p. 130; Caldwell, PCM, p. 156; McLean, PCM, p. 225; Hall, PCM, pp. 265–66.

64. Bullock to Friend, Dec. 6, 1813, *Richardson's War of 1812*. pp. 230–34.

65. Probably many of the Indians also possessed British muskets, but some of them would have obtained American weapons in trade or war. The American backcountrymen made considerable use of the Pennsylvania rifle, which fired a .55- to .60-caliber ball and had greater accuracy and therefore range than the musket. Its disadvantage as against the Brown Bess was the even slower loading.

66. Elliott to Claus, Oct. 24, 1813, PAC MG 19/fl/10:111–13; Baynes, General Orders, Nov. 24, 1813, Wood, *British Documents*, 2:294–97; Evans, PCM, p. 73; Caldwell, PCM, p. 161; Cochran Narrative, pp. 63–64.

67. Fraser, PCM, pp. 286–87.

68. William Caldwell, PCM, p. 155; Fraser, PCM, p. 286.

69. Harrison to Armstrong, Oct. 9, 1813, Esarey, *William Henry Harrison*, 2:558–65.

70. Theobald to Lossing, Jan. 16, 1861, Draper Mss., 7YY33–43; Wall to Butler, Aug. 30, 1834, Butler, *Commonwealth of Kentucky*, pp. 547–48.

71. Account by the editor of the *Frankfort Commentator*, based upon interviews given by James and Michael Davidson, and published on December 6, 1831. A copy was supplied by Davidson to Charles Scott Todd. Davidson statement, 1831, Draper Mss., 7YY141; Todd to Drake, Apr. 25, 1836, Nov. 27, 1840, Draper Mss., 7YY142, 8U3.

72. Map enclosed in Johnson to Armstrong, Nov. 21, 1813, Sec. of War, LR, Reg.

73. John Richardson, "A Canadian Campaign, by a British officer," 19:254.

74. Caldwell, PCM, p. 155; Harrison to Armstrong, Oct. 9, 1813, Esarey, *William Henry Harrison*, 2:558–65; Elliott to Claus, Oct. 24, 1813, PAC MG 19/fl/10:111–13.

75. Harrison to Armstrong, Oct. 9, 11, 1813, Esarey, *William Henry Harrison*, 2:558–65, 576–77; Johnson to Armstrong, Nov. 21, 1813, Sec. of War, LR, Reg.; Procter to de Rottenburg, Oct. 23, 1813, Wood, *British Documents*, 2:323–27; Elliott to Claus, Oct. 24, 1813, PAC MG 19/fl/10:111–13; Caldwell, PCM, p. 155; Fraser, PCM, pp. 286–87; McAfee, *Late War*, pp. 391–93; Brown, *Authentic History*, 1:127–35; John Speed Smith to M.B. Corwin, Mar. 6, 1840, *Kentucky Gazette*, Apr. 9, 1840; Captain James Mason to General J.M. McCalla, Oct. 13, 1840, *Kentucky Gazette*, Nov. 12, 1840; James Davidson to C.A. Wickliffe, Sept. 7, 1840, *Scioto Gazette*, Sept. 24, 1840; C.S. Todd to M.B. Corwin, Feb. 29, 1840, Isaac R. Jackson, *A Sketch of the Life and Public Services of William Henry Harrison*, pp. 36–37; Samuel Boone interviewed by Draper (1868), Draper Mss., 22S267.

76. Warburton, PCM, p. 14; Evans, PCM, p. 73; Muir, PCM, pp. 77, 82; Chambers, PCM, p. 85.

77. Caldwell, PCM, p. 155.

78. Johnson to Armstrong, Nov. 21, 1813, Sec. of War, LR, Reg.; Charles A. Wickliffe, "Tecumseh and the Battle of the Thames," p. 46; "McAfee Papers," p. 128.

79. There has been much confusion about the American casualties at Moraviantown and published details are unreliable. Clarence Stewart Peterson, *Known Military Dead During the War of 1812*, scarcely touches the problem, and the Report of the Adjutant-General of the State of Kentucky, *Soldiers of the War of 1812*, misprints the muster rolls for Johnson's regiment. The earliest estimates of the casualties by or derived from participants vary: 10 killed and 35 wounded, McAfee diary, Oct. 5, 1813, "McAfee Papers," p. 128; 7 or 8 killed outright, 4 fatally wounded, and about 20 injured, Shelby to his wife, Sept. [Oct.] 8, 1813, Shelby Papers, vol. 4, LOC; 14 killed and about 20 wounded, Peter Trisler, Jr. to his father, Oct. 8, 1813, Durrett Miscellaneous Manuscripts, University of Chicago Library; 7 killed outright, 5 fatally wounded, and 17 injured, Harrison to Armstrong, Oct. 9, 1813, Esarey, *William Henry*

Harrison, 2:558–65; 13 killed and others wounded, letter to the *Chillicothe* (Ohio) *Fredonian*, Oct. 11, 1813, *The Weekly Register*, Nov. 6, 1813, 5:174; 15 killed and some wounded, Bond Journal, LOC, p. 79; 8 or 10 killed, *The Weekly Register*, Nov. 13, 1813, 5:184; 15 killed and 30 wounded, Samuel R. Brown, *Views of the Campaigns of the North-western Army*, p. 73; 25 killed or fatally wounded and 50 injured in Johnson's regiment, and 2 killed and 6 or 7 wounded in the infantry, Brown, *Authentic History*, 1:130; and 17 killed and 30 wounded among Johnson's regiment and slighter casualties from the infantry, McAfee, *Late War*, p. 394.

The disparity between some of these figures—for example, the two sets provided by McAfee—may be partly accounted for by the inclusion in the later estimates of the killed those men who lingered for some time before dying of their wounds. Mortality was generally high in the army, for a number of reasons, and although Sherman's barn was used as a hospital, not all of the injured seem to have been adequately treated. Shelby to his wife, Oct. 28, 1813, Shelby Papers, Vol. 4, LOC; Brown, *Views*, p. 114. The muster and pay rolls were examined in an effort to resolve this problem, and they show, as McAfee's diary states, that ten men were killed or died of their wounds on October 5 itself. One, G.W. Carter, belonged to Mason's company in Trotter's brigade of infantry; the others to the Second Battalion of Johnson's regiment: William Whitley, Zachariah Eastham, Joshua Brown, Abraham Banta, James Turner, John L. Mansfield, John McGunnigal, George Tangler, and Robert Scott. Harrison's dispatch shows that the death toll had risen to twelve by October 9. One of the names required to satisfy this figure is James Sutton of Johnson's Second Battalion, who died on October 7, and the other must have been either Zachariah Jameson of the mounted regiment or William Grigg of the infantry, whose enlistments terminated on October 6, and October 9, respectively. To Harrison's tally must be added those who died of wounds after October 9. There were at least three of them: Samuel Logan (died October 10) and William Guthrie (October 21) of the Second Battalion of Johnson's regiment, and Thomas Graham (October 10) of the infantry. A number of other soldiers died in October and November, but their deaths cannot unequivocally be attributed to the battle. Pay and muster rolls of Johnson's regiment, Voluntary Organizations and State Militia, War of 1812, Record Group 94, National Archives, Washington, D.C.

80. These details are drawn from British compensation records. On July 20, 1813, a board of officers recommended that the Indians be compensated for death or injury incurred during sevice. A chief losing an eye or a limb would recieve $100 per annum in money or presents, and a similarly injured warrior $70 per annum. The widows of chiefs and warriors killed in action were respectively entitled to a gift in cash or goods of $200 and $140. Prize money was also to be paid for the capture of Detroit, chiefs on the scale of British subalterns, and warriors as privates. Baynes, General Orders, July 26, 1813, PAC RG 10, 28:16484–85. As a consequence detailed lists of Indians killed in action were compiled, and on April 25, 1815, bounties were paid at Burlington to the widows, who acknowledged receipt by signing with crosses. Tecumseh's wife, his sister Tecumapeace, and other widows of chiefs were awarded $50 and those of warriors $35, considerably less than the amounts mentioned in the General Orders of 1813. Return of Indians killed in service, Sept. 1, 1813–Sept. 1, 1814, PAC RG 10, 12:10524; bounties paid, PAC RG 10, 28:16504–05; supplementary list, Apr. 29, 1815, PAC RG 10, 30:17883; Indian speeches, Apr. 26–27, 1815, PAC RG 10, 12:10562–69.

To complicate the matter, the Shawnee prophet (Tecumseh's brother) stated in 1814 that before the retreat from Amherstburg the British had promised that if Tecumseh was killed his widow would receive a pension of $700, the widow of the next most important chief would be awarded $600, and the widows of any other chiefs and warriors $500. Tenskwatawa to Colonel William Caldwell, Nov. 20, 1814, PAC RG 10, 29: 17381–82. In addition to the casualties mentioned in these documents, it has been necessary to add the names of Winepegon and Andrew Clark, of whom more later. George Williams map, Aug. 9, 1814, PAC H2/410/ Thames/1814.

81. Brown, *Authentic History*, 1:314.

82. Shadrach Byfield, "A Narrative of a Light Company Soldier's Service, in the 41st Regiment of Foot, During the Late American War," *The Magazine of History with Notes and Queries* 11 (1910):80.

83. "McAfee Papers," p. 128.

84. Peter Trisler, Jr. to his father, Oct. 8, 1813, Durrett Miscellaneous Manuscripts, University of Chicago Library.

85. *The Weekly Register*, Oct. 9, 16, 1813, 5:98, 120.

86. Lewis Cass to Armstrong, Oct. 28, 1813, Sec. of War, LR, Reg.

This testimony is significant because Cass was one of the few Americans on the field of Moraviantown who may have known Tecumseh by sight. He had been captured with Hull's army at Detroit in 1812 and in the days following his surrender could often have seen the chief.

87. Procter to de Rottenburg, Oct. 23, 1813, Wood, *British Documents*, 2:323–27

88. *The War . . .*, Nov. 2, 1813, no. 72, vol. 2: 83; letter to the *Chillicothe* (Ohio) *Fredonian,* Oct. 11, 1813, *The Weekly Register,* Nov. 6, 1813, 5:174.

89. *The Weekly Register*, Nov. 13, 1813, 5:174.

90. Rowland to a friend, Oct. 9, 1813, *The War . . .* Nov. 16, 1813, no. 74, 2:91.

91. Richardson, "Canadian Campaign," 19:254.

6
Who Killed Tecumseh?

1. Bernard Mayo, "The Man Who Killed Tecumseh," *The American Mercury* 19 (1930):446. The more common variant of this banal ditty, chanted by Richard M. Johnson's political supporters, was "Rumpsey, dumpsey, Colonel Johnson killed Tecumseh."

2. Thomas D. Clark, *Frontier America*, p. 277.

3. Arthur M. Schlesinger, *The Age of Jackson*, pp. 141, 212; Leland Winfield Meyer, *The Life and Times of Richard M. Johnson of Kentucky*, pp. 393–429; Robert Bolt, "Vice President Richard M. Johnson of Kentucky: Hero of the Thames—or the Great Amalgamator?", *Register of the Kentucky Historical Society* 75 (1977):191–203.

4. Dorothy B. Goebel, *William Henry Harrison*, chs. 7–12; Claude H. Hall, "The Fabulous Tom Ochiltree," *Southwestern Historical Quarterly* 71 (1967–68):375–76.

5. Samuel R. Brown, *Views of the Campaigns of the Northwestern Army*, pp. 71–72, 105. This book was first published in 1814 and was quoted in the press as early as March of that year. *Kentucky Reporter*, Mar. 19, 1814.

6. Samuel R. Brown, *Authentic History of the Second War for Independence*, 1:128–29, 135.

7. *The Weekly Register*, Apr. 16, 1814, 6:111–12; *An Impartial and Correct History of the War Between the United States of America, and Great*

Britain, p. 123, John Lewis Thomson, *Historical Sketches of the Late War Between the United States and Great Britain*, p. 174; *The Times*, Aug. 11, 1814, quoted in Glenn Tucker, *Poltroons and Patriots. A Popular Account of the War of 1812*, 2:490; Nathaniel Atcheson, "A Compressed View of the Points to be Discussed in Treating with the United States of America," *The Pamphleteer* 5 (1815):117; John Strachan, Jan. 30, 1815, William F. Coffin, *1812: The War, and its Moral: A Canadian Chronicle*, p. 283.

8. Robert B. McAfee, *The Late War in the Western Country*, p. 394.

9. Harrison to John Tipton, May 2, 1834, Logan Esarey, ed., *Messages and Letters of Willilam Henry Harrison*. 2:749–55; Charles A. Wickliffe, "Tecumseh and the Battle of the Thames," *Register of the Kentucky Historical Society* 60 (1962):46.

10. Brown, *Authentic History*, 1:220; note by Draper in B.F.H. Witherell, "Reminiscences of the North-west," *Collections of the State Historical Society of Wisconsin* 3 (1857):314.

11. *Kentucky Gazette*, Aug. 6, 1840; speech of Oct. 17, 1840, quoted in William Albert Galloway, *Old Chillicothe: Shawnee and Pioneer History*, pp. 155–58; Thomas L. McKenney, *Memoirs, Official and Personal*, 1:182.

12. William Emmons, *Authentic Biography of Colonel Richard M. Johnson of Kentucky*, pp. 33–37. The work is dated July, 1834. On September 18, 1834, the Reverend Obediah B. Brown addressed Mann Butler giving the same account but implying that it was his own. Mann Butler, *A History of the Commonwealth of Kentucky*, pp. 548–50. Both Emmons and Brown collaborated with Johnson during his political campaigns.

13. Wall to Butler, Aug. 30, 1834, Butler, *Commonwealth of Kentucky*, pp. 547–48.

14. Alfred Brunson, "Death of Tecumseh at the Battle of the Thames in 1813," *Report and Collections of the State Historical Society of Wisconsin* 4(1859):371.

15. Emmons, for example, states that Johnson had passed around the top of the tree and was riding along its other side when his horse stumbled and warned the Indian of his approach; but Johnson told McKenney that he was entangled in the tree's branches when he observed the Indian aiming at him.

16. Interview with Theobald by John Peck, *Kentucky Gazette*, Jan. 23, 1836; Theobald to C.S. Todd, Nov. 27, 1840, Draper Mss., 7YY144; Theobald to B.J. Lossing, Jan. 16, 1861, Draper Mss., 7YY33–43.

17. Wall to Butler, Aug. 30, 1834, Butler, *Commonwealth of Kentucky*, pp. 547–48; Davidson to C.A. Wickliffe, Sept. 7, 1840, *Kentucky Gazette*, Oct. 1, 1840; James Davidson, "Who Killed Tecumseh?", *Historical Magazine* (July, 1866):205.

18. Dudley to C.S. Todd, Sept. 2, 1840, *Scioto Gazette*, Sept. 24, 1840. A.P. Stewart said that his father, an infantryman in Trotter's brigade recalled seeing Johnson retiring badly wounded. His horse collapsed after he was taken down, but the battle continued for at least another thirty minutes. "Recollections of Aura P. Stewart," *MPHC* 4 (1883):331.

19. Affidavit of Knaggs, Sept. 22, 1853, B.F.H. Witherell, "Reminiscences of the Northwest," pp. 313–14.

20. Talcott E. Wing, "History of Monroe County, Michigan," *MPHC* 4 (1883):322; *Toledo Blade*, Apr. 1, 1874, reprinting material from the *Detroit Free Press* supposedly based upon an interview given by Navarre; *Kentucky Gazette*, July 30, Oct. 29, 1840.

21. *Indiana State Journal*, Sept. 20, 1859, reprinted in note to John T. Kingston, "Death of Tecumseh," *Report and Collections of the State Historical Society of Wisconsin* 4 (1859):376.

22. *New York Spectator*, May 14, 1828; *Columbus Sentinel*, Jan. 3, 1832; clipping evidently taken from the *Cleveland Herald*, 1878, Draper Mss., 7YY75.

23. *Cincinnati Daily Gazette*, May 29, 1873; *Cincinnati Times-Star*, July 27, 1886.

24. Navarre told Draper that Tecumseh often visited the Navarre family at their home on the Maumee, giving and receiving presents. Interview with Navarre by Draper (1863), Draper Mss., 17S144–45, 17S148; Bert J. Griswold, *The Pictorial History of Fort Wayne*, p. 222.

25. William Gaines to Draper, Dec. 4, 1881, Draper Mss., 5YY47; Interview with Navarre by Draper (1863), Draper Mss., 17S144–45, 17S148. It is worth mentioning that the original of Trisler's letter has been lost, and that only a typewritten copy remains.

26. Wickliffe, "Tecumseh," p. 47.

27. Davidson, "Who Killed Tecumseh?"

28. Account supplied by the Davidsons to the editor of the *Frankfort Commentator* (1831), Draper Mss., 7YY141; Interview with Mary Logan Smith by Draper (1863), Draper Mss., 18S153; Davidson, "Who Killed Tecumseh?"

29. Benjamin Drake, *Life of Tecumseh and of his Brother the Prophet*, p. 218.

30. William B. Allen lodged with Davidson about 1830 and received from him the story of King's shooting of Tecumseh. As Allen remembered it, King did not use Whitley's gun but had loaded his own weapon with two balls. Moreover, the victim was "not distinguished by his dress from the other Indians . . . ." William B. Allen, *History of Kentucky*, pp. 324–25. It is impossible to set this secondhand version, recalled so late, against Davidson's own narratives. The captain was probably also the informant mentioned by Butler, *Commonwealth of Kentucky*, p. 546, but here it was Tecumseh's tomahawk that King kept as a memento. Davidson was not alone in broadcasting the deed of King. John Booth was reported to have said that King told him how he fired through a bush or a fallen tree to kill an Indian, and W.L. Floyd also claimed to have had King's account of the shooting. Alfred Brunson, *A Western Pioneer, or, Incidents in the Life and Times of Rev. Alfred Brunson*, 1:143; Allen, *Kentucky*, pp. 324–25. Coleman C. Spiller of Simrall's regiment informed W.R. Galt that a red-haired man ("I am very sure that he said that his name was King") pointed out Tecumseh, who lay with two other Indians, as the man he had killed. Galt to Henry B. Dawson, Aug. 15, 1866, "Who Killed Tecumseh?" *Historical Magazine* (Oct. 1866):318.

31. Scribner to B. Drake, Sept. 8, 1840, Draper Mss., 7YY143; Dudley to Drake, Feb. 24, 1841, Drake, *Tecumseh*, pp. 215–16.

32. Charles G. Talbert, "William Whitley, 1749–1813," *Filson Club History Quarterly* 25 (1951):115; Interview with Whitaker by Draper (1863), Draper Mss., 18S141–43.

33. Among accounts recording that Tecumseh and Whitley were discovered close together are Theobald to Lossing, Jan. 16, 1861, Draper Mss., 7YY33–43; Major Nesbitt, cited by Mark Hardin in interview by Draper (1863), Draper Mss., 18S185–86; Interview with George W. Chambers by Draper (1868), Draper Mss., 25S237; Brunson, "Death of Tecumseh," p. 372; "Recollections of Aura P. Stewart," p. 331; Joseph Sullivant, *A Genealogy and Family Memorial*, pp. 316–17.

34. Interview with Joseph Bisseau, a relative of Labadie, by Draper (1863), Draper Mss., 17S174; statement of John S. Herndon, *Louisville Weekly Journal*, Dec. 9, 1859.

35. Thomas D'Arcy McGee, *A History of the Irish Settlers in North America*, p. 103; annotation to John Dorival lithograph of the Battle of

the Thames, registered in 1833 by William Emmons, LOC, print
number LC–USZ62–122 (lot 44131); *Western Citizen*, Dec. 11, 1824;
Cincinnati Daily Gazette, June 6, 1873; Nancy Wright to Draper, Feb.
18, Mar. 4, 1879, Draper Mss., 6YY18–19; Interview with J.S. Whitaker by Draper (1863), Draper Mss., 18S141–43.

36. Jamieson to Draper, Apr. 22, May 2, 1882, Draper Mss.,
7YY68–70. Benson J. Lossing, *The Pictorial Field-book of the War of
1812*, p. 551, credited this chief with commanding the Indian right at
Moraviantown, erroneous information that was probably supplied by
G.H.M. Johnson, an acquaintance of Sha-wah-wan-noo who was interviewed by Lossing in 1860.

37. Shawano to Richardson, Oct. 23, 1848, A.H.U. Colquhoun,
ed., *Tecumseh and Richardson: The Story of a Trip to Walpole Island and Port
Sarnia*, pp. 52–55.

38. Bond Journal, LOC, p. 79; Harrison to John O'Fallon, Apr. 9,
1834, Galloway, *Old Chillicothe*, pp. 160–61; Harrison to Tipton, May 2,
1834, Esarey, *William Henry Harrison*, 2:749–55. Clark's history is
interesting. He was identified by Draper, who obtained a statement of
Andrew's brother, John, and corresponded with the latter's daughter,
Mrs. W.H. Millen. Memorandum of John Clark, Draper Mss., 8YY10;
Mrs. Millen to Draper, May 15, June 8, 11, 1884, Draper Mss., 8YY3,
8YY5–6. John Clark died in December 1865. J.H. Kinzie to Draper,
June 20, 1866, Draper Mss., 8YY11. From these materials it appears
that Shawnees raided the home of Mr. McKenzie on the Kanawha River,
Virginia, and carried off his two daughters, Margaret and Elizabeth,
aged—John Clark says—ten and eight, respectively. Clark's memorandum dates the incident in 1778 and asserts that the girls were adopted in
the family of Tecumseh at Piqua. Mrs. Millen, prompted by Draper,
could only admit to a "faint recollection" of hearing her father refer to the
Indians who adopted the girls as relatives to Tecumseh. A later historian
maintained that Isaac McKenzie's home was possibly attacked as early as
1774 and that "the girls were carried captive to the great village of the
tribe, at Chillicothe, where they were kept in charge of the chief." A.T.
Andreas, *History of Chicago*, 1:73. Piqua and Chillicothe, it must be said,
were the head towns of different bands of Shawnee to neither of which
Tecumseh belonged.

Both girls remained on the frontier and married British traders.
Margaret bore three children to John Kinzie, while Elizabeth married

John Clark, by whom she produced two sons and a daughter. These last were John Clark, born about June, 1782, and Andrew and Sarah, twins, about five years later. In 1797, after the Treaty of Greenville, Mr. McKenzie (named by Milo M. Quaife as Moredock O. McKenzie) visited the West and was reunited with his daughters. He returned to Virginia with both of them and Elizabeth's children, John and Sarah, the latter only a few months old. Andrew stayed with the Indians and supposedly acted as aide and intepreter to Tecumseh at Moraviantown. Both Margaret and Elizabeth remarried after their return to the East, the former to Benjamin Hall, and the latter to Jonas Clybourne. Elizabeth eventually died in Laporte County, Indiana, at the home of her daughter, then Mrs. Willliam Eahart. Her son John also moved West and became an Indian trader about Chicago. J. H. Kinzie, *Wau-Bun, The 'Early Day' in the North-West*, ed. Milo M. Quaife, pp. xxix–xxxvi, xlii–xlvii; Milo M. Quaife, *Chicago and the Old North-west, 1673–1835*, pp. 146–47, which suggests further references. The John Clark memorandum contains a story of Tecumseh's death that was said to have been transmitted by a half-brother of Andrew who had also been at Moraviantown. It tells how the chief was mortally wounded and fell upon his hands and knees before he was dispatched by a Kentucky horseman.

Andrew Clark's attachment to Tecumseh survived difficulties between the chief and John Kinzie, probably the same who married Clark's aunt. Kinzie was employed by the British Indian Department in 1813, but was discovered by Tecumseh "to be acting a treacherous part with the Indians who told General Procter in council that if he was not hung the Indians themselves would put him to death." Kinzie was charged with corresponding with the enemy and misleading the Indians and was sent to Quebec in irons. Evidence of Captain Nelson of the schooner *Vermillion* and of Michel Coursolle, British Court of Inquiry, Oct. 1815, *MPHC* 16 (1890):331, 333.

39. Warfield to Todd, Nov. 27, 1840, Draper Mss., 2YY199.

40. Brunson, "Death of Tecumseh," pp. 371–72.

41. Brunson, *Western Pioneer*, 1:140–41; Brunson to Draper, May 1, 1882, Draper Mss., 7YY30–31.

42. Dudley to Drake, Feb. 24, 1841, Drake, *Tecumseh*, pp. 215–16. Brunson suggests that remarks passed by Clark indirectly led the Kentuckians to Tecumseh's body. The privilege of claiming that Clark specifically identified Tecumseh was reserved for yet another statement,

and that the least meritorious of the whole. Sullivant, whose father received an account from Captain James Coleman in 1823, alleged that Coleman found young Clark, a wounded Indian, sitting by a tree He was asked the name of a nearby warrior "lying on his face, who, from his dress, we thought might be a chief . . . ," and answered that it was Tecumseh. Sullivant, *Genealogy*, pp. 316–17. Unfortunately, Tecumseh was discovered on the fifth not on the sixth when Clark was located, and the Shawnee's outfit was not so pretentious that it would have attracted notice.

43. Caleb Atwater, *Remarks Made on a Tour to Prairie du Chien . . . in 1829*, p. 119.

44. Caleb Atwater, *A History of the State of Ohio*, p. 236.

45. *Army and Navy Chronicle* 7 (1838):295–96, reprinted from the *Baltimore American*.

46. Benson J. Lossing, "Was Tecumtha Skinned?", 1:285.

47. Brunson to Draper, Apr. 26, 1882, Draper Mss., 7YY29; William Gaines to Draper, Apr. 26, 1882, Draper Mss., 7YY71.

48. Trowbridge to Draper, Mar. 14, 1874, Draper Mss., 5YY6; G.C. Johnston to Draper, July 28, 1874, Draper Mss., 11YY2; A.H. Edwards to J. Wentworth, June 10, 1881, John Wentworth, *Early Chicago: Fort Dearborn: An Address*, pp. 56–59.

49. Interview with Captain Caldwell by Draper (1863), Draper Mss., 17S224–27.

50. Peter D. Clarke, *Origin and Traditional History of the Wyandotts*, p. 114; letter to Draper, Apr. 17, 1874, Draper Mss., 9YY27. James A. Clifton has shown that Billy Caldwell romanticized his military career in his later years. He said, for example, that he had helped to rescue the Kinzie family after a massacre near Fort Dearborn in 1813, but contemporary records do not sustain the claim.

51. Caldwell certificate, William Hickling, "Caldwell and Shabonee," *Addresses Delivered at the Annual Meeting of the Chicago Historical Society . . . 1868 . . . Together with . . . Sketches of Billy Caldwell and Shabonee*, p. 29; John Wentworth, *Early Chicago: A Lecture, Delivered . . . on . . . April 11, 1875*, pp. 22–23.

52. *Army and Navy Chronicle* 6 (1838):349–50.

53. *Kentucky Gazette*, Jan. 30, 1840.

54. Kingston, "Death of Tecumseh."

55. Perry Armstrong, *The Sauks and the Black Hawk War*, p. 576; Armstrong to Draper, Dec. 23, 1881, Draper Mss., 9YY71.

56. Hickling to Draper, Sept. 1, Oct. 13, 1875, Draper Mss., 9YY109–11.

57. Hunt to C. C. Trowbridge, Mar. 13, 1874, Draper Mss., 5YY7; Interview with Hunt by Draper (1866), Draper Mss., 21S70.

58. Hubbard to Draper, Sept. 4, 1875, Draper Mss., 9YY104.

59. Gordon S. Hubbard, "Col. G.S. Hubbard's Narrative," *Addresses Delivered at the Annual Meeting of the Chicago Historical Society . . . 1868 . . . Together with . . . Sketches of Billy Caldwell and Shabonee*, p. 41.

60. Hickling, "Caldwell and Shabonee," p. 36.

61. Chamblee and Billy Caldwell to Harrison's friends, Mar. 23, 1840, Wentworth, *Fort Dearborn*, p. 61. Forsyth's son, Robert, heard Shabbona and his brother inform Forsyth that a rider of a dun or elk-colored horse shot Tecumseh, but this was in Peoria in the spring of 1824. Shabbona may have frequently visited Forsyth. Interview with Forsyth by Draper (1868), Draper Mss., 22S106–07.

62. Forsyth to Ninian Edwards, Mar. 31, 1816, Reuben G. Thwaites, ed., "Letter Book of Thomas Forsyth, 1814–1818," *Collections of the State Historical Society of Wisconsin* 11 (1888): 345–47. Nesscottin-nemeg or Nuscotomeg (Bad Sturgeon) was a belligerent Potawatomi war chief from the junction of the Iroquois and Kankakee rivers, a brother-in-law to Main Poc. He was held responsible for the murder of Captain William T. Cole's party on Salt Creek (July 20, 1810) and of two families near Vincennes in the spring of 1811. Wounded during the capture of the Fort Dearborn garrison in the following year, he was said to have stolen thirty horses from the Vincennes area in the winter of 1813–14. Forsyth to Edwards, July 5, 1814, Thwaites, "Letter Book," pp. 320–23; R David Edmunds, *The Potawatomis: Keepers of the Fire*, p. 185–87.

63. Drake, *Tecumseh*, p. 200. An interesting sequel to this story reposes in a letter of Maria Harlan, whose father, she said, participated in the Battle of the Thames. He was Daniel Kenshalo, who died in 1872. Harlan had it that her father claimed to have been fighting Tecumseh hand-to-hand and had been struck in the arm by the chief's tomahawk. As the axe was raised for a second blow, Tecumseh, a man fully six feet with a high forehead and piercing black eyes, was shot from close by and fell against Kenshalo. Harlan to Draper, June 30, 1884, Draper Mss., 7YY122.

64. The conversation was recalled by a mixed-blood Ottawa, Alexander Robinson. Interview with Robinson by Draper (1866), Draper Mss., 21S278–79.

65. Foster to Draper, Dec. 9, 30, 1884, Draper Mss., 7YY19–20.

66. Bourassa interviewed by Draper (1868), Draper Mss., 23S185–89.

67. The medal believed to have been taken from Tecumseh's body could long be seen at the Museum of the Mint in Philadelphia. An inventory described it as a silver disk, three inches in diameter, inscribed with the crest and arms of Britain on one side and a bust of George III with the words *Georgius III Dei Gratia* on the reverse. James Ross Snowden, *A Description of the Medals of Washington . . . in the Museum of the Mint*, p. 118. Such medals were issued in the period between the Revolution and the War of 1812 and are depicted in Melvill Allan Jamieson, *Medals Awarded to North American Indian Chiefs, 1714–1922*.

68. Nehemiah Matson, who knew Shabbona in 1836, pirates other accounts for his *Memories of Shaubena*, pp. 26–29.

69. Cook to the editor, Dec. 24, 1884, "The Death of Tecumseh," *The Century Magazine* 30 (1885):332; Cook to Draper, 1889, Draper Mss., 7YY3.

70. Letter from Sangamo, Illinois, Jan. 11, 1824, *Western Citizen*, Feb. 7, 1824.

71. Drake, *Tecumseh*, 201; McKenney, *Memoirs*, 1:181–82.

72. William Oliver to Drake, Dec. 23, 1840, Drake, *Tecumseh*, pp. 218–19; Interview with John M. Ruddell by Draper (1868), Draper Mss., 22S51–52.

73. Carl F. Klinck and James T. Talman, eds., *The Journal of Major John Norton 1816*, p. 343.

74. Wickliffe, "Tecumseh," pp. 47–49.

75. Interview with Whitaker by Draper (1863), Draper Mss., 18S141–43.

76. Harrison to Tipton, May 2, 1834, Esarey, *William Henry Harrison*, 2:749–55; Harrison to O'Fallon, Apr. 9, 1834, Galloway, *Old Chillicothe*, pp. 160–61; account of Harrison's officers, Draper Mss., 7YY146–47; J. Scott Harrison to Draper, June 30, 1873, Draper Mss., 7YY74. Lieutenant Stephen Clever told T.S. Woodward that Tecumseh was found at least three hundred yards from where Johnson had been shot. Harrison had the body washed and identified it by the uneven length of the legs, the smallness of the foot on the shorter limb, and a bluish cast of one of the teeth. Woodward to J.J. Hooper, Oct. 20, 1858, *Woodward's Reminiscences of the Creek, or Muscogee Indians*, pp. 82–88. The general is

also said to have recognized Tecumseh by a burn scar received as a boy the length of his left hip (interview with Pierre Navarre by Draper [1863], Draper Mss., 17S144–45, 17S148; *Toledo Blade*, Apr. 1, 1874) and by a wound in the wrist obtained at Chatham and a scar on the face (Samuel Boone interview by Draper [1868], Draper Mss., 22S265–67). All of these accounts are demonstrably confused. Tecumseh was apparently injured in the arm, not the wrist, at Chatham; and while attempts were made to identify him by leg wounds, they related to a thigh he had broken as a young man and possibly to an injury he sustained at the battle of Monguagon in 1812.

77. Wall to Butler, Aug. 30, 1834, Butler, *Commonwealth of Kentucky*, pp. 547–48. Shane is generally described as a mixed-blood Shawnee, but John Johnston, Indian agent at Fort Wayne, thought that his mother was an Ottawa. He later emigrated to the West and during the last four years of his life served as interpreter to the Shawnees. He died on June 11, 1834. McAfee, *Late War*, p. 378; Johnston to Draper, Apr. 27, 1849; May 23, 1852, Draper Mss., 11YY37, 11YY42; Richard W. Cummins to Butler, Oct. 27, 1834, Butler, *Commonwealth of Kentucky*, p. 547.

78. Interview with Shane by Drake (1821), Draper Mss., 2YY57; Emmons, *Johnson*, p. 37.

79. Theobald to Todd, Nov. 27, 1840, Draper Mss., 7YY144; Theobald to Lossing, Jan. 16, 1861, Draper Mss., 7YY33–43.

80. Interview with Thomas and Arrowsmith by Draper (1858), Draper Mss., 7S143–44, 8S46–47; Interview with Francis Cassidy by Draper (1866), Draper Mss., 21S186; George Randall to Draper, Sept. 2, 185? Draper Mss., 5BB46; Edna Kenton, *Simon Kenton: His Life and Period, 1755–1836*, p. 285.

81. F.M. Finch to Draper, June 8, 1891, Draper Mss., 8YY18; Statement of R.J. Conner, June 19–20, 1891, Draper Mss., 8YY21; Conner to Draper, Aug. 18, 1887, Draper Mss., 8YY32; Charles N. Thompson, *Sons of the Wilderness: John and William Conner*.

82. *Western Citizen*, Nov. 19, 1831.

83. Robert B. Duncan to Draper, June 9, 1887, Draper Mss., 8YY27.

84. William James, *A Full and Correct Account of the Military Occurrences of the Late War Between Great Britain and the United States of America*, 1:294.

85. Harrison to Tipton, May 2, 1834; Esarey, *William Henry Harrison*, 2:749–55.

86. Interview with O'Fallon by Draper (1851), Draper Mss., 5S85.

87. John Richardson, *Richardson's War of 1812*, pp. 212–14; Interview with David Todd by Draper (1851), Draper Mss., 5S80.

88. Cochran Notes, p. 124; Cochran Narrative, pp. 64–65.

89. Warburton, PCM, p. 43.

90. Gaines to Draper, Apr. 26, 1882, Draper Mss., 7YY71; Gaines to Draper, Nov. 25, Dec. 4, 1881, Draper Mss., 5YY46–47.

91. Samuel Baker in the *Cincinnati Times-Star*, July 27, 1886; Gaines to Draper, Nov. 25, 1881, Apr. 26, 1882, Draper Mss., 5YY46, 7YY71; Interview with Bentley by Draper (1863), Draper Mss., 17S178–79; Interview with Thomas Shelby, son of Isaac Shelby, by Draper (1863), Draper Mss., 18S228–29; Dudley to Drake, Feb. 24, 1841, Drake, *Tecumseh*, pp. 215–16.

92. James Mason to J.M. McCalla, Oct. 13, 1840, *Kentucky Gazette*, Nov. 12, 1840; Interview with Bentley by Draper (1863), Draper Mss., 17S178–79.

93. George Williams map, Aug. 9, 1814, PAC H2/410/Thames/1814.

94. Gaines, Dr. Benjamin Logan, and Isaac Thomas believed that the head wounds were the result of bullets. Interview with Logan by Draper (1863), Draper Mss., 18S177; Interview with Thomas by Draper (1858), Draper Mss., 7S143–44. The former also claimed that part of the hip was shot away. Pierre Navarre informed Draper that the body was bullet-ridden, tomahawked, and bayoneted in the face. Interview with Navarre by Draper (1863), Draper Mss., 17S144–45, 17S148.

95. Samuel Baker said that a Colonel Miller identified Tecumseh by a scar on his right calf, the product of a wound received in a battle variously given as Brownstown (1812) and Fort Meigs (1813). Inasmuch as Tecumseh was thought to have been injured at Monguagon, there may be some truth in Baker's story. *Cincinnati Daily Gazette*, May 29, 1873; *Cincinnati Times-Star*, July 27, 1886.

96. Brunson, "Death of Tecumseh," p. 372; account of a soldier, Elkins, reprinted from the *Mobile Register* of 1852 by Lossing, "Was Tecumtha Skinned?"

97. *Cleveland Herald Supplement*, Nov. 18, 1871. Sanderson's material is manifestly inaccurate. His comment that Tecumseh "was a man of huge

frame, powerfully built, and . . . about six feet two inches in height" is as fallacious as his description of Isaac Brock, a British general, as "the ugliest officer I ever saw."

7

An Epilogue: 1813–1815

1. Chambers, PCM, p. 87; Bullock, PCM, p. 119; Gilmore, PCM, p. 183; Le Breton, PCM, pp. 174–75.

2. Harrison to Armstrong, Oct. 9, 1813, Logan Esarey, ed., *Messages and Letters of William Henry Harrison*, 2:558–65.

3. Return of the Right Division, Nov. 10, 1813, PCM, pp. 430–32.

4. Printed return, CP 42/152:59.

5. A.C. Whitehorne, *The History of the Welch Regiment*, pp. 106–07.

6. R. Gourlay, *Statistical Account of Upper Canada*, pp. 140–41.

7. Elliott to Claus, Oct. 24, 1813, PAC MG 19/fl/10:111–13

8. Return of the western Indians, Oct. 26, 1813, PAC RG 8, C681:9–10; P.B. Porter to Harrison, Nov. 3, 1813, Harrison Papers, LOC.

9. Baynes, General Orders, Nov 24, 1813, William Wood, ed., *Select British Documents of the Canadian War of 1812*, 2:294–97.

10. The prosecution witnesses were Warburton, Evans, Muir, Chambers, Hill, Bullock, Fitzgerald, Bent, and White of the Forty-first; Dixon of the Royal Engineers; Troughton of the Royal Artillery; Holmes and Coleman of the Canadian Light Dragoons; Billy Caldwell of the Indian Department; and Assistant Commissary Gilmore. Caldwell, Gilmore, and Holmes also appeared for the defense, along with Crowther, McLean, Brooks, and Grant of the Forty-first; Captain William and Colonel William Caldwell, Jones and Fraser of the Indian Department; Lamb of the Royal Artillery; Lefevre and Benac of the Canadian Light Dragoons; Le Breton of the Royal Newfoundland Regiment; La Rocque of the Canadian Chasseurs; Hall of the Canadian Fencibles; Talbot, Baby, and Dolsen of the militia; Wood, clerk of the ordnance stores, and Richard Pattinson.

11. Bathurst to the Duke of York, Feb. 21, 1814, PAC RG 8, C682:132–34; Duke of York to Prevost, Feb. 22, 1814, PAC RG 8, C682:135–37.

12. PCM, pp. 2–5.

13. PCM, pp. 323–27.

14. Shelby to his wife, Oct. 1, 1813, Shelby Papers, vol. 4, LOC; Armstrong to Harrison, Sept. 22, 1813, Esarey, *William Henry Harrison*, 2:544–45; McArthur to Armstrong, Oct. 6, 1813, Sec. of War, LR, Unreg.

15. Bathurst to Prevost, Dec. 27, 1813, CO 43/23:137–39.

16. Cass to Armstrong, Oct. 21, Nov. 28, 1813, Sec. of War, LR, Reg.

17. Cass to Armstrong, Dec. 17, 1813, Sec. of War, LR, Reg.

18. Lieutenant Henry Medcalf to H. Bostwick, Dec. 25, 1813, PAC RG 8, C682: 44–48; Drummond to Noah Freer, Feb. 14, Sept. 5, 19, 1814, PAC RG 8, C682:111–13, C685:168–69, 208–10; Drummond to Prevost, Mar. 5, 1814, PAC RG 8, C682:157–62; Drummond to Prevost, June 7, 1814, Wood, *British Documents*, 3:106; Captain Alexander Stewart to Major General P. Riall, Mar. 5, 6, 1814, PAC RG 8, C682:184–85, 188–89, 191; Basden to Stewart, Mar. 13, 1814, Wood, *British Documents*, 2:352–54; Holmes to Captain R. Butler, Mar. 10, 1814, Esarey, *William Henry Harrison*, 2:632–36; Thomas Talbot to Riall, May 16, 1814, Wood, *British Documents*, 3:88–90; John Bostwick to commander at Long Point, Nov. 3, 1814; PAC RG 8, C686:13: Major General L. de Watteville to J. Harvey, Nov. 10, 1814, PAC RG 8, C686:181–83; Captain P.L. Chambers to de Watteville, Nov. 10, 1814, PAC RG 8, C686:187; Lieutenant-Colonel W. James to Harvey, Nov. 21, 1814, PAC RG 8. C686:190–93; Drummond to Yeo, Nov. 13, 1814, Wood, *British Documents*, 3: 290–91; J.I. Poole, "The Fight at Battle Hill," reprinted in Morris Zaslow and Wesley B. Turner, eds., *The Defended Border: Upper Canada and the War of 1812*, pp. 130–42.

19. Armstrong to Harrison, Dec. 29, 1813, Jan. 1, 1814, Esarey, *William Henry Harrison*, 2:612–15.

20. Drummond to Prevost, Mar. 5, 1814; PAC RG 8, C682:163–69.

21. Chambers to de Watteville, Nov. 10, 1814, PAC RG 8, C686:187.

22. Drummond to Prevost, Dec. 22, 1813, Wood, *British Documents*, 2:500–05.

23. Drummond to Prevost, Jan. 21, 1814, CO 42/156:77–81; Drummond to Prevost, Feb. 19, 1814, PAC RG 8, C682:120–22.

24. Lieutenant Colonel R. Nichol to Drummond, May 30, 1814,

PAC RG 8, C683:251–54; Drummond to Prevost, June 7, Nov. 9, 1814, Wood, *British Documents*, 3:92–93, 245–48; Drummond to Freer, Nov. 14, 1814, ibid., 3:289–90.

25. Bullock to Freer, Feb. 26, 1814, Wood, *British Documents*, 3:268–70; Bullock to Freer, Oct. 23, Dec. 30, 1813, PAC RG 8, C680:255–58, C681:331–33; McDouall to Drummond, May 26, 1814, Wood, *British Documents*, 3:271–73; McDouall to Prevost, July 20, 1814, CO 42/157:130–31; Drummond to Prevost, Jan. 19, July 2, 1814, PAC RG 8, C682:27–28, C257:295–97; Drummond to Prevost, Jan. 28, Nov. 9, 1814, Wood, *British Documents*, 3:266–68, 245–48; Prevost to Bathurst, July 10, 1814, CO 42/157:7–9; Bathurst to Prevost, Dec. 5, 1813, PAC RG 8, C681:197–206; Dickson to Freer, Jan. 17, 1815, PAC RG 8, C258:4–8.

26. McDouall to Drummond, July 17, Sept, 9, 1814, PAC RG 8, C685:66–69, CO 42/157:244–45; McDouall to Freer, Aug. 14, 1814, CO 42/157:195–98; G. Crookshank to Major General Grant, Aug. 21, 1814, PAC RG 8, C685:143–44: A.H. Bulger to McDouall, Sept. 7, 1814, CO 42/157:246–48. McDouall subsequently became a major general and died on November 15, 1848.

27. Dickson to Freer, Oct. 23, 1813, PAC RG 8, C257:162–63; Bullock to Freer, Feb. 26, 1814, Wood, *British Documents*, 3:268–70; Dickson's correspondence in "Dickson and Grignon Papers, 1812–1815," *Collections of the State Historical Society of Wisconsin* 11 (1888):271–315.

28. McDouall to Drummond, July 16, 1814, Wood, *British Documents*, 3:253–56; McKay to McDouall, July 27, 1814, ibid., 3:257–65. Thomas G. Anderson, who commanded some volunteers in the expedition to Prairie du Chien, provided a retrospect impression in which he claimed extravagant credit for himself. "Personal Narrative of Capt. Thomas G. Anderson," *Report and Collections of the State Historical Society of Wisconsin* 9 (1882):193–96. Fort Madison, an American post on the Mississippi some miles above the mouth of the Des Moines, was evacuated after Indian attack in 1813. It was not rebuilt, and Fort Clark was erected in its stead.

29. Parke to T. Posey, Nov. 18, 1814, Esarey, *William Henry Harrison*, 2:670–72.

30. McDouall to Bulger, Feb. 26, 1815, "The Bulger Papers," *Collections of the State Historical Society of Wisconsin* 13 (1895):94–97.

31. Elliott to J.B. Glegg, Jan. 31, 1814, PAC RG 8, C682:100–03b.

32. Returns of western Indians, Mar. 4, June 7–14, 22, July 20, Oct. 11, 1814, Jan. 14, 1815, PAC RG 10, 28:16710, 16995, 17033–34; 29:17126; 3:1526; 30:17584.

33. William Claus to Edward McMahon, Nov. 4, 1813, PAC RG 8, C257:176–77; speech of the Shawnee King, Nov. 21, 1814, PAC RG 10, 29:17384–85; speech of Tenskwatawa, 1814, PAC RG 10, 29:17518–21.

34. Return of troops under J. Murray, Dec. 12, 1813, PAC RG 8, C681:237; J. Harvey to Elliott, Dec. 17, 1813, Wood, *British Documents*, 2:484; Drummond to Prevost, Dec. 18, 20, 22, 1813, ibid., 2:486–88, 492–93, 500–05; Riall to Drummond, Jan 1, 1814, PAC RG 8, C682:5–8; Charles Askin Diary, "Askin Papers," *MPHC* 32 (1903):513–15.

35. Elliott to Glegg, Jan. 31, 1814, PAC RG 8, C682:100–03b.

36. C.L.L. Foster to Claus, Jan. 3, 1814, PAC RG 10, 28:16633–34; Claus to Foster, Feb. 14, 1814, PAC RG 10, 28:16693; Drummond to Freer, Feb. 5, 16, 1814, PAC RG 8, C257:211–12, 217–19; John Fergusson to Claus, Oct. 1814, PAC RG 10, 29:17327; Claus, Dec. 8, 1815, PAC RG 10, 4:1839; Post's petition, Dec. 2, 1815, with receipts, PAC RG 10, 4:1841–42, 1845–48; *Quebec Gazette*, Mar. 17, 1814. Since much nonsense has been written about Tecumseh's immediate relations, it is worth mentioning that the chief had but one full sister (Tecumapeace) and one son (Paukeesaa).

37. *Quebec Gazette*, Mar. 24, 1814; speech of Prevost, PAC RG 10, 12:10308–12.

38. Freer to R.R. Loring, Apr. 12, 1814, PAC RG 10, 3:1327–29; Foster to Claus, Apr. 12, 1814, PAC RG 10, 28:16782–83; James Givens to Claus, May 21, 1814, PAC RG 10, 28:16892–94; William Caldwell and Ironside to Claus, Oct. 22, 1814, PAC RG 10, 29:17306–08; list of presents given in Montreal, March to April, 1814, PAC RG 8, C257:230; *Montreal Gazette*, Apr. 5, 1814.

39. Elliott to Claus, Feb. 24, 1814, PAC RG 10, 28:16701–02; Ironside to Claus, Mar. 2, 1814, PAC RG 10, 28:16707–08; Elliott to Alexander Stewart, Mar. 4, 1814, PAC RG 8, C682:190; Stewart to Riall, Mar. 11, 1814, PAC RG 8, C682:208–10; Basden to Stewart, Mar. 13, 1814, Wood, *British Documents*, 2:352–54; John Le Breton to Foster, Mar. 8/10, 1814, ibid., 2:354–56.

40. Drummond to Prevost, Apr. 13, 19, 1814, PAC RG 8, C683:30–33, C257:233–36.

41. Indian council, May 20, 1814, PAC RG 10, 3:1376–84; Givens to Claus, May 11, 15, 21, 1814, PAC RG 10, 28:16862–63, 16872, 16892–94; Lieutenant Colonel W. James to Foster, Mar. 11, 1815, PAC RG 10, 4:1692–94.

42. Freer to Drummond, Mar. 1, 1814, PAC RG 10, 3:1299–1301; Freer to Loring, July 9, 1814, PAC RG 10, 3:1463–64; Claus to Loring, June 22, 1814, PAC RG 10, 3:1416–18; Caldwell to Claus, June 22, 1814, PAC RG 10, 28:17030–31; returns of the Indians, June 14, 1814, PAC RG 10, 28:16995; speech of Naiwash, June 14, 1814; PAC RG 8, C257:303–04. Colonel William Caldwell became deputy superintendent of the Indian Department after the death of Elliott. The obvious alternative to the latter, Thomas McKee, was in poor health and had a drinking problem; he died on October 20, 1814. Drummond to Prevost, Mar. 31, 1814, PAC RG 8, C682:285–88.

43. Loring to Claus, May 21, June 7, 1814, PAC RG 10, 28:16896, 16950–53; Indian speeches, May 30, 1814, PAC RG 10, 28:16913, 16915–16; extract of letter of Givens, May 30, 1814, PAC RG 10, 28:16932–33; return of the western Indians, June 22, 1814, PAC RG 10, 28:17033–34; Glegg to Caldwell, June 16, 1814; PAC RG 10, 3:1408; Drummond to Prevost, July 10, 1814, Wood, *British Documents*, 3:120–23; Riall to Drummond July 6, 1814, ibid., 3:115–20; diary of Captain W.H. Merritt, ibid., 3:614.

44. Caldwell to Claus, July 2, 1814, PAC RG 10, 29:17082; Glegg to Caldwell, July 1, 1814, PAC RG 10, 29:17083; Loring to Caldwell, July 7, 1814, PAC RG 10, 29:17090–91; Carl F. Klinck and James T. Talman, eds., *The Journal of Major John Norton, 1816*, p. 352; Drummond to Prevost, July 13, 1814, PAC RG 8, C684:90–93.

45. Riall to Caldwell, July 12, 1814, PAC RG 10, 29:17096; Ironside to Duncan Cameron, July 15, 1814, PAC RG 10, 29:17114–15; Riall to Drummond, July 19, 1814, PAC RG 8, C684:179; Drummond to Prevost, Aug. 21 1814, PAC RG 8, C685:123–28; Klinck and Talman, *John Norton*, pp. 356–57, 363–64.

46. Speech of Naiwash Oct. 6, 1814, PAC RG 10, 29:17250–52.

47. Report of Waanoos, Ottawa chief, Oct. 11, 1814, PAC RG 10, 29:17265–66; Ironside to Claus, Oct. 28, 1814, PAC RG 10, 29:17316; return of the Indians, Nov. 1, 1814, PAC RG 10, 29:17328; Elliott to Claus, Oct. 14, 1814, PAC RG 10, 29:17271–72.

48. Drummond's reply to Naiwash, Nov. 2, 1814, PAC RG 10, 3:1570–72; letter of Lieutenant Colonel W. Smelt, Nov. 8, 1814, PAC RG 8, C686:165–69; Drummond to Yeo, Nov. 13, 1814, Wood, *British Documents*, 3:290–91.

49. Samuel R. Brown, *An Authentic History of the Second War for Independence*, 1:138–39.

50. McArthur to Armstrong, Oct. 6, 1813, Sec. of War, LR, Unreg.

51. Harrison to Armstrong, Oct. 10, 16, 1813, Esarey, *William Henry Harrison*, 2:573–75; 579–81; armistice, Oct. 14, 1813, ibid., 2:577–79.

52. Armstrong to Harrison, Dec. 29, 1813, Esarey, *William Henry Harrison*, 2:612–15; Cass to Armstrong, Oct. 21, 28, Dec. 17, 1813, Sec. of War, LR, Reg.

53. Cass to Armstrong, Dec. 4, 1813, Sec. of War, LR. Reg.

54. Elliott to Glegg, Jan. 31, 1814, PAC RG 8, C682:100–03b; Drummond to Prevost, Dec. 22, 1813, Wood, *British Documents*, 2:500–05.

55. Elliott to Claus, Mar. 25, 1814, PAC RG 10, 28:16747–50; Ojibwa message, Mar. 27, 1814, PAC RG 10, 28:16752—53; William Claus, May 14, 1814, PAC RG 8, C683:186–87; Drummond to Prevost, Apr. 13, May 31, 1814, PAC RG 8, C683:30–33, 209–18.

56. Speech of Ottawa chief, May 20, 1814, records of Indian council, PAC RG 10, 3:1376–84.

57. George C. Chalou, "The Red Pawns Go To War: British-American Indian Relations, 1810–15," Ph.D. diss., Indiana University, 1971, pp. 327–29.

58. Forsyth to Ninian Edwards, Mar. 31, 1816, Reuben G. Thwaites, ed., "Letter Book of Thomas Forsyth, 1814–1818," *Collections of the State Historical Society of Wisconsin* II (1888): 345–47: McDouall to Bulger, Feb. 26, 1815, "The Bulger Papers," pp. 94–97; Joseph Barron to Thomas Posey, Nov. 12, 1814, Esarey, *William Henry Harrison*, 2:666–67; R. David Edmunds, *The Potawatomis: Keepers of the Fire*, pp. 198–205; minutes of Indian councils at Michillimackinac, Oct. 28, 1814, Jan. 29, 1815, PAC RG 10, 29:17302–04, 30:17658–60.

59. Speech of Little Crow, CO 42/157:12–13.

60. Bulger to McDouall, Nov. 14, Dec. 30, 1814, "Bulger Papers," pp: 20–22, 25–35.

61. Dickson to Lieutenant John Lawe, Jan. 23, Feb. 4, Mar. 31, 1814, "Dickson and Grignon Papers," pp. 285–87, 289–92, 300–02.

62. Speech of McDouall to Indians at Michillimackinac, June 5, 1814, CO 42/157:15–18.

63. McDouall to Bulger, Feb. 18, 1815, "Bulger Papers," pp. 74–78.

64. McDouall to Freer, Aug. 14, 1814, CO 42/157:195–98.

65. McDouall to Drummond, July 16, 1814, Wood, *British Documents*, 3:253–56; McKay to McDouall, July 27, 1814, ibid., 3:257–65. McDouall's estimate of Teté de Chien, which Prevost passed to Bathurst, was inaccurate, for Bulger later looked him up and reported that he was "thought to be a worthless fellow & has very little influence over his nation." Bulger to McDouall, Dec. 30, 1814, "Bulger Papers," pp. 25–35; Prevost to Bathurst, Aug. 2, 1814, CO 42/157:97–99.

66. William T. Hagan, *The Sac and Fox Indians*, contains a thorough account of this phase of the warfare.

67. Anderson to McDouall, Aug. 29, Sept. 4, 1814, "Capt. T.G. Anderson's Journal, 1814," *Report and Collections of the State Historical Society of Wisconsin* 9 (1882): 220–21, 230–32; Graham to Anderson, Sept. 3, 7, 1814, ibid., pp. 224–28.

68. McDouall to officer commanding Fort McKay, Aug. 21, 1814, "Anderson's Journal," pp. 228–30.

69. A.M. Gibson, *The Kickapoos, Lords of the Middle Border*, pp. 74–75.

70. Brock to Liverpool, Aug. 29, 1812, Wood, *British Documents*, 1:506–09; Brock to Prevost, Sept, 18, 28, 1812, ibid., 1:592–94, 596–98; Prevost to Bathurst, Oct. 5, 1812, CO 42/147:207–11; Bathurst to Prevost, Dec. 9, 1812, June 3, 1814, CO 42/147:237–41, CO 43/23:150–55; correspondence printed in *Kingston Gazette*, Oct. 16, 1813.

71. For the Treaty of Ghent, see Frank A. Updyke, *The Diplomacy of the War of 1812*; Charles M. Gates, "The West in American Diplomacy, 1812–1815," *Mississippi Valley Historical Review* 26 (1940):499–510; G.G. Hatheway, "The Neutral Indian Barrier State," Ph.D. diss., University of Minnesota, 1957; Frederick Louis Engelman, *The Peace of Christmas Eve*; and Bradford Perkins, *Castlereagh and Adams: England and the United States, 1812–1823*.

72. McDouall to Bulger, Feb. 26, 1815, "Bulger Papers," pp. 94–97; speech of McDouall to the Indians, ibid., pp. 97–100; Prevost to Drummond, Oct. 27, 1814, PAC RG 10, 3:1558–59.

73. Bathurst to Prevost, Dec. 27, 1814, PAC MG 19/f1/10:145, 147–48.

74. Prevost to Drummond, Mar. 4, 1815, PAC RG 10, 4:1667–68; speech of Prevost, Mar. 1815, PAC RG 10, 4:1669–71; Claus to Loring, Mar. 21, 30, 1815, PAC RG 10, 4:1714–15, 1739–40; speech of Claus, PAC RG 10, 4:1716–19; speeches at Burlington, Apr. 24–27, 1815, PAC RG 10, 12:10557–69.

75. McDouall to Bulger, May 1, Mar. 19, Apr. 25, 1815, "Bulger Papers," pp. 135–39, 118–22, 133–34; Bulger to McDouall, June 19, 1815, ibid., 149–51; Bulger to Governor William Clark or officer commanding at Saint Louis, May 23, 1815, Douglas Brymner, "Capture of Fort M'Kay, Prairie du Chien, in 1814," *Collections of the State Historical Society of Wisconsin* 11 (1888):259–60.

76. The best account of the sink-hole affair can be found in Frank E. Stevens, *The Black Hawk War*, pp. 55–57.

77. Caldwell, instructions, May 1815, PAC RG 10, 30:17904–05.

Appendix
The Dispute Over Tecumseh's Burial

1. Gaines to Draper, Apr. 26, 1882, Draper Mss., 7YY71; T.K. Holmes to Draper, Apr. 20, 1882, Draper Mss., 7YY67; Interview with Pierre Navarre by Draper (1863), Draper Mss., 17S144–45, 17S148; *Toledo Commercial*, Mar. 21, 1874.

2. Thaddeus S. Arnold, "Battle of the Thames and Death of Tecumseh," *Annual Transactions of the United Empire Loyalists Association of Ontario, 1901–02* 4 (1903):32–33.

3. Benson J. Lossing, *The Pictorial Field-book of the War of 1812*, p. 560; Katherine B. Coutts, "Thamesville and the Battle of the Thames," (1908), reprinted in Morris Zaslow and Wesley B. Turner, eds., *The Defended Border: Upper Canada and the War of 1812*, p. 119; Norman St. Clair Gurd, *The Story of Tecumseh*, p. 181. Every Shawnee belonged to a clan with its animal totem. Tecumseh, it should be noted, was a member of the panther, not the turtle, clan.

4. Arnold, "Battle of the Thames," p. 33.

5. *Toronto Globe*, Sept. 3, 1913.

6. William B. Allen, *A History of Kentucky*, p. 324; Colin C. Ironside to Draper, May 4, 1885, Draper Mss., 7YY76.

7. *Columbus Sentinel*, Jan. 3, 1832. B.B. Thatcher and George Jones, among others, copied the story.

8. John Charles Dent, "Tecumseh," *The Canadian Portrait Gallery*, 2:155; H.P. Chase and I. Reynolds to Department of Indian Affairs, July 12, 1876, PAC RG 10, vol. 1993, file 6828; J.D. McLean to Gordon Cascaden, Aug. 21, 1902, PAC RG 10, vol. 1993, file 6828; *Brantford Expositor*, May 14, 1926.

9. Dent, "Tecumseh," 2:155; Scobie H. Logan to Minister of the Interior, Mar. 20, 1912, PAC RG 10, vol. 1993, file 6828; G.N. Weekes to Superintendent of Indian Affairs, Mar. 18, 1931, PAC RG 10, vol. 1993, file 6828; *Toronto Globe*, Mar. 10, 1931; *Sarnia Canadian Observer*, Feb. 26, 1931.

10. Margaret A. Brown to D.C. Scott, Nov. 24, 1913, PAC RG 10, vol. 1993, file 6828, *The Free Press* (London, Ontario), July 31, 1926; Lynn Hetherington, "Tecumseh," *The University Magazine* 8 (1909):147.

11. Duncan Campbell Scott, general superintendent of Indian Affairs, to Ross Gray, Feb. 23, 1931, PAC RG 10, vol. 1993, file 6828.

12. J.E. Middleton and Fred Landon, *The Province of Ontario*, 1:192; Gurd, *Tecumseh*, pp. 183–84; Norman Gurd, "Notes and Comments," *Canadian Historical Review*, 12 (1931):117–18; *Sarnia Canadian Observer*, Feb. 26, 1931; Gurd to Ross Gray, Jan. 29, 1931, PAC RG 10, vol. 1993, file 6828; police report of Thomas Corless, Jan. 18, 1931, PAC RG 10, vol. 1993, file 6828; H.B. Williams and Samson Sands to D.C. Scott, Feb. 4, 1931, PAC RG 10, vol. 1993, file 6828.

13. In addition to the above, consult reports of Corless, Jan. 27, Feb. 27, 1931, PAC RG 10, vol. 1993, file 6828; *Montreal Gazette*, Jan. 19, 1931.

14. Nelson Stone to Department of Indian Affairs, Mar. 9, 1931, PAC RG 10, vol. 1993, file 6828; Cruikshank to Scott, May 11, 1931, PAC RG 10, vol. 1993, file 6828; J.B. Harkin to Scott, July 2, 1931, PAC RG 10, vol. 1993, file 6828.

15. Walpole Island Soldiers' Club circular, PAC RG 10, vol. 1993, file 6828; W.D. Herridge to the Secretary of State for External Affairs, Aug. 17, 1934, PAC RG 10, vol. 1993, file 6828; *Amherstberg Echo*, Aug. 29, 1941; *Life*, Sept. 1, 1941, pp. 22–23.

16. Interview with Shane by B. Drake (1821), Draper Mss., 2YY59, 12YY36; Stephen Ruddell to Drake, Jan. 1822, Draper Mss., 2YY120–32; Charles A. Wickliffe, "Tecumseh and the Battle of the Thames," *Register of the Kentucky Historical Society* 60 (1962):48. Miller and his

younger brother Adam were captured as boys by the Indians and spent many years with them, Christopher among the Shawnees and Adam with the Delawares. On March 13, 1794, Christopher was captured by the Americans and briefly served General Anthony Wayne as a scout or a spy. Wickliffe met him in 1812 when he commanded the third regiment of Kentucky detached militia. There is evidence that Tecumseh's first biographer, Benjamin Drake, planned to interview Miller, but failed to do so. Miller died on May 16, 1828.

BIBLIOGRAPHY

Manuscripts

Public Record Office, Kew, England
  War Office Papers
    WO 1/96 (War Office in-letters)
    WO 71/243 (Court-martial of Henry Procter)
    WO 42/38/294–95 (Certificates relating to Procter)
  Admiralty Papers .
    Adm. 1/503–504 (Despatches of the Commander-in-Chief, North
      American station)
  Colonial Office Papers
    CO 42/147–48, 151–52, 156–57 (Despatches from Canada)
    CO 43/23 (Bathurst's letters to Prevost)
Welch Regiment Museum, Cardiff Castle, Cardiff, Wales
  James Cochran, "The War in Canada, 1812–15."
  Copy of Richardson's *War of 1812* (1842) annotated by James Cochran
  Major A. C. Whitehorne, "Roll of Officers 41st and 69th, 1719–
    1838."
Public Archives of Canada, Ottawa, Canada
  Indian Affairs Papers (RG 10)
    Lieutenant-Governor's Office, Upper Canada, vols. 3–4 (microfilm
      C–10996 to C–10997)
    Superintendent-General's Office, vol. 12 (microfilm C–11000 to
      C–11001)
    Deputy Superintendent-General's Office, vols. 28–30 (microfilm
      C–11007 to C–11009)
    Department of Indian Affairs, Headquarters File, vol. 1993, file
      6828 (microfilm C–11130)

Military Papers (RG 8)
- Records of the 41st Regiment, 1811–15, vols. C911–14 (microfilm C–3278)
- Records of the War of 1812, vols. C257–58, C679–87 (microfilm C–2852 to C–2853, C–3172 to C–3174, C–3231)

Miscellaneous
- Claus Papers, MG 19/f1, vols. 10, 17 (microfilm C–1480, C–1482)
- Kent Historical Society, "Some Historical Notes on the County of Kent" (1948), MG 9, D8–67
- Ontario Department of Lands and Forests, Surveys Branch Town Plans (microfilm M–308)

National Map Collection
- Map of Amherstburg, 1808: H3/440/Amh. 1808
- "Part of the River Thames, Upper Canada," a map by George Williams, Aug. 9, 1814, forwarded with a letter of Lieutenant Colonel Hughes to General Mann, Aug. 16, 1814: H2/410/Thames/1814
- "Frontiers of North Shores of Lake Erie…," 1815: V30/410/Thames/1815 (in two sections)

National Archives, Washington, D.C.
- Letters Received by the Secretary of War, Registered and Unregistered (microfilm M 221–222)
- Letters Received by the Secretary of War relating to Indian Affairs (microfilm M 271)
- War of 1812 Papers of the Department of State, 1789–1815 (microfilm M 588, reel 7)
- Voluntary Organizations and State Militia, War of 1812, Muster and Pay Rolls (Record Group 94)

Library of Congress, Washington, D.C.
- Isaac Shelby Papers
- William Henry Harrison Papers
- Duncan McArthur Papers
- Journal of Lewis Bond
- Henry Onderdonk, "Life and Times of Tecumseh" (1842)

State Historical Society of Wisconsin, Madison, Wisconsin
- Lyman C. Draper Papers
  - Tecumseh Papers (YY series)
  - Draper Tours and Interviews (S series)
  - Simon Kenton Papers (BB series)
  - William Henry Harrison Papers (X series)
  - Charles Scott Todd Papers (U series)

Burton Historical Collection, Detroit Public Library, Detroit, Michigan
  Mary Ruth Lacey Papers
University of Chicago Library, Chicago, Illinois
  Durrett Miscellaneous Manuscripts, Box 8

Books and Articles

Adams, Henry. *History of the United States of America, 1801–17.* 9 vols.
  New York: Antiquarian Press, 1962, first published, 1891–1896.
Adjutant-General of the State of Kentucky. *Soldiers of the War of 1812.*
  Frankfort: Legislature of Kentucky, 1891.
Allen, William B. *A History of Kentucky.* Louisville: Bradley & Gilbert,
  1872.
Anderson, Thomas G. "Personal Narrative of Capt. Thomas G. An-
  derson." *Report and Collections of the State Historical Society of Wisconsin* 9
  (1882):137–206.
Anderson, Thomas G. "Capt. T. G. Anderson's Journal, 1814." *Report
  and Collections of the State Historical Society of Wisconsin* 9 (1882):207–61.
Andreas, A. T. *History of Chicago.* 3 vols. Chicago: Andreas, 1884–1886.
*An Impartial and Correct History of the War Between the United States of
  America, and Great Britain.* New York: J. Low, 1815.
Anson, Bert. *The Miami Indians.* Norman: University of Oklahoma Press,
  1970.
Armstrong, John. *Notices of the War of 1812.* 2 vols. New York: Wiley &
  Putnam, 1840.
Armstrong, Perry. *The Sauks and the Black Hawk War.* Springfield, Ill.:
  H. W. Rokker, 1887.
Arnold, Thaddeus S. "Battle of the Thames and Death of Tecumseh."
  *Annual Transactions of the United Empire Loyalists Association of Ontario,
  1901–02* 4 (1903):30–35.
"Askin Papers," *MPHC* 32 (1903):474–515.
Atcheson, Nathaniel. "A Compressed View of the Points to be Discussed
  in Treating with the United States of America." Mar. 2, 1814, *The
  Pamphleteer* 5 (1815):105–39.
Atwater, Caleb. *Remarks Made on a Tour to Prairie de Chien . . . in 1829.*
  Columbus, Ohio: I. N. Whiting, 1831.
———. *A History of the State of Ohio.* Cincinnati: Glezen & Shepard,
  1838.
Berton, Pierre. *Flames Across the Border, 1813–1814.* Toronto: McClel-
  land & Stewart, 1981.

Bolt, Robert. "Vice President Richard M. Johnson of Kentucky: Hero of the Thames—Or the Great Amalgamator?" *Register of the Kentucky Historical Society* 75 (1977):191–203.

Brown, Samuel R. *Views of the Campaigns of the North-western Army.* Philadelphia: W. G. Murphey, 1815, first published, 1814.

———. *An Authentic History of the Second War for Independence.* 2 vols. Auburn, N.Y.: J. G. Hathaway, 1815.

Brunson, Alfred. "Death of Tecumseh at the Battle of the Thames in 1813." *Report and Collections of the State Historical Society of Wisconsin* 4 (1859):369–74.

———. *A Western Pioneer, or, Incidents in the Life and Times of Rev. Alfred Brunson.* 2 vols. Cincinnati: Hitchcock & Walden, 1872–1879.

Brymner, Douglas. "Capture of Fort M'Kay, Prairie du Chien, in 1814." *Collections of the State Historical Society of Wisconsin* 11 (1888):254–70.

Bulger, Andrew H. "Bulger Correspondence, 1810–1816." *MPHC* 23 (1895):445–523.

———. "The Bulger Papers." *Collections of the State Historical Society of Wisconsin* 13 (1895):10–153.

Burt, A. L. *The United States, Great Britain and British North America, 1783–1815.* New York: Russell & Russell, 1961, first published, 1940.

Butler, Mann. *A History of the Commonwealth of Kentucky.* Cincinnati: J. A. James & Co., 1836.

Butterfield, Consul W. *History of the Girtys.* Columbus, Ohio: Long's College Book Co., 1950, first published, 1890.

Byfield, Shadrach. "A Narrative of a Light Company Soldier's Service, in the 41st Regiment of Foot, During the Late American War." *The Magazine of History with Notes and Queries* 11 (1910):57–96, first published, 1840.

"Campaigns in the Canadas." *Quarterly Review* 27 (1822):405–49.

Cass, Lewis. "Indians of North America." *North American Review* 22 (1826):53–119.

———. "Policy and Practise of the United States and Great Britain in Their Treatment of Indians." *North American Review* 24 (1827):365–442.

Clark, Thomas D. *Frontier America.* New York: C. Scribner, 1959.

Clarke, Peter D. *Origin and Traditional History of the Wyandotts.* Toronto: Hunter, Rose & Co., 1870.

Cleary, Francis. "History of Fort Malden or Amherstburg." *Essex Historical Society Papers and Addresses* 2 (1915):34–50.

Cleaves, Freeman. *Old Tippecanoe: William Henry Harrison and His Times.* Port Washington, N.Y.: Kennikat Press, 1969, first published, 1939.

Clifton, James A. "Merchant, Soldier, Broker, Chief. A Corrected Obituary of Captain Billy Caldwell." *Journal of the Illinois State Historical Society* 71 (1978):185–210.

Coffin, William F. *1812: The War, and Its Moral: A Canadian Chronicle.* Montreal: J. Lovell, 1864.

Coles, Harry L. *The War of 1812.* Chicago & London: University of Chicago Press, 1965.

Colquhoun, A. H. U., ed. *Tecumseh and Richardson: The Story of a Trip to Walpole Island and Port Sarnia.* Toronto: Ontario Book Co., 1924.

Commemorative Biographical Record of the County of Kent Ontario. Toronto:J. H. Beers, 1904.

Cook, D. B. to the editor, Dec. 24, 1884. "The Death of Tecumseh." *The Century Magazine* 30 (1885):332.

"Copies of Papers on File in the Dominion Archives at Ottawa . . . Pertaining to the Relations of the British Government with the Indian Tribes . . . and to the Military Posts and Marine Interests of the Great Lakes, 1762–1799," *MPHC* 12 (1888):1–315.

"Copies of Papers on File in the Dominion Archives . . . Pertaining to the Relations of the British Government with the United States During the Period of the War of 1812," *MPHC* 15 (1890): *passim.*

"Copies of Papers on file in the Dominion Archives . . . Pertaining to the Relations of the British Government with the United States During and Subsequent to the Period of the War of 1812," *MPHC* 16 (1890): *passim.*

Coutts, Katherine B. "Thamesville and the Battle of the Thames" (1908), reprinted in Zaslow, Morris, and Turner, Wesley B., eds. *The Defended Border: Upper Canada and the War of 1812.* Toronto: Macmillan, 1964, pp. 14–20.

———. "The Tecumseh Memorial Boulder." *Kent Historical Society* 6 (1924):85–87.

Cruikshank, Ernest A. "Robert Dickson, the Indian Trader." *Collections of the State Historical Society of Wisconsin* 12 (1892):133–53.

———. "The Contest for the Command of Lake Erie in 1812–13" (1899), reprinted in Zaslow, Morris, and Turner, Wesley B., eds. *The Defended Border: Upper Canada and the War of 1812.* Toronto: Macmillan, 1964, pp. 84–104.

———. "The County of Norfolk in the War of 1812" (1923), reprinted in Zaslow, Morris, and Turner, Wesley B., eds. *The Defended Border: Upper Canada and the War of 1812*. Toronto: Macmillan, 1964, pp. 224–40.

Cullum, George W., ed. *Campaigns of the War of 1812–15, Against Great Britain*. New York: J. Miller, 1879.

Davidson, James, to the editor of the Louisville *Journal*, Oct. 22, 1859. "Who Killed Tecumseh?" *Historical Magazine* (July, 1866):205.

Dawson, Moses. *Historical Narrative of the Civil and Military Services of Major-General William Henry Harrison*. Cincinnati: Cincinnati Advertiser, 1824.

Defence Major General Proctor, Tried at Montreal by a General Court Martial . . . . Montreal: J. Lovell 1842.

Dent, John Charles. "Tecumseh." *The Canadian Portrait Gallery*. 4 vols. Toronto: J. B. Magurn, 1880–1881, 2:144–57.

Dickson, Robert. "Dickson and Grignon Papers, 1812–1815." *Collections of the State Historical Society of Wisconsin* 11 (1888):271–315.

Drake, Benjamin. *Life of Tecumseh and of his Brother the Prophet*. Cincinnati: Anderson, Gates & Wright, 1841.

Edmunds, R. David. *The Potawatomis: Keepers of the Fire*. Norman: University of Oklahoma Press, 1978.

———. *The Shawnee Prophet*. Lincoln: University of Nebraska Press, 1983.

———. *Tecumseh and the Quest for Indian Leadership*. Boston: Little, Brown & Co., 1984.

Emmons, William. *Authentic Biography of Colonel Richard M. Johnson of Kentucky*. Boston: A. Langworthy, 1834.

Engelman, Frederick Louis. *The Peace of Christmas Eve*. London, England: R. Hart-Davis, 1962.

Ermatinger, Charles O. Z. "The Retreat of Proctor and Tecumseh." *Ontario Historical Society Papers and Records* 18 (1919):11–21.

Esarey, Logan, ed. *Messages and Letters of William Henry Harrison*. 2 vols. Indianapolis: Indiana Historical Collections of the Indiana Historical Commission, 1922.

"Extracts from the Diary of John Askin," *MPHC* 32 (1903):468–74.

Finley, James B. *Autobiography of Reverend James B. Finley*. Edited by W. P. Strickland. Cincinnati: Methodist Book Concern for the author, 1857.

Galloway, William Albert. *Old Chillicothe: Shawnee and Pioneer History*. Xenia, Ohio: The Buckeye Press, 1934.

Galt, William R. to H. B. Dawson, Aug.15, 1866. "Who Killed Tecumseh?" *Historical Magazine* (October, 1866):318.

Gates, Charles M. "The West in American Diplomacy, 1812–1815." *Mississippi Valley Historical Review* 26 (1940):499–510.

Gibson, A. M. *The Kickapoos: Lords of the Middle Border.* Norman: University of Oklahoma Press, 1963.

Gilpin, A. R. *The War of 1812 in the Old Northwest.* East Lansing: Michigan State University Press, 1958.

Goebel, Dorothy B. *William Henry Harrison.* Indianapolis: Historical Bureau of the Indiana Library and Historical Department, 1926.

Gourlay, R. *Statistical Account of Upper Canada.* Toronto: McClelland & Stewart, 1974, first published, 1822.

Griswold, Bert J. *The Pictorial History of Fort Wayne.* Chicago: R. O. Law, 1917.

Guillet, Edwin C. *Early Life in Upper Canada.* Toronto: University of Toronto Press, 1969, first published, 1933.

Gurd, Norman St. Clair. *The Story of Tecumseh.* Toronto: Briggs, 1912.

———. "Notes and Comments." *Canadian Historical Review* 12 (1931):117–18.

Hagan, William T. *The Sac and Fox Indians.* Norman: University of Oklahoma Press, 1958.

Hall, Claude H. "The Fabulous Tom Ochiltree." *Southwestern Historical Quarterly* 71 (1967–68):347–76.

Hall, Francis. *Travels in Canada, and the United States, in 1816 and 1817.* London, England: Longman, Hurst, Rees, Orme & Brown, 1818.

Hamil, Fred Coyne. *The Valley of the Lower Thames, 1640 to 1850.* Toronto: University of Toronto Press, 1951.

Hatch, William S. *A Chapter of the History of the War of 1812 in the Northwest.* Cincinnati: Miami Printing & Publishing Co. 1872.

Henderson, J. L. H. ed. *John Strachan: Documents and Opinions.* Toronto: McClelland & Stewart, 1969.

Hetherington, Lynn. "Tecumseh." *The University Magazine* 8 (1909):135–47.

Hickerson, H. *The Chippewa and Their Neighbours.* New York: Holt, Rinehart & Winston, 1970.

Hickling, William. "Caldwell and Shabonee." *Addresses Delivered at the Annual Meeting of the Chicago Historical Society . . . 1868 . . . Together with . . . Sketches of Billy Caldwell and Shabonee.* Chicago: Fergus Printing Co., 1877, pp. 29–41.

Hodge, Frederick W., ed. *Handbook of American Indians,* 2 vols. Washington, D.C.: Smithsonian Institution, 1907–1910.

Horsman, Reginald. "The Role of the Indian in the War." Philip P. Mason, ed. *After Tippecanoe.* East Lansing & Toronto: Michigan State University Press & Ryerson Press, 1963, pp. 60–77.

————. *Matthew Elliott, British Indian Agent.* Detroit: Wayne State University Press, 1964.

————. *The War of 1812.* London, England: Eyre & Spottiswoode, 1969.

Hubbard, Gordon S. "Col. G. S. Hubbard's Narrative." *Addresses Delivered at the Annual Meeting of the Chicago Historical Society . . . 1868 . . . Together with . . . Sketches of Billy Caldwell and Shabonee.* Chicago: Fergus Printing Co., 1877, pp. 41–46.

Illustrated Historical Atlas of the Counties of Essex and Kent. Toronto: H. Beldon & Co., 1880.

Irving, L. Homfray. *Officers of the British Forces in Canada During the War of 1812–15.* Toronto: Canadian Military Institute, 1908.

Jackson, Donald, ed. *Black Hawk: An Autobiography.* Urbana: University of Illinois Press, 1964.

Jackson, Isaac R. *A Sketch of the Life and Public Services of William Henry Harrison.* Columbus, Ohio: I. N. Whiting, 1840.

James, William. *A Full and Correct Account of the Military Occurrences of the Late War Between Great Britain and the United States of America.* 2 vols. London, England: W. James, 1818.

Jamieson, Melvill Allan. *Medals Awarded to North American Indian Chiefs, 1714–1922.* London, England: Spink & Son, 1936.

Johnston, Charles M. "William Claus and John Norton: A Struggle for Power in Old Ontario." *Ontario History* 57 (1965): 101–08.

Kenton, Edna. *Simon Kenton: His Life and Period, 1755–1836.* Garden City, New York: Doubleday, Doran & Co., 1930.

King, Rufus. *Ohio.* Boston: Houghton Mifflin, 1888.

Kingston, John T. "Death of Tecumseh." *Report and Collections of the State Historical Society of Wisconsin* 4 (1859): 375–76.

Kinzie, J. H. *Wau-Bun, The 'Early Day' in the North-West.* Edited by Milo M. Quaife. Chicago: R. R. Donnelley, 1932.

Klinck, Carl F., ed. *Tecumseh: Fact and Fiction in Early Records.* Englewood Cliffs, N.J.: Prentice Hall, 1961.

————. and Talman, James T., eds. *The Journal of Major John Norton, 1816.* Toronto: Champlain Society, 1970.

Lajeunesse, Ernest J. ed. *The Windsor Border Region.* Toronto: Champlain Society, 1960.

Lauriston, Victor. "The Case for General Proctor" (1951), reprinted in Zaslow, Morris, and Turner, Wesley B., eds. *The Defended Border: Upper Canada and the War of 1812.* Toronto: Macmillan, 1964, pp. 121–29.

————. *Romantic Kent.* Chatham, Ontario: County of Kent and City of Chatham, 1952.

The Letters of Veritas, Re-published from the Montreal Herald. Montreal: W. Gray, 1815.

Lomax, D. A. N. *A History of the Services of the 41st (Welch) Regiment.* Devonport, England: Hiorns & Miller, 1899.

Lorrain, Alfred M. *The Helm, the Sword, and the Cross: A Life Narrative.* Cincinnati: Poe & Hitchcock, 1862.

Lossing, Benson J. *The Pictorial Field-book of the War of 1812.* New York: Harper & Bros., 1896, first published, 1868.

————. "Was Tecumtha Skinned?" *American Historical Record* 1 (1872):285.

The Lucubrations of Humphrey Ravelin. London, England: G. & W. B. Whittaker, 1823.

McAfee, Robert B. *The Late War in the Western Country.* Ann Arbor, Mich.: University Microfilms, 1966, first published, 1816.

————. "The McAfee Papers." *Register of the Kentucky State Historical Society* 26 (1928):4–23, 108–36, 236–48.

McGee, Thomas D'Arcy. *A History of the Irish Settlers in North America* Boston: P. Donahoe, 1852.

McKenney, Thomas L. *Memoirs, Official and Personal.* 2 vols. New York: Paine & Burgess, 1846.

Mahan, Alfred Thayer. *Sea Power in its Relations to the War of 1812.* 2 vols. Boston: Little, Brown, 1905.

Mahon, John K. *The War of 1812.* Gainesville: University of Florida Press, 1971.

Marshall, John. *Royal Navy Biography.* 12 vols. London, England: Longman, Rees, Orme, Brown & Green, 1823–1835.

Mason, Philip P., ed. *After Tippecanoe: Some Aspects of the War of 1812.* East Lansing, Mich., & Toronto: Michigan State University Press & Ryerson Press, 1963.

Matson, Nehemiah. *Memories of Shaubena.* Chicago: D. B. Cooke, 1878.

Mayo, Bernard. "The Man Who Killed Tecumseh." *The American Mercury* 19 (1930):446–53

Meyer, Leland Winfield. *The Life and Times of Richard M. Johnson of Kentucky.* New York: Columbia University Press, 1932.

Michigan Pioneer and Historical Society Historical Collections. 40 vols. Lansing: George, Thorp, Godfrey, Smith et al. 1877–1929.

Middleton, J. E. and Landon, Fred. *The Province of Ontario.* 4 vols. Toronto: Dominion Publishing Co., 1927.

"Papers from the Canadian Archives, 1767–1814." *Collections of the State Historical Society of Wisconsin* 12 (1892):23–132.

Perkins, Bradford. *Prologue to War: England and the United States, 1805–1812.* Berkeley: University of California Press, 1961.

———. *Castlereagh and Adams: England and the United States, 1812–1823.* Berkeley: University of California Press, 1964.

Peterson, Clarence Stewart. *Known Military Dead During the War of 1812.* Baltimore: Peterson, 1955.

Peterson, Harold L. "Lock, Stock and Barrel." *American History* 2 (no. 10, 1968):27–46.

Poole, J. I. "The Fight at Battle Hill" (1911), reprinted in Zaslow, Morris, and Turner, Wesley B., eds. *The Defended Border: Upper Canada and the War of 1812.* Toronto: Macmillan, 1964, pp. 130–42.

"Prairie du Chien Documents, 1814–15." *Report and Collections of the State Historical Society of Wisconsin* 9 (1882):262–81.

Quaife, Milo M. *Chicago and the Old North-west, 1673–1835.* Chicago: University of Chicago Press, 1913.

———, ed. *The John Askin Papers,* 2 vols. Detroit: Detroit Library Commission, 1928–1931.

———, ed. *War on the Detroit: The Chronicles of Thomas Verchères de Boucherville.* Chicago: R. R. Donnelley, 1940.

Quisenberry, Anderson Chenault. *Kentucky in the War of 1812.* Frankfort: Kentucky State Historical Society, 1915.

Richardson, John. "A Canadian Campaign, by a British Officer." *The New Monthly Magazine and Literary Journal* 17 (1826):541–48, and 19 (1827):162–70, 248–54, 448–57, 538–51.

———, *Tecumseh; or, the Warrior of the West: a Poem in Four Cantos, with Notes.* London, England: R. Glynn, 1828.

———. *Richardson's War of 1812.* Toronto: Historical Publishing Co., 1902, first published, 1842.

———. *The Canadian Brothers; or, The Prophecy Fulfilled.* 2 vols. Toronto: University of Toronto Press, 1976, first published, 1840.

Robinson, Doane. *A History of the Dakota or Sioux Indians.* Minneapolis: Ross & Haines, 1967, first published, 1904.

Scharf, J. Thomas. *History of Saint Louis City and County.* 2 vols. Philadelphia: L. H. Everts & Co., 1883.

Schlesinger, Arthur M. *The Age of Jackson*. London, England: Eyre & Spottiswoode, 1947.

Schoolcraft, Henry Rowe. *Personal Memoirs of a Residence of Thirty Years with the Indian Tribes*. Philadelphia: Lippincott, Grambo & Co. 1851.

Snowden, James Ross. *A Description of the Medals of Washington . . . in the Museum of the Mint*. Philadelphia: J. B. Lippincott, 1861.

Stacey, C. P. "Another Look at the Battle of Lake Erie" (1958), reprinted in Zaslow, Morris, and Turner, Wesley B., eds. *The Defended Border: Upper Canada and the War of 1812*. Toronto: Macmillan, 1964, pp. 105–13.

Stagg, J. C. A. *Mr. Madison's War: Politics, Diplomacy, and Warfare in the Early American Republic, 1783–1830*. Princeton, New Jersey: Princeton University Press, 1983.

Stanley, George F. G. "The Contribution of the Canadian Militia During the War." P. P. Mason, ed. *After Tippecanoe*. East Lansing, Mich., & Toronto: Michigan State University Press & Ryerson Press, 1963, pp. 28–48.

Stevens, Frank E. *The Black Hawk War*. Chicago: Stevens, 1903.

Stewart, Aura P. "Recollections of Aura P. Stewart." *MPHC* 4 (1883):324–55.

Sullivant, Joseph. *A Genealogy and Family Memorial*. Columbus, Ohio: Sullivant, 1874.

Talbert, Charles G. "William Whitley, 1749–1813." *Filson Club History Quarterly* 25 (1951):101–21, 210–16, 300–16.

Thompson, Charles N. *Sons of the Wilderness: John and William Conner*. Indianapolis: Indiana Historical Society, 1937.

Thomson, John Lewis. *Historical Sketches of the Late War Between the United States and Great Britain*. Philadelphia: T. Desilver, 1816.

Thwaites, Reuben G. ed. "Letter Book of Thomas Forsyth, 1814–1818." *Collections of the State Historical Society of Wisconsin* 11 (1888):316–55.

Tucker, Glenn. *Poltroons and Patriots. A Popular Account of the War of 1812*. 2 vols. Indianapolis: Bobbs-Merrill, 1954.

―――. *Tecumseh; Vision of Glory*. Indianapolis: Bobbs-Merrill, 1956.

Updyke, Frank A. *The Diplomacy of the War of 1812*. Gloucester, Mass.: P. Smith, 1965, first published, 1915.

Wallace, A. F. C. *The Death and Rebirth of the Seneca*. New York: A. A. Knopf, 1973.

War Office. *A List of all the Officers of the Army and Royal Marines*. London, England: War Office, 1813–14.

Wentworth, John. *Early Chicago: A Lecture, Delivered . . . on . . . April 11, 1875.* Chicago: Fergus Printing Co., 1876.

————. *Early Chicago: Fort Dearborn: An Address.* Chicago: Fergus Printing Co., 1881.

Whitehorne, A. C. *The History of the Welch Regiment.* Cardiff, Wales: Western Mail & Echo, 1932.

Wickliffe, Charles A. to the editor of the *Bardstown Gazette*, Nov. 25, 1859. "Tecumseh and the Battle of the Thames." *Register of the Kentucky Historical Society* 60 (1962):45–49.

Williams, Samuel. *Sketches of the War Between the United States and the British Isles.* Rutland, Vermont: Fay & Davison, 1815.

Wing, Talcott E. "History of Monroe County, Michigan," *MPHC* 4 (1883):318–24.

Witherell, B. F. H. "Reminiscences of the North-west." *Collections of the State Historical Society of Wisconsin* 3 (1857):297–337.

Woehrmann, Paul John. "The American Invasion of Western Upper Canada in 1813." *Northwest Ohio Quarterly* 38 (nos. 2–4, 1966):74–88, 39 (no. 2, 1967):61–73; 39 (no. 4, 1967):39–48; 40 (no. 1, 1968):27–44.

Wood, William, ed. *Select British Documents of the Canadian War of 1812.* 3 vols. in 4. Toronto: Champlain Society, 1920–1928.

Woodward, Thomas S. *Woodward's Reminiscences of the Creek, or Muscogee Indians.* Montgomery, Ala.: Barrett & Wimbush, 1859.

Wright, J. Leitch. *Britain and the American Frontier, 1783–1815.* Athens: University of Georgia Press, 1975.

Young, Bennett H. *The Battle of the Thames.* Louisville, Kentucky: Filson Club, 1903.

Zaslow, Morris, and Turner, Wesley B., eds. *The Defended Border: Upper Canada and the War of 1812.* Toronto: Macmillan, 1964.

Newspapers and Serials

Canada
  Amherstburg Echo (1941)
  Brantford Expositor (1926)
  Toronto Globe (1913, 1931)
  Kingston Gazette (1813)
  London Free Press (1926)
  Montreal Gazette (1813–14, 1931)

Quebec Gazette (1805, 1811, 1813–14)
Sarnia Canadian Observer (1931)
United States of America
  Army and Navy Chronicle (1838)
  Cleveland (Ohio) *Herald Supplement* (1871)
  Columbus (Ohio) *Sentinel* (1832)
  New York Commercial Advertiser (1813)
  Cincinnati (Ohio) *Daily Gazette* (1873)
  Kentucky Gazette (1835–41)
  Kentucky Reporter (1814)
  Life (1941)
  New York Spectator (1828)
  Scioto (Chillicothe, Ohio) *Gazette* (1840)
  Cincinnati (Ohio) *Times-Star* (1886)
  Toledo (Ohio) *Blade* (1874)
  Toledo (Ohio) *Commercial* (1874)
  The War, Being a Faithful Record of the Transactions of the War Between the United States of America and the United Kingdom of Great Britain and Ireland (New York: S. Woodworth & Co., 1813–1814), a weekly gathered into two volumes.
  Louisville (Ky.) *Weekly Journal* (1859)
  The Weekly Register, Baltimore: H. Niles, 1813–1814, vols. 5–6.
  Western Citizen. Paris, Kentucky, 1824, 1831.

Unpublished Manuscripts

Calloway, Colin Gordon. "British Relations with the North American Indians, 1783–1815." Ph.D. dissertation, Leeds University, England, 1978.

Chalou, George C. "The Red Pawns Go to War: British-American Indian Relations, 1810–1815." Ph.D. dissertation, Indiana University, 1971.

Goltz, Herbert C. W. "Tecumseh, the Prophet and the Rise of the Northwestern Indian Confederacy." Ph.D. dissertation, University of Western Ontario, 1973.

Hatheway, G. G. "The Neutral Indian Barrier State." Ph.D. dissertation, University of Minnesota, 1957.

Hauser, Raymond E. "An Ethno-history of the Illinois Indian Tribe, 1673–1832." Ph.D. dissertation, Northern Illinois University, 1973.
Heath, Herschell. "The Indians as a Factor in the War of 1812." Ph.D. dissertation, Clark University, Worcester, Mass., 1926.
Smith, Dwight L. "Indian Land Cessions in the Old Northwest, 1795–1809." Ph.D. dissertation, Indiana University, 1949.

INDEX

Allen, James: 124

Allen, William B.: 255n.

Amherstburg, Upper Canada: 3–4, 18–19, 26, 37, 45–47, 62, 76, 89, 102, 158, 184, 190, 216, 234n., 251n.; described, 9–10; communications, 10, 26–30, 34, 38, 40–41, 44, 57, 67; blockaded, 30, 34, 36–37; councils, 53–58, 62, 64, 85, 88, 233–34n.; British troops evacuate, 62–64, 67–71; U.S. garrison, 187–89, 212; regained by British, 211

Ancaster, Upper Canada: 182

Anderson, Robert: 163

Anderson, Thomas G: 265n.

Armstrong, John: 39–40, 186, 189, 202

Army, American (West): composition and strength, 38, 69–71, 87, 109–10, 124, 187; arms and artillery, 87, 107, 110, 141, 248n.; battle formations 87, 124–25; battle losses, 87, 127–28, 133, 249–50n.; drilling, 109–10; *see also* William Henry Harrison, Richard Mentor Johnson, United States of America

Army, British (Centre Division): 17, 26–30, 39, 44, 46–47, 49–50, 96, 112, 182, 185–86

Army, British (Right Division): composition and strength, 10, 14, 108–109; Royal Newfoundland Regiment, 10, 14, 109: Forty-first Regiment of Foot, 10, 14–15, 28–29, 108, 232n.; Canadian Artillery, 10, 108–109; Royal Artillery, 10, 108–109: Tenth Royal Veteran Battalion, 10, 109; Canadian Light Dragoons, 10, 109, 121, 126; discord in, 14, 51–52, 77, 81, 83, 96, 121–22, 128–29; condition, 14, 72, 128; arms and artillery, 15, 91, 105, 107–108, 121, 126, 129; Indian Department, 16–18, 113–14, 176, 196, 198–201, 267n.; Royal Engineers, 48; militia, 68–69; battle losses, 84, 92, 108, 127, 182; loss of stores, ordnance and ammunition, 89, 91–92, 96, 184; inadequately provisioned, 91–92, 128, 184; defeated at Moraviantown, 112, 121–30; censured, 129, 183; retreat to Lake Ontario, 182;